Committees and Commissions in India
1979

Concepts in Communication
Informatics & Librarianship-55

General Editor : **S.P. Agrawal**

Committees and Commissions in India 1979

Volume 17

PART A

A Concept's Project

Compiled by a team of professionals
under the guidance of
VIRENDRA KUMAR

CONCEPT PUBLISHING COMPANY, NEW DELHI 110059

ISBN 81-7022-508-6 (Vol. 17, Part A)

First Published 1994

Published and Printed by
Ashok Kumar Mittal
Concept Publishing Company
A/15-16, Commercial Block, Mohan Garden
NEW DELHI 110059 (India)

Lasertypeset by
Printing Express
H-13, Bali Nagar
NEW DELHI 110015

GENERAL EDITOR'S INTRODUCTION

In the context of the changing world, the role of the government – be it at central, state or local level – is becoming more pervasive in the modern society. Everyday, it has to encounter new problems and face new issues which demand quite a new thinking and novel strategies to overcome them. Thus, the increasing role of the government in every sphere of people's life has broadened its functions and responsibilities tremendously and enlarged its activities to such an extent that the government machinery of its own can hardly manage its affairs. Moreover, its functions are becoming more complicated and complex requiring the assistance of outside specialists, technocrats and specialized agencies.

In view of this, the modern government has to set-up committees and commissions and working or study groups on various problems and issues from time to time. In the light of the recommendations of these committees and commissions, the government take decisions on key issues and problems. Often the government is obliged to seek the assistance of a committee to evaluate some of its schemes in operation so that on the basis of the evaluation reports of the committee, it may either continue, modify or scrap the on-going schemes. In other words, the committees or commissions, etc., exercise a great deal of pivotal force in shaping the policies and programmes of the government and for this purpose submit a large number of reports.

In these volumes of *Committees and Commissions in India*, now being published under the *Concepts in Communication Informatics and Librarianship (CICIL)* series, an attempt has been made to cover the period from 1974 onwards. The volumes include the vital data about only those reports of the committees and commissions which have been constituted by the Central Government. We have made every endeavour to include the digest of all the important reports on various vital issues of great importance and on major areas of national development.

We have also an ambitious plan to publish the digests of the important reports of the committees and commissions appointed by different state governments, the semi-government organisations and the learned bodies as also the reports published during the period of the British Government.

The publication has been brought out under the guidance of Shri Virendra Kumar, specialist in his own right with vast experience of working in Government Documents Section in the Central Secretariat Library and having the privilege of the blessings of Dr. S.R. Ranganathan – the father of Indian Library Science. I also put on record the collaborative help provided by Shri M.W.K. Sherwani.

We are sure that this compilation will prove a very useful reference tool for researchers, serious students and scholars of the public administration and political science, administrators, policy-makers, educationists and historians.

S.P. AGRAWAL

PREFACE

This volume of *Committees and Commissions in India* attempts to understand the activities of the various Committees and Commissions during the period 1974.

A 'Commission' is a governmental agency created to perform a particular function such as special investigations or on governmental regulations of business. It is appointed mainly when it is thought that a matter involves some financial questions. There are other reasons for which a Commission is appointed, e.g., in matters pertaining to welfare of the State and its citizens and/or improving the efficiency in an administration. The status of a 'Committee' is also the same as that of a 'Commission', but it does not possess as wide powers as are enjoyed by a Commission and has to limit itself to specific work assigned to it under its terms of reference. While arriving at decisions in the form of recommendations, a Commission or Committee ensures that such decisions are representative of interests of various types of people and also a safeguard against abuse of power.

A Committee or a Commission comprises a Chairman, the Members and Member Secretary (sometimes there is also an Assistant Secretary). In some cases, there are even One-man Commissions and the enquiry in such Commissions is entrusted to an Officer-on-Special Duty.

The Chairman of a Commission is a person well-versed mostly in legal matters and is often a retired judge of a High Court or the Supreme Court of India. Occasionally, a Member of Parliament is also appointed as the Chairman of a Commission. On the other hand, the Chairman of the Committee is mostly a specialist in the subject of the Committee. He can be a Leader or a Convenor also, if he heads a Panel, a Study Group or a Delegation, etc.

The Members of a Commission, Committee, Panel, Study Group etc., are specialists in their respective fields and provide valuable guidance to the Commission or the Committee in making recommendations.

The Member-Secretary or Secretary is generally nominated from among the experienced officials who have the requisite competent knowledge of the subject on which the Commission or the Committee is appointed.

Committees and Commissions in India provides in chronological order vital information about Committees and Commissions appointed by the Government from time to time. Information for each Committee or Commission is presented in a compact form in four parts, namely; Constitution; Appointment; Terms of Reference and Recommendations.

CONTENTS

PART B

BACKWARD CLASSES COMMISSION, 1979 — REPORT[1]

Chairman Shri B.P. Mandal

Members Shri R.R. Bhole; Shri Dewan Mohan Lal; Shri Dina Bandhu Sahu replaced by Shri L.R. Naik; Shri K. Subramaniam

M. Secy. Shri S.S. Gill

Appointment

On the 20th December, 1978, Shri Morarji Desai the then Prime Minister of India announced on the floor of the Parliament the decision to appoint a Backward Classes Commission. So the President in exercise of the Powers conferred by the Article 340 of the Constitution appointed a Backward Classes Commission to investigate the conditions of socially and educationally backward classes within the territory of India on January 1, 1979.

Terms of Reference

(i) To determine the criteria for defining the socially and educationally backward classes;

(ii) To recommend steps to be taken for the advancement of the socially and educationally backward classes of citizens so identified;

(iii) To examine the desirability or otherwise of making provisions for the reservation of appointments or posts in favour of such backward classes of citizens which are not adequately represented in public services and posts in connection with the affairs of the Union or of any State; and

1. Delhi, Controller of Publications 1981, Vols. I & II, 129 p. First Part; Vols. III & VII, 273 p. Second Part.

(iv) Present to the President a report setting out the facts as found by them and making such recommendations as they think proper.

In connection, the Commission may also examine the recommendations of the Backward Classes Commission appointed earlier and the considerations which stood in the way of the acceptance of its recommendations by Government.

Contents

Part I. Vol. I: Main Report and Recommendations; Forwarding Letter to the President; Composition and Terms of Reference of the Commission; Preface; The First Backward Classes Commission; Status of other Backward Classes in some States; Methodology and Data Base; Social Backwardness and Caste; Social Dynamics of Caste; Social Justice, Merit and Privilege; Social Justice, Constitution and the Law; North-South Comparison of Other Backward Classes Welfare (A Case Study of Four States); Evidence by Central and State Governments (A review); Evidence by the Public; Socio-Educational Field Survey and Criteria of Backwardness; Identification of O.B.Cs.; Recommendations; Summary of Report.

Part I. Vol II: Appendices 1 to 21.

Part II. Vol. III: Study prepared by the Indian Law Institute.

Part II. Vol. IV: Study Prepared by the Tata Institute of Social Sciences, Bombay.

Part II. Vol. V: Socio-Educational Survey Tables.

Part II. Vol. VI: Statewise list of Other Backward Classes.

Part II. Vol. VII: Minutes of Dissent by Shri Naik (Ex-M.P.) Member; Annexures.

Summary of the Report

The First Backward Classes Commission (Chapter I)

The First Backward Classes Commission was set up on January 29th, 1953, and it submitted its report on March 31st, 1955. On the basis of criteria evolved by it, the Commission listed 2,399 castes as socially and educationally backward. It recommended various welfare measures for OBCs including reservation in Government services and educational institutions.

The Central Government did not accept the recommendations of the Commission on the ground that it had not applied any objective tests for identifying Backward Classes. Five out of the 11 Members of the Commission had given notes of dissent. The Government felt that the Commission had classified a very large section of the population as backward and if special assistance had to be extended to all these people, "the really needy will be swapped by the multitude". The Government was also opposed to the adoption of caste as one of the criterion for backwardness and preferred the application of economic tests.

As Article 340 of the Constitution speaks of "socially and educationally backward classes", the application of 'economic tests' for their identification seems to be misconceived.

Status of OBCs in Some States (Chapter II)

It is for nearly 100 years that Provincial Governments in India have been implementing special programmes for the welfare of depressed and backward classes. Madras Government took the lead by framing Grant-in-Aid Code in 1885 to regulate financial aid to educational institutions for backward classes students. Mysore State was the next to follow and, by now, all the Southern States are implementing fairly comprehensive programmes for OBCs. As on date 16 States and 2 Union Territories are providing special assistance of varying degrees to Other Backward Classes. Ten State Governments are doing so on the basis of recommendations made by Backward Classes Commission specially set up by them in this behalf and the others are doing in an *ad hoc* manner.

Special concessions like reservation of jobs in Government employment and seats in educational institutions; financial assistance; subsidised educational facilities, etc., are being given by several State Governments to OBCs. Southern States have done much more work in this connection as compared to the rest of the country. Karnataka has reserved 48 per cent of all Government jobs for OBC candidates in addition to 18 per cent for SCs and STs. In the case of Tamil Nadu, these figures stand 50 per cent and 18 per cent respectively.

Methodology and Data Base (Chapter III)

One serious defect noticed by the Government in the report of first Backward Classes Commission was that it had not formulated any objective criteria for classifying Other Backward Classes. The need for field surveys and formulation of objective tests has also been repeatedly emphasised by the Supreme Court in several cases. In view of this, the Commission has taken special care to tap a number of independent sources for the collection of primary data. Some of the important measures taken in this connection were: seminar of sociologists on social backwardness; issue of three sets of questionnaires to State Governments, Central Government and the public; extensive touring of the country by the Commission, taking evidence of legislators, eminent publicmen, sociologists, etc.; undertaking a country-wide socio-educational survey; preparation of reports on some important issues by specialised agencies; analysis of census data, etc.

By adopting this multilateral approach the Commission was able to cast its net far and wide and prepared a very firm and dependable data base for its Report.

Social Backwardness and Caste (Chapter IV)

Castes are the building bricks of the Hindu social structure. They have kept Hindu society divided in a hierarchical order for centuries. This has resulted in a close linkage between the caste ranking of a person and his social, educational and economic status.

The manner of stratification of society gave the higher castes deep-rooted vested interests in the perpetuation of the system. The priestly castes evolved an elaborate and subtle scheme of scripture, ritual and mythology and perpetuate their supremacy and hold the lower castes in bondage for ages. Most of our Shastras uphold the four-fold Varna system and, because of this religious sanction, caste system has lasted longer than most other social institutions based on inequality and inequity.

In view of the permanent stratification of society in hierarchical caste order, members of lower castes have always suffered from discrimination in all walks of life and this has resulted in their social, educational and economic backwardness. In India, therefore, the low ritual caste status of a person has a direct bearing on his social backwardness.

Social Dynamics of Caste (Chapter V)

Caste system has been able to survive over the centuries because of its inherent resilience and its ability to adjust itself to the ever changing social reality. The traditional view of caste system, as contained in Chapter IV, is based more on Hindu Shastras than the actual state of social reality. Moreover, caste restrictions have loosened considerably as a result of the rule of law introduced by the British, urbanisation, industrialisation, spread of mass education and, above all, the introduction of adult franchise after independence. But all the above changes mark only shift of emphasis and not any material alteration is the basic structure of caste.

It is generally agreed that whereas certain caste taboos have weakened as a result of the above changes, the importance of casteism in Indian politics is on the increase. This perhaps, was inevitable, caste system provided the political leadership with readymade channels of communication and mobilisation and, in view of this, the importance of caste was bound to increase in Indian politics. As Rajni Kothari has observed, "those in India who complain of 'casteism' in politics are really looking for a sort of politics which has no basis of society."

The pace of social mobility is no doubt increasing and some traditional features of caste system have inevitably weakened. But what caste has lost on the ritual front, it has more than gained on the political front. In view of this it will be unrealistic to assume that the institution of caste will wither away in the foreseeable future.

Social Justice, Merit and Privilege (Chapter VI)

Equality before the law is a basic Fundamental Rights guaranteed under Article 14 of the Constitution. But the principle of 'equality' is a double edged weapon. It places the strong and the handicapped on the same footing in the race of life. It is a dictum of social justice that there is equality only among equals. To treat unequals as equals is to perpetuate inequality. The humaneness of a society is determined by the degree of protection it provides to its weaker, handicapped and less gifted members.

'Equality of opportunity' and 'equality of treatment' places the weak and the strong on par and, to that extent, it amounts to denial of social justice. In fact, it is 'equality of results' which is the acid test of society's egalitarian pretensions. In a highly unequal society like ours, it is only by giving special protection and privileges to the underprivileged section of society that we can enable the weak to resist exploitation by the strong.

It was in view of these considerations that our Constitution makers made special provisions under Articles 15(4), 16(4) and 46, etc., to protect the interests of SCs, STs and OBCs. Some people consider provisions like reservation of posts for backward classes, etc., as a violation of their Fundamental Rights and denial of meritorious person's legitimate due. In fact, 'merit' itself is largely a product of favourable environmental privileges and higher rating in an examination does not necessarily reflect higher intrinsic worth of the examine. Children of socially and educationally backward parents coming from rural background cannot compete on an equal footing with children from well to do homes. In view of this 'merit' and 'equality' should be viewed in proper perspective and the element of privilege should be duly recognised and discounted for when 'unequals' are made to run the same race.

Social Justice, Constitution and the Law (Chapter VII)

The element of conflict between the Fundamental Rights and the Directive Principles of State Policy has been the subject-matter of numerous Parliamentary debates and judicial pronouncements. In pursuance of Articles 15(4) and 16(4) a number of State Governments made reservations in Government services and educational institutions for OBCs and several petitions were filed before the High Courts and the Supreme Court against such orders. Gradually a sizeable body of case law has grown on the subject and a gist of it is given below.

Caste is an important factor in the identification of Other Backward Classes among Hindu communities. Backwardness must be both social and educational and not either social or educational. Caste is also a class of citizens and if the caste as a whole is socially and educationally backward, reservation can be made in favour of such a caste on the ground that it is a socially and educationally backward class of citizens within the meaning of Article 15(4). The further division of backward classes into 'backward' and 'most backward' is not warranted by Article 15(4). The aggregate reservation of posts under Article 15(4) should be less than 50 per cent. Objective criteria should be evolved on the basis of field survey, etc., for identifying OBCs.

North South Comparison of OBC Welfare (Chapter VIII)

Southern States have done much more for the welfare of Other Backward Classes than Northern States. Moreover, in the South the whole operation was conducted quite smoothly whereas in the North even modest welfare measures for OBCs have given rise to sharp resistance. The Commission approached Tata Institute of Social Sciences, Bombay, to prepare a comparative study of the 4 States of Tamil Nadu, Karnataka, Bihar and Uttar Pradesh, so as to have better appreciation of this phenomenon.

Tata Institute Study formulated a number of hypotheses in this regard. They are: Reservation scheme had a much longer history in the South; forward castes were more divided among themselves in the South; OBCs were not getting along very well with SCs/STs in the North and thus divided the backward classes movement; backward classes were more politicised in the South; reservation scheme was introduced too suddenly in the North; the capacity of backward classes to retaliate depends upon their numbers, political consciousness, dominance and perceived lack of alternative opportunities; more rapid expansion of tertiary sector gave opening to forward castes in the South which was not available to the same extent in the North, etc.

Tata Institute Study supports the above hypotheses by citing a number of examples and historical developments in the 4 States under consideration.

Evidence by Central and State Governments (Chapter IX)

Two sets of questionnaires were circulated to all State Governments, Union Territories and Ministries and Departments of Central Government for eliciting information on various aspects of our inquiry. These questionnaires were designed to obtain a comparative picture of status of backward classes in various States, steps taken for their welfare, views of various Government agencies on the question of social and educational backwardness and any useful suggestions regarding the Commission's terms of reference.

Most of the State Governments favoured caste as an important criteria for determining social and educational backwardness. Some States preferred economic criteria and some a combination of caste and means-test. Eighteen State Governments and Union Territories have taken special steps for the welfare of Other Backward Classes, though there is wide variation in the quantum of assistance provided by them. For instance, reservation in Government services for OBCs ranges from 50 per cent in the case of Karnataka and Tamil Nadu and 5 per cent in Punjab and nil in the case of Rajasthan, Orissa, Delhi, etc. Representation of OBCs in local bodies, State Public Service Commissions, High Courts, etc., is also negligible. Social discrimination is still practised against OBCs. There are a number of castes and communities which are treated as untouchables though they have not been included in the list of Scheduled Castes. All the State Governments which have launched programmes for the welfare of backward classes have to fund the same from their own resources as no separate Plan allocation is made by the Centre for this purpose.

Most States have reported loss of employment by village artisans owing to the introduction of machines, change in consumption patterns, etc.

From the information supplied by the Central Government Ministries and Departments it is seen that Other Backward Classes constitute 12.55 per cent of the total number of Government employees, whereas their aggregate population is 52 per cent. Their representation in Class I jobs is only 4.69 per cent, i.e., less than 1/10th of their proportion to the country's total population.

Evidence by the Public (Chapter X)

Nearly 2/3rd of the respondents to our questionnaire for General Public felt that no material changes have taken place in the country's caste structure since Independence. Regarding criterion for identifying backwardness, nearly 3/4th of the respondents favoured caste. More than 3/4th of the respondents also complained of various disabilities suffered by backward classes and many felt that no concrete steps have been taken to remove them. They wanted job reservation quotas to be enhanced and more educational concessions to be given to the children of OBC. Ameliorative measures suggested for OBCs were: reservation in Government employment and educational institutions; grant of interest free loans, free distribution of agricultural land and house sites; etc.

In their evidence before the Commission, Members of Sixth and Seventh Lok Sabha also expressed views similar to those summarised above. Some MPs warned against malicious propaganda being carried on by vested interests to create conflict between OBCs and SCs and STs. Some stated that the Commission should adopt those criteria for determining backwardness which have been tested before the Courts. They also suggested that the lists of OBCs prepared by State Governments and accepted by the courts should be adopted by the Commission *in toto*.

During the Commission's tour to various States, a large number of representations were received for including particular castes in the list of OBCs. Most of the other respondents expressed similar views on the criteria for identifying backward classes and measures to be taken for their upliftment as already indicated above.

Socio-Educational Field Survey — Criteria for Backwardness (Chapter XI)

A country-wide socio-educational survey covering 405 out of 407 Districts was conducted with the help of Bureau of Economics and Statistics of various states from February to June, 1980. Voluminous data gathered from the Survey was computerised and 31 primary tables were generated from this data in respect of each State and Union Territory. On the basis of these tables, 11 Indicators or Criteria for social and educational backwardness were derived and they were grouped under 3 broad heads, i.e., Social, Educational and Economic. In view of their relative importance, 3 points were assigned to each one of the Social Indicators, 2 to Educational Indicators and 1 to Economic Indicators. This added up to a total score of 22 points. All these 11 indicators were applied to each one of the castes covered by the Survey in each State. Castes obtaining a minimum score of 11 points on this scale were listed as socially and educationally backward.

Identification of OBCs (Chapter XII)

A large number of castes were identified as backward in each State as a result of the Socio-Educational Survey. As this Survey covered only 2 villages and one urban block per district, a large number of castes were naturally left out. Moreover, in some cases, the size of the sample was so small that the results were not dependable.

In view of this, two supplementary approaches were adopted to prepare complete lists of OBCs for each State. First, State-wise list of the 11 groups of primitive tribes, exterior castes, criminal tribes, etc., contained in the Registrar General of India's compilation of 1961 were culled and included in the Commission's lists or OBCs. This was done as the social and educational status of these castes and communities was more or less akin to Scheduled Castes and Scheduled Tribes. Secondly, based on the public evidence and personal knowledge of the

Members of the Commission, Statewise list of those OBCs were drawn up which could not be covered by the socio-educational survey.

It was as a result of this three pronged approach that State lists of OBCs (Volume-III) were prepared.

From the results of the field survey it was seen that some of the well-known OBCs which were also included in the lists of backward classes notified by various State Governments were not ranked as 'backward' in the survey. This is unavoidable in any sociological survey based on Statistical methods. Such aberrations were corrected in the light of the other field evidence available with the Commission.

The set of eleven Indicators (criteria), being caste-based, could not be applied to non-Hindu communities. In view of this, a separate set of 3 criteria was evolved for the identification of non-Hindu backward communities.

On the basis of the available census data, the population of Hindu and non-Hindu, OBCs was estimated to be 52 per cent of the total population of India. This is in addition to the population of Scheduled Castes and Scheduled Tribes which amounts to 22.5 per cent.

Recommendations (Chapter XIII)

Reservation for SCs and STs is in proportion to their population, i.e., 22.5 per cent. But as there is a legal obligation to keep reservations under Article 15(4) and 16(4) of the Constitution below 50 per cent, the Commission recommends a reservation of 27 per cent for OBCs. This reservation should apply to all Government services as well as technical and professional institution, both in the Centre and the States.

Special educational facilities designed at upgrading the cultural environment of the students should be created in a phased manner in selected areas containing high concentration of OBCs. Special emphasis should be placed on vocational training. Separate coaching facilities should be provided in technical and professional institutions to OBC students to enable them to catch up with students from open quota.

Special programmes for upgrading the skills of village artisans should be prepared and subsidised loans from financial institutions granted to them for setting up small scale industries. To promote the participation of OBCs in the industrial and business life of the country, a separate network of financial and technical institutions should be created by all State Governments.

Under the existing scheme of production-relations, Backward Classes comprising mainly small landholders, tenants, agricultural labour, village artisans, etc., are heavily dependent on the rich peasantry for their sustenance. In view of this OBCs continue to remain in mental and material bondage of the dominant castes and classes. Unless these production-relations are radically altered through structural changes and progressive land reforms implemented rigorously all over the country, OBCs will never become truly independent. In view of this, highest priority should be given to radical land reforms by all the States.

At present no Central assistance is available to any State for implementing any welfare measures for Other Backward Classes. Several State Governments expressed their helplessness in undertaking more purposeful development programmes for backward classes in view of lack of resources. It is, therefore, recommended that welfare programmes specially designed for OBCs should be financed by the Central Government in the same manner and to the same extent as done in the case of SCs and STs.

Recommendations

13.1 It may appear that the upliftment of Other Backward Classes is part of the larger national problem of the removal of mass poverty. This is only partially correct. The deprivation of OBCs is a very special case of the larger national issue: here the basic question is that of social and educational backwardness and poverty is only a direct consequence of these two cripplings caste-based handicaps. As these handicaps are embedded in our social structure, their removal will require far-reaching structural changes. No less important will be changes in the perception of the problems of OBCs by the ruling classes of the country.

Reservations

13.2 One such change in the attitude of the ruling elite pertains to the provision of reservation in Government services and educational institutions for the candidates of Other Backward Classes. It is generally argued that looking to the large population of OBCs (52%), recruitment of a few thousand OBCs every year against reserved vacancies is not going to produce any perceptible impact on their general condition. On the other hand, the induction of a large proportion of employees against reserved vacancies will considerably impair the quality and efficiency of the Government services. It is also stated that the benefits of such reservations will be skimmed off by those sections of OBCs which are already well off and the really backward sections will be left high and dry. Another argument advanced against this approach is that the policy of large scale reservations will cause great heart burning to those meritorious candidates whose entry into services will be barred as a result thereof.

13.3 All the above arguments are based on fairly sound reasoning. But these are also the arguments advanced by the ruling elite which is keen on preserving its privileges. Therefore, like all such reasoning, it is based on partisan approach. By the same token, while illuminating some immediate areas of concern it tends to ignore much larger issues of national importance.

13.4 It is not at all our contention that by offering a few thousand jobs to OBC candidates we shall be able to make 52 per cent of the Indian population as forward. But we must recognise that an essential part of the battle against social backwardness is to be fought in the minds of the backward people. In India, Government service has always been looked upon as a symbol of prestige and power. By increasing the representation of OBCs in Government services, we give them an immediate feeling of participation in the governance of this country. When a backward class candidate become a Collector or a Superintendent of Police, the material benefits accruing from his position are limited to the members of his family only. But the psychological spin off of this phenomenon is tremendous; the entire community of that backward class candidate feels socially elevated. Even when no tangible benefits flow to the community at large, the feeling that now it has its "own man" in the "corridors of powers" acts as a morale booster.

13.5 In a democratic set-up every individual and community has a legitimate right and aspiration to participate in ruling this country. Any situation which results in a near-denial of this right to nearly 52 per cent of the country's population needs to be urgently rectified.

13.6 Apprehensions regarding drop in the quality of Government services owing to large scale induction of SC/ST and OBC candidates against reserved posts may be justified only up to a point. But is it possible to maintain that all candidates selected on merit turn out to be honest, efficient, hard-working and dedicated? At present, top echelons of all the Government services are manned predominantly by open competition candidates and if the performance of our bureaucracy is any indication, it has not exactly covered itself with glory. Of course, this does not imply that candidates selected against reserved posts will do better. Chances are that owing to their social and cultural handicaps they may be generally a shade less competent. But, on the other hand, they will have the great advantage of possessing first hand knowledge of the sufferings and problems of the backward sections of society. This is not a small asset for field workers and policy-makers even at the highest level.

13.7 It is no doubt true that the major benefits of reservation and other welfare measures for Other Backward Classes will be cornered by the more advanced sections of the backward communities. But is not this a universal phenomenon? All reformist remedies have to contend with a slow recovery along the hierarchical gradient; there are no quantum jumps in social reform. Moreover, human nature being what it is, a "new class" ultimately does emerge even in classless societies. The chief merit of reservation is not that it will introduce egalitarianism amongst OBCs when the rest of the Indian society is seized by all sorts of inequalities. But reservation will certainly erode the hold of higher castes on the services and enable OBCs in general to have a sense of participation in running the affairs of their country.

13.8 It is certainly true that reservation for OBCs will cause a lot of heart burning to others. But should the more fact of this heart burning be allowed to operate as a moral veto against social reform. A lot of heart burning was caused to the British when they left India. It burns the hearts of all whites when the black protest against apartheid in South Africa. When the higher castes constituting less than 20 per cent of the country's population subjected the rest to all manner of social injustice, it must have caused a lot of heart burning to the lower castes. But now that the lower castes are asking for a modest share of the national cake of power and prestige, a chorus of alarm is being raised on the plea that this will cause heart burning to the ruling elite. Of all the spacious arguments advanced against reservation for backward classes, there is none which beats this one about 'heart burning' in sheer sophistry.

13.9 In fact the Hindu society has always operated a very rigorous scheme of reservation, which was internalised through caste system. Eklivya lost his thumb and Shambhuk his neck for their breach of caste rules of reservation. The present furore against reservations for

OBCs is not aimed at the principle itself, but against the new class beneficiaries, as they are now clamouring for a share of the opportunities which were all along monopolised by the higher castes.

Quantum and Scheme of Reservations

13.10 Scheduled Castes and Scheduled Tribes constitute 22.5 per cent of the country's population. Accordingly, a *pro-rata* reservation of 22.5 per cent has been made for them in all services and public sector undertakings under the Central Government. In the States also, reservation for SCs and STs is directly proportional to their population in each State.

13.11 As stated in the last Chapter (para 12.22) the population of OBCs, both Hindu and non-Hindu, is around 52 per cent of the total population of India. Accordingly, 52 per cent of all posts under the Central Government should be reserved for them. But this provision may go against the law laid down in a number of Supreme Court judgements wherein it has been held that the total quantum of reservation under Articles 15(4) and 16(4) of the Constitution should be below 50 per cent. In view of this the proposed reservation for OBCs would have to be pegged at a figure which, when added to 22.5 per cent for SCs and STs, remains below 50 per cent. In view of this legal constraint, the Commission is obliged to recommend a reservation of 27 per cent only, even though their population is almost twice this figure.

13.12 States which have already introduced reservation for OBCs exceeding 27 per cent, will remain unaffected by this recommendation.

13.13 With the above general recommendations regarding the quantum of reservation, the Commission proposes the following overall scheme of reservation for OBCs:

(1) Candidates belonging to OBCs recruited on the basis of merit in an open competition should not be adjusted against their reservation quota of 27 per cent.
(2) The above reservation should also be made applicable to promotion quota at all levels.
(3) Reserved quota remaining unfilled should be carried forward for a period of three years and dereserved thereafter.
(4) Relaxation in the upper age limit for direct recruitment should be extended to the candidates of OBCs in the same manner as done in the case of SCs and STs.

(5) A roster system for each category of posts should be adopted by the concerned authorities in the same manner as presently done in respect of SC and ST candidates.

13.14 The above scheme of reservation in its total should also be made applicable to all recruitment to public sector undertakings both under the Central and State Governments, as also to nationalised banks.

13.15 All private sector undertakings which have received financial assistance from the Government in one form or the other should also be obliged to recruit personnel on the aforesaid basis.

13.16 All universities and affiliated colleges should also be covered by the above scheme of reservation.

13.17 To give proper effect to these recommendations, it is imperative that adequate statutory provisions are made by the Government to amend the existing enactments, rules, procedures, etc., to the extent they are not in consonance with the same.

Educational Concessions

13.18 Our educational system is elitist in character, results in a high degree of wastage and is least suited to the requirements of an over-populated and developing country. It is a legacy of the British rule which was severely criticised during the independence struggle and yet, it has not undergone any structural changes. Though it is least suited to the needs of backward classes, yet, they are forced to run the rat-race with others as no options are available to them. As 'educational reform' was not within the terms of reference of this Commission, we are also forced to trend the beaten track and suggest only the palliative measure within the existing framework.

13.19 Various State Governments are giving a number of educational concessions to Other Backward Class students (Chapter IX, paras 9.30 to 9.33) like exemption of tuition fees, free supply of books and clothes, mid-day meals, special hostel facilities stipends, etc. These concessions are all right as far as they go. But they do not go far enough. What is required is, perhaps, not so much the provision of additional funds as the framing of integrated scheme for creating the proper environment and incentives for serious and purposeful studies.

13.20 It is well known that most backward class children are irregular and indifferent students and their drop-out rate is very high.

There are two main reasons for this. First, these children are brought up is a climate of extreme social and cultural deprivation and, consequently, a proper motivation for schooling is generally lacking. Secondly, most of these children come from very poor homes and their parents are forced to press them into doing small chores from a very young age.

13.21 Upgrading the cultural environment is a very slow process. Transferring these children to an artificially upgraded environment is beyond the present sources of the country. In view of this it is recommended that this problem may be tackled on a limited and selective basis on two fronts.

13.22 First, an intensive and time bound programme for adult education should be launched in selected pockets with high concentration of OBC population. This is a basic motivational approach, as only properly motivated parents will take serious interest in educating their children. Secondly, residential schools should be set up in these areas for backward class students to provide a climate specially conducive to serious studies. All facilities in these schools including board and lodging, will have to be provided free of cost to attract students from poor and backward homes, separate Governments hostels for OBC students with the above facilities will be another step in the right direction.

13.23 A beginning on both these fronts will have to be made on a limited scale and selective basis. But the scope of these activities should be expanded as fast as the resources permit. Adult education programme and residential schools started on a selective basis will operate as growing-points of consciousness for the entire community and their multiplier effect is bound to be substantial. Whereas several States are extended a number of *ad hoc* concessions to backward class students, few serious attempts have been made to integrate these facilities into a comprehensive scheme for a qualitative upgradation of educational environment available to OBC students.

13.24 After all, education is the best catalyst of change and educating the backward classes is the surest way to improve their self-image and raise their social status. As OBCs cannot afford the high wastage rates of our educational system, it is very important that their education is highly biased in favour of vocational training. After all reservation in services will absorb only a very small percentage of the educated backward classes and the rest should be suitably equipped with vocational skills to enable them to get a return on having invested several years in education.

13.25 It is also obvious that even if all the above facilities are given to OBC students, they will not be able to compete on an equal footing with others in securing admission to technical and professional institutions. In view of this it is recommended that seats should be reserved for OBC students in all scientific, technical and professional institutions run by the Central as well as State Governments. This reservation will fall under Article 15(4) of the Constitution and the quantum of reservation should be the same as in the Government services, i.e., 27 per cent. Those States which have already reserved more than 27 per cent seats for OBC students will remain unaffected by this recommendation.

13.26 While implementing the provision for reservation it should also be ensured that the candidates who are admitted against the reserved quota are enabled to derive full benefit of higher studies. It has been generally noticed that these OBC students coming from an impoverished cultural background, are not able to keep abreast with other students. It is, therefore, very essential that special coaching facilities are arranged for all such students in our technical and professional institutions. The concerned authorities should clearly appreciate that their job is not finished once candidates against reserved quota have been admitted to various institutions. In fact the real task starts only after that. Unless adequate follow-up action is taken to give special coaching assistance to these students, not only these young people will feel frustrated and humiliated but the country will also be landed with ill-equipped and sub-standard engineers, doctors and other professionals.

Financial Assistance

13.27 Vocational communities following hereditary occupations have suffered heavily as a result of industrialisation. Mechanical production and introduction of synthetic materials has robbed the village potter, oil crusher, black-smith, carpenter, etc., of their traditional means of livelihood and the pauperisation these classes is a well known phenomenon in the country-side.

13.28 It has, therefore, become very necessary that suitable institutional finance and technical assistance is made available to such members of village vocational communities who want to set-up small scale industries on their own. Similar assistance should also be provided to those promising OBC candidates who have obtained special vocational training.

13.29 Of course, most State Governments have created various financial and technical agencies for the promotion of small and medium scale industries. But it is well known that only the more influential members of the community are able to derive benefits from these agencies. In view of this, it is very essential that separate financial institutions for providing financial and technical assistance are established for the backward classes. Some State Governments such as Karnataka and Andhra Pradesh have already set-up separate financial corporations, etc., for OBCs.

13.30 Cooperative Societies of occupational groups will also help a lot. But due care should be taken that all the office-bearers and members of such societies belong to the concerned hereditory occupational groups and outsiders are not allowed to exploit them by infiltrating into such cooperatives.

13.31 The share of OBCs in the industrial and business life of the country is negligible and this partly explains their extremely low income levels. As a part of its overall strategy to uplift the backward classes, it is imperative that all State Governments are suitably advised and encouraged to create a separate network of financial and technical institutions to foster business and industrial enterprise among OBCs.

Structural Changes

13.32 Reservations in Government employment and educational institutions, as also all possible financial assistance will remain mere palliatives unless the problem of backwardness is tackled at its root. Bulk of small land-holders, tenants, agricultural labour, impoverished village artisans, unskilled workers, etc., belong to Scheduled Castes, Scheduled Tribes and Other Backward Classes. "Apart from social traditions, the dominance by the top peasantry is exercised through recourse to informal bondage which arises mainly through money-lending, leasing out of small bits of land and providing house-sites and dwelling space to poor peasants. As most of the functionaries of Government are drawn from the top peasantry, the class and caste linkage between the functionaries of Government and the top peasantry remain firm. This also tilts the socio-political balance in favour of the top peasantry and helps it in having its dominance over others."

* Rising Middle Peasantry in North India by Pradhan M. Prasad, *Economic and Political Weekly*, Annual Number 1980.

13.33 The net outcome of the above situation is that notwithstanding their numerical preponderance, backward classes continue to remain in mental and material bondage of the higher castes and rich peasantry. Consequently, despite constituting nearly 3/4th of the country's population, Scheduled Castes, Scheduled Tribes and Other Backward Classes have been able to acquire a very limited political clout, even though adult franchise was introduced more than three decades back. Through their literal monopoly of means of production the higher castes are able to manipulate and coerce the backward classes into acting against their own interests. In view of this, until the stranglehold of the existing production relations is broken through radical land reforms, the abject dependence of under privileged classes on the dominant higher castes will continue indefinitely. In fact there is already a sizeable volume of legislation on the statute books to abolish zamindari, place ceilings on land-holdings and distribute land to the landless. But in actual practice its implementation has been halting, half-hearted and superficial. The States such as Karnataka, Kerala and West Bengal which have gone about the job more earnestly have not only succeeded in materially helping the backward classes, but also reaped rich political dividends into the bargain.

13.34 It is the Commission's firm conviction that a radical transformation of the existing production relations is the most important single step that can be taken for the welfare and upliftment of all backward classes. Even if this is not possible in the industrial sector for various reasons, in the agricultural sector a change of this nature is both feasible and overdue.

13.35 The Commission, therefore, strongly recommends that all the State Governments should be directed to enact and implement progressive land legislation so as to effect basic structural changes in the existing production relations in the countryside.

13.36 At present surplus land is being allotted to SCs and STs. A part of the surplus land becoming available in future as a result of the operation of land ceiling laws, etc., should also be allotted to the OBC landless labour.

Miscellaneous

13.37 (i) Certain sections of some occupation communities such as Fishermen, Banjaras, Bansforas, Khatwes, etc., still suffer from the stigma of untouchability in some parts of the country. They have been listed as OBCs by the Commission, but their inclusion in the lists of Scheduled Castes/Scheduled Tribes may be considered by the Government;

(ii) Backward Classes Development Corporation should be set-up both at the Central and State level to implement various socio-educational and economic measures for their advancement;

(iii) A separate Ministry/Department for OBCs at the Centre and the States should be created to safeguard their interests; and

(iv) With a view to giving better representation to certain very backward sections of OBCs like the Gaddis in Himachal Pradesh, Neo-Buddhists in Maharashtra, Fishermen in the Coastal areas, Gujjars in J&K, it is recommended that areas of their concentration may be carved out into separate constituencies at the time of delimitation.

Central Assistance

13.38 At present no Central Assistance is available to any State Government for implementing any welfare measures for Other Backward Classes. The 18 States and Union Territories which have under taken such measures have to provide funds from their own resources. During the Commission's tour practically every State Government pointed out that unless the Centre is prepared to liberally finance at special schemes for the upliftment of OBCs, it will be beyond the available resources of the States to undertake any worthwhile programme for the benefit of Other Backward Classes.

13.39 The Commission fully shares the views of the State Governments in this matter and strongly recommends that all development programmes specially designed for Other Backward Classes should be financed by the Central Government in the same manner and to the same extent as done in the case of Scheduled Castes and Scheduled Tribes.

13.40 Regarding the period of operation of the Commission's recommendations, the entire scheme should be reviewed after twenty years. We have advisedly suggested this span of one generation, as the raising of social consciousness is a generational progress. Any review at a shorter interval would be rather arbitrary and will not give a fair indication of the impact of our recommendations on the prevailing status and life-styles of OBCs.

Summary and Conclusions

The hypotheses given in Chapter I essentially aim at explaining the phenomenon of violent backlash to the reservation scheme promulgated in U.P. and Bihar in 1977 and 1978 respectively. Various political sociological and political economic factors have been examined mainly in terms of the evolution of the balance of power among the caste groups. The following conclusions emerge.

1. In Tamil Nadu and Karnataka, the reservation schemes have had a long history. In the beginning only the Brahmins were kept out. They were too weak to protest and slowly learnt to live with reservation schemes. They sought and obtained alternative avenues of employment. In 1950, substantial sections of the Vellalas, Naidus, Modaliars, Gounders, Chettiyars were kept out. But by then they had established their political ascendancy. They had sufficiently infiltrated into the power structure to do without the protection of the reservations. Moreover, only a few of the really backwards offered them any serious competition.

In U.P. and Bihar, the job and seat reservation schemes came as a bolt from the blue for the forward castes. Had they been covered by the reservation schemes earlier and slowly shunted off to the open competition pool, it would have been a different matter. The historical circumstances did not necessitate this.

2. In Tamil Nadu and Karnataka, the forward communities have been divided either by the classification schemes or politically, or both. As discussed in the Tamil Nadu chapter, the Vellalas, Chettiars and Naidus have all been divided into forward sub-castes and backward sub-castes. They cannot make a common cause of the reservation issue. The possibility of any alliance among them has been pre-empted or prevented. Similarly in Karnataka, 70 per cent of the Lingayat castes find themselves forward and the rest backward. The 15 per cent reservation for the special weaker group irrespective of caste has also divided the Lingayat community. The forward Lingayats are the only group highly agitated over the issue. But, they cannot convert their disaffection into political clout. Also, the Karnataka G.O. has put all the Vokkaligas, another dominant landed gentry caste, into the backward

list. Just until ten years ago, both the castes had formed a duopoly and ruled the State. Now, no alliance can take place between them. All the political parties there have to reckon with this changed situation.

In Bihar, and U.P. the G.Os. have not divided the forward castes. In Bihar, despite a long history of the feuds between the Bhumihars and Rajputs, these castes find themselves united on the issue of reservation. In U.P. where caste feuds were muted the Yadav G.O. has united twenty per cent of the articulate, organised and powerful section of the population. The Rajputs are particularly upset. Only recently they had begun to make their entry into echelons of power and were suddenly thwarted.

The reservation of three per cent for the economically weaker section is just a drop in the ocean, for the Bihar forward castes. Had this share been larger, probably, the forward castes would have found themselves divided and too weak to resort to backlash.

3. Both Tamil Nadu and Karnataka have witnessed cases of Harijan baiting and atrocities on them at the hands of the middle order castes. But such instances are few. In Tamil Nadu, the DK movement welded the non-Brahmin upper castes and the Harijans into one camp. In fact non-Sanskritic area, the ritual and cultural distances between these two groups was less than that between the brahmins and non-Brahmins. In Karnataka, the Harijan and the OBCs find themselves in one camp due to their resentment of the Brahmins in the beginning, and Lingayats later on.

In U.P. and Bihar the Harijans and other landless castes, on the one hand, and the landed backward castes on the other have never had mutuality of economic, social and political interests. If the forward castes fear rank disequilibrium at the hands of the upper peasant castes in the OBC category, the latter also feel threatened by the rising political consciousness on the part of the Harijans. The latter are driven hard by their Kurmi, Koeri, Yadav employers. Atrocities on the Harijans have been committed by the members belonging to these peasant castes. Harijans have generally gone with Brahmins in voting for Congress. This fundamental cleavage between the upper peasant castes and the Harijans has rendered the backward class movement weak and hence has facilitated the forward castes backlash. As long as the OBC castes are in the grip of Sanskritisation, they cannot lead the Harijans.

4. In Tamil Nadu and Karnataka, the non-Brahmins made a solid, united and well organised entry into politics and the higher echelons of the Congress party. Their politicisation began a long time

ago. This has imparted considerable strength of the backward classes movement. In Karnataka particularly, Devaraj Urs went on encouraging the holding of the conferences of the minor weaker non-dominant castes, between 1972 and 1978. He had inducted their leaders into the corridors of power. After preparing the political ground and organising the weaker OBCs, he got his famous G.O. issued in 1978. The organisation and mobilisation were sufficient to deter any potential backlash.

In U.P. and Bihar the ground had not been adequately prepared. In a sense, the Yadav and Thakur G.Os. were planted from above, when the ground had not been cleared. In Bihar, the backward castes entered politics (and the Congress) divided. Their entry depended on the mercy of the forward caste leaders. They have not been held together as an autonomous coherent political force. Witness the contest for the Chief Ministership in 1963 between Birchand Patel and K.B. Sahay. (Patel's abilities had attracted the attention of even Pandit Nehru). Both the backwards and Harijans deserted Patel. In U.P. also the rise of the backward classes was belated. As said earlier, both Thakur and Yadav attempted to telescope the backward castes mobilisation into a decade. Even today the backward castes are politically divided. The weakness of the backward castes is evident from the fact their share of cabinet posts and the assembly seats has been waxing and waning. The elections of 1967 and 1977 did not signify a permanent and abiding resurgence of the backward castes on the political scene of U.P. and Bihar. Karpoori Thakur and Ram Naresh Yadav definitely erred in thinking that they did.

5. There is no doubt that in Tamil Nadu, the Youth belonging to the non-Brahmin forward castes must be experiencing the cruch of the reservation scheme. But quite a few of them can take advantage of the vagueness and fluidity of the classification based on sub-castes. The seriousness of this rampant misuse has been statistically proved by the Tamil Nadu Backward Classes Commission Report. As long as such misuse is possible, the propensity for frustration and aggression is relatively reduced. In Karnataka, too, this is happening, but not to the same extent. In this State, misuse of the provision for the special group whose income does not exceed, Rs. 4,800 per annum, has been reported.

The Bihar and U.P. classifications do not permit any falsification of castes, as the classification is based on the broad caste lines, and not on sub-caste lines. A Rajput cannot pass off as a Kurmi or Koeri and remain undetected for a long time.

6. A second stage of the resurgence of the weaker among the backward castes has been delayed in Tamil Nadu. The non-Brahmin forward castes dominate the services and professions, because of the earlier head start. Nine castes in the list of the OBCs have gained a lot from the operation of the reservation scheme. The situation, theoretically, is ideal for a second stage of the movement. If this develops, and if these OBC castes which have gained disproportionately are excluded from the list, we may expect a backlash. But the weaker backward castes have not even protested against the inclusion of the Sozhia Vallalal Gounders, etc., in the list in 1973. This absence of resentment and protest is in a large measure due to the Tamil revivalism and sub-nationalism.

In Karnataka, there has been no such revivalism movement to delay the upsurge of the weaker among the backward castes.

7. Owing to the classification in Tamil Nadu along the sub-caste lines, it is difficult to fix the percentage of the population which is classified as forward. In Karnataka, it is really the forward Lingayats, constituting about 10 to 12 per cent of the population who are really adversely affected and feel agitated. In that State the Christians, Vaishyas and Brahmins have written off the government service.

In Uttar Pradesh the population classified as forward is considerable, i.e., around 20 per cent. In Bihar, the numerically small strength of the forwards, i.e., around 13 per cent is more than made up by its control over the countryside. The legacy of semi-feudalism in these two States has enabled these forward castes to fight bitterly against the reservation scheme.

8. The economies of Tamil Nadu and Karnataka have been expanding relatively faster. The private tertiary sector appears to be growing. It can shelter many forward caste youths. Also, they are prepared to migrate outside the State.

The private tertiary sectors in Bihar and U.P. are stagnant. The forwarded caste youths in these two States have to depend heavily on government jobs. Driven to desperation, they have reacted violently.

Minute of Dissent by Shri L.R. Naik, Ex-M.P. (Member)
Backward Classes Commission

I have endeavoured to the best of my ability and understanding of the socio-educational problems of the backward classes of citizens of India to assist the Chairman and other Members of the Backward Classes Commission in carrying out the arduous task entrusted to them by the President of India in terms of reference prescribed. I am happy that I received full co-operation and encouragement from them, especially Shri B.P. Mandal, Chairman of the Commission. It is, therefore, not without feelings of regret and reluctance that I write a separate minute of dissent only with reference to categorisation of socially and educationally backward classes of citizens, identified by the Commission in terms of reference made to them.

The Commission have, on certain criteria as delineated in Chapter XI prepared a common list of socially and educationally backward classes of citizens and I suggest its modifications in the following manner:

> I held very sincerely that castes/classes mentioned in the common list, each having homogeneous and cohesive characteristics, are not at the same degree or level of social and educational backwardness and I fear that the safeguards recommended for their advancement will not percolate to less unfortunate sections among them and the constitutional objectives proclaiming an establishment of an egalitarian society will remain a myth. Some of the communities in the common list who would be called hereinafter as 'Intermediate Backward Classes' on the lines delineated in the report of the Tata Institute of Social Studies (Volume IV) have made their presence felt in the caste hierarchical society in India, either on their numerical strength or their age-old co-existence along with other advance communities in villages and towns. Given better opportunities and encouragement in future, I have, no doubt, in my mind that they would integrate with the general populace sooner than later. But there are number of castes and classes in the common list who are incapable of making such a dent, in the near future, being extremely backward, both socially and educationally and also economically. Their economical backwardness is evidently the consequence of their age-old social and educational backwardness. By way of clarity they would be hereinafter, called 'Depressed Backward Classes' as distinct from the 'Intermediate Backward Classes'. I am of the opinion that these unfortunate classes of people, i.e., 'Depressed Backward Classes' steeped as they are in massive backwardness would take time for their enlightenment and advancement, unless, of course, concerted efforts, at national

levels, are made by way of sagacious inputs of safeguards the benefits of which should be percolated to them in a large measure. So there is a compelling need to sift them carefully from the main common list and create a separate entity of equals or near-equals to bring about a healthy competition among them for the benefits of safeguards. The rest of the communities in the common list should then form a distinct category for the same reason of creating an atmosphere for competition among equals for the safeguards. This device is necessary in the interest of the nation as a whole.

The 'Intermediate Backward Classes', in my opinion, are those whose traditional occupation had been agriculture, market gardening, beatle-leaves growers, pastoral activities, village industries such as artisans, tailors, dyers and weavers, petty business-cum-agricultural activities, heralding, temple service, toddy selling, oil mongering, combating, astrology, etc. etc., who have co-existed since times immemorial with upper castes and had, therefore, some scope to embibe better association and what all it connotates than many unfortunate 'Depressed Backward Classes' whose intermingling with the Indian society was either denied, prohibited and even segregated obviously on account of stigma of their traditional occupations, stigma of criminality, stigma of nomadism resulting in their abysmally low social status. They, generally, are ex-criminal tribes, nomadic and wandering tribes, earth diggers, fishermen, boatmen and palanquin bearers, salt makers, washermen, shepherds, barbers, scavengers, basket makers, furriers and tanners, landless agricultural labourers, watermen toddy tappers, camel-hardsmen, pig keepers, pack bullock carriers, collectors of forest produce, hunters and fowlers, corn parchers, primitive tribes (not specified as Scheduled Tribes), exterior classes (not specified as Scheduled Castes), and begging communities, etc. etc.

These very names amply connote their social and educational backwardness and, therefore, should have been postulated by the Founding Fathers of our Constitution as in the case of the Scheduled Castes and Scheduled Tribes for the purpose of specification. Thing that are obvious need no proof. I sincerely consider that this lapse on the part of our Constitution makers has resulted in a serious constraint in establishing an egalitarian society based on justice; social, economical and political. Three decades of Independence and the dawn of freedom is yet to bestow a willing smile on many a hamlet and slum of these unfortunate segments of the Indian society. They continue to submit to the decrees of fate rather than have the benefits of the decrees of our basic laws. Liberty, Equality and Fraternity so richly enshrined in the Constitution of our country have still to acquire meaningful proposition for all of them. Most of these communities are either Scheduled Tribes, Scheduled Castes depending on their characteristics in relation to some States, but not so in other States.

During the course of my extensive tours throughout the length and breadth of India, I observed that a tendency is fast developing among 'Intermediate Backward Classes' to repeat the treatments or rather ill-treatments, they themselves have received from times immemorial at the hands of the upper castes, against their brethren, I mean, 'the Depressed Backward Classes'. In an unequal society like ours, it is necessary that the Commission take all precautions so that the more helpless and needy segments are not deprived of the benefits of the various safeguards by avoiding cut-throat competition among unequals. The casteism is still very much in our midst and this is assuming new forms without showing much loss of its original vitality. In fact, several observers feel that the logic of democratic politics and mass mobilisation has brought casteism to the Centre of the stage. It is with regret, I affirm that political leaders belonging to 'Intermediate Backward Classes' are not immune from such aberration nor they are imaginative enough to bring about the advancement of the people who are at the bottom of our society, such as these 'Depressed Backward Classes'. All that they seem to be doing is to emulate some disgruntled upper castes in userping economic and political power in the name of backward classes. This is a mental aberration which deserves outright condemnation from whatever quarters it may emanate — whether from Upper Castes or Intermediate Backward Classes.

The ancient adage that 'if a big fish and a small fish are put together, the former will swallow the latter', is still very apt in the context of the caste hierarchical society of India. Care should, therefore, be taken with all emphasis at our command that the benefits of safeguards are dispersed equitably and rationally, as far as possible, among all sections of the backward classes. This, I consider, can happen by avoiding competition for benefits among unequals or by bringing about competition among equals. I, therefore, propose that the common fist should be categorised into two parts, 'A' and 'B'; 'A' consisting of those classes whom I have described as 'Depressed Backward Classes' and 'B' the rest of the communities in the list to be described as 'Intermediate Backward Classes'. The list of 'Depressed

Backward Classes' in relation to States and Union Territories is given in Annexure II.

Quantum of Reservation

A percentage distribution of Indian population by castes and religious groups has been indicated in the body of the main Report. It is seen therefrom that the percentage population of Other Backward Classes including non-Hindu communities is derived at 52. It is further seen that the population percentage of Hindu backward castes/groups is 43.70, whereas that of non-Hindu communities is 8.40. Now on categorisation of Other Backward Classes into 'Intermediate Backward Classes' and 'Depressed Backward Classes', a fresh statement of percentage distribution of Indian population is prepared and is at Annexure I.

It is seen therefrom that the percentage population of 'Depressed Backward Classes' is 25.56 and that of 'Intermediate Backward Classes' is 26.44. It is undoubtedly safe to assume that these two categories are equal to each other from their population point of view.

After good deal of discussions with which I am in full agreement, the Commission has recommended reservations to the extent of 27 per cent in all services under the Central Government. It has further recommended that seats should be reserved in all scientific, technical and professional institutions run by the Central as well as State Governments and the quantum of reservation should be the same as in public services, i.e., 27 per cent.

In all fairness and in view of the fact that the 'Depressed Backward Classes' are comparable in matters of backwardness to those of the Scheduled Castes and Scheduled Tribes, I recommend 15 per cent reservation for them out of 27 per cent both in public services and educational institutions as mentioned above. For all other concessions they should be treated on par with SC/ST. I refrain from recommending political reservation. I, however, urge them to unite and organise. They have nothing to lose except their chains of age-old degradation, social, economical and political. Hatred towards none and love and affection for all should be their motto. They should recognise that an essential part of their battle against their social backwardness is to be fought in their own minds for their own salvation. At the same time, I have a work of caution for the ruling elite in our country that there cannot be an egalitarian society unless the depressed are enabled to be on par with them. They should, therefore, refrain from agitating against any reservation for the backwards and if they do so it is at their own peril and that of the nation.

Acknowledgement

I am quite aware that Shri B.P. Mandal, Chairman of the Commission is mainly responsible for my induction in the Commission. I am grateful to him. His encouragement and profound kindness that he showered on me will be ever cherished. I am also grateful to my other esteemed and distinguished colleagues for their co-operation.

I must put on record the invaluable co-operation and assistance I received from Dr. S. Bheemappa, Professor of Surgery, Bangalore Medical College, Bangalore (Karnataka) in identifying the 'Depressed Backward Classes' from all over India and in deriving their population figures. It has been his second habit to understand the problems of the underdog at their depth. His expert advice on the subject to the Commission deserves all appreciation.

I am also grateful to all Co-opted Members from all the States and Union Territories for their co-operation and advice.

ANNEXURE II

STATEWISE LISTS OF THE DEPRESSED BACKWARD CLASSES

ANDHRA PRADESH

1. Achukatalavandhu
2. Adi Karnataka
3. Aryakshatriya, Chittari, Chitrakara, Giniyar, Nkha
4. Bandara
5. Balasanthu, Bahurupi
6. Banda
7. Bandara
8. Bathini
9. Battada
10. Begari
11. Bellara
12. Bestha, Jelare, Vade-Balaji, Neyyalu, Agnikula-Kshatriya, Palli, Gangaputragoondla, Parvatharajakulam, Gangavar
13. Bhamta
14. Bhettadas-Bodo, Bhottads, Muriabhattada and Sano Bhottads
15. Bissoy-Barangi Jodia, Bannangi, Daduva, Godo Jodia, Hollar, Jheriya, Kollai, Konde, Paranga, Pergajodia, Prangi, Takora
16. Boya, Valmiki
17. Badabukkala
18. Budbukk
19. Bukka
20. Burbook
21. Chakala, Chawla, Dhobi, Rajaka, Chakali, Vannar
22. Chopemari
23. Chatri-Agnikulaksatryaya, Bombili
24. Cheruman
25. Chintala
26. Damala
27. Dasari
28. Dasari (Donga & Gudu)
29. Dhakkada
30. Dher
31. Dommara
32. Dombo
33. Dombs-Andhiya Dombs, Audiniya Dombs, Chonel Dombs, Christian Dombs, Nirgani Dombs, Oriya Dombs, Ponaka Dombs, Telaga Dombs, Ummia Dombs
34. Dongayatha
35. Dommara
36. Gangani
37. Garodi
38. Godaba

38A. Gavara

39. Godala
40. Goudus-Bato (Bhirithya) Dudhokuria, Hata, Jatako and Joria
41. Gudala
42. Hasla
43. Irula
44. Jogi

44A. Joshinadidala

45. Kadan
46. Kaikadi (or Koracha or Korwa)
47. Kalladi, Kalwar
48. Kanakkan
49. Kandra
50. Kaniyan
51. Kanjar
52. Kanjara-Bhatta
53. Kampmare or Reddika
54. Kapumaries
55. Karimpalan
56. Katipamula
57. Koraga
58. Khond
59. Kochi
60. Kodalo

61. Kond (Kui)
62. Koosa
63. Kota
64. Koti
65. Krishnabalija (Dasari Bukka)
66. Kudiya
67. Kudubi
68. Kudumban
69. Kurakula
70. Kuravan
71. Kurichchan
72. Madri
72Á. Mandula
73. Maila
74. Malasar
75. Mondi Patta
76. Mali (excluding the areas where treated as Scheduled Tribe)
77. Malis-Kerchia Malis, Paiko Malis and Peddamali
77A. Maugala
78. Medari or Mahendra
79. Moger
80. Mondiwar
81. Mondivaru, Mondi Banda, Banda
82. Manula
83. Muliya
84. Muria
85. Nagavaddilu
86. Naik
87. Naikappu
88. Nakkalas
89. Nayadi
90. Neelakanthi
91. Neyyala
92. Nhavi
93. Nirshikaris
94. Nokkar
95. Nolakeyava
96. Nolli
97. Oddars (or Waddars)
98. Odde, Odder, Vadde, Oddilu, Vaddi, Vadde
99. Omanaito
100. Pacha Bhotla
101. Pachabotla
102. Padampari
103. Pagadai
104. Paigarapu
105. Painda
106. Palakari
107. Pallan
108. Pambala
109. Pamula
110. Panan
111. Paniyan
112. Panniandi
113. Pareiyan
114. Pardhi (Nirshikari)
115. Paravan
116. Perika
117. Pariki Muggula
118. Passi
118A. Pondara
119. Petias
120. Picharis
121. Pitchiguntala
122. Poligars
123. Poroja-Bado, Perojaor Sodia, Jodia Peroja, Pareng Peroja and Sono Poroja
124. Poosala
125. Pulayan
126. Puthiraj Vannan
127. Rachkoya
128. Raneyar
129. Raulo
130. Saora
131. Sapari
132. Sare
133. Senatal
134. Sholaga
135. Sholager
136. Sindhor
137. Singalu
138. Sore
139. Sunna
140. Taleyari
141. Thottia Naicks
142. Yoda
143. Uppar, Sagar
144. Valluvan
145. Valmiki
146. Valmiki Boya (Boya, Bedar,

Kirataka, Nishadi, Yellapi Pedda Boya) Talayari and Ghundu Vallu

147. Thogra, Bholla Baliga
148. Vadder-Bevi, Upparilu
149. Vettuvan
150. Waddar or Kala Waddars or Pathrods
151. Wadla
152. Yueruleu
153. Yaras
154. Yata
155. Yetla

ASSAM

1. Barjubi
2. Baria
3. Bhumij
4. Bhuyan
5. Choudang
6. Chutia, Chutiya
7. Dhamai
8. Ghatuar
9. Gor
10. Kandhai
11. Karbi
12. Maria
13. Moran, Matak
14. Mukhi
15. Munda
16. Mura
17. Nai, Bij, Hajjam, Napit
18. Nonia, Nunia
19. Oraon
20. Santhal, Santal
21. Sudra Das, Dey
22. Sut, Soot
23. Tipara, Tipera
24. Arya Mala
25. Asur
26. Baiga
27. Baijara
28. Basor
29. Basphor
30. Bauri
31. Bedia
32. Beldar
33. Bharaik
34. Bhil
35. Bhokta
36. Bhumij
37. Bhuiyan
38. Binjia
39. Birhor
40. Birjia
41. Bondo
42. Bowri
43. Chamar
44. Chere
45. Chick Banik
46. Dandari
47. Dandasi
48. Dhanwar
49. Dusad
50. Ganda
51. Ghansi
52. Ghatowar
53. Gonda
54. Gonds
55. Gorait
56. Hari
57. Holra
58. Kalahandi
59. Kalihandi
60. Karmali
61. Kashan
62. Kawar
63. Keot
64. Kharia
65. Kherwar
66. Khodal
67. Khond
68. Khonyor
69. Kohor
70. Kol
71. Kondpan
72. Kormakar
73. Korwa
74. Kotwal
75. Koya
76. Madari
77. Mahli
78. Majwar
79. Malpaharia

80. Manki
81. Mirdhar
82. Mohli
83. Mundas
84. Nagasia
85. Nath
86. Oraon
87. Paidi
88. Panika
89. Pans
90. Parja
91. Pasi
92. Sahora
93. Santhals (Santal)
94. Severas
95. Tausa
96. Turi

BIHAR

1. Abdal
2. Agariya
3. Adhiri
4. Amaat
5. Bagdo
6. Bajigar
7. Banpur
8. Bangalo
9. Bari
10. Basphor
11. Bekhada
12. Beldar, Bachgotra, Sapera
13. Beldiya
14. Bentkar
15. Bhar
16. Bharbhuja
17. Bhuihar, Bhuiyar, Bhubhalia
18. Bind
19. Binjina
20. Chandrabhanshi (Kahar)
21. Chain, Chayeen
22. Chanou
23. Chapota
24. Chatwal
25. Devhar
26. Dhamin
27. Dhankar
28. Dhanwar
29. Dhari
30. Dhekaru
31. Dheha
32. Dhimar
33. Dhunia, Dhumian
34. Gadaba
35. Gandharb
36. Ghatwar
37. Ghusuria
38. Godo (Chhavo), Godhi
39. Godra
40. Goskha
41. Gonrh, Gorh, Godh, Gothahum
42. Goud
43. Gulgaliya
44. Irika
45. Jadup
46. Jogi, Jogo, Jugi
47. Juang
48. Kabari
49. Kadar
50. Kahar, Chandraborai, Chatrapati, Chotra-Bansi, Ramani, Rawani, Paneri
51. Kalwar
52. Kamkar
53. Kandra
54. Kapadia
55. Karwalnut
56. Kawar
57. Kela
58. Keet
59. Khadwar
60. Khangar
61. Khatik
62. Koli
63. Korku
64. Kumarbhag Pahadia
65. Kanjra Ghara
66. Kritiria
67. Lalbegi, Bhangi (Muslim)
68. Madar
69. Mahuria
70. Majhwar
71. Malnar (Malhor)
72. Mali (Malakar)
73. Mallah, Birha, Goyatri, Ghetwel,

Jalwar, Kewat, Kurwaha Maheta, Majhi Muriyoni, Masuria, Phutant, Purhia, Nisad, Goshi, Dhiwar, Jhiwar, Jhimar
74. Mangan
75. Mangar (Magar)
76. Markande
77. Marwari Bauria
78. Muriaro
79. Namshudra
80. Nonia, Kharwat, Nunia
81. Pahira
82. Pal (Bherihar-Gaderi)
83. Parya
84. Pathekut, Bachigolia
85. Patwa
86. Pinganiya
87. Rajdhobi
88. Rangwa
89. Sangastrash
90. Sauta (Sota)
91. Soir, Soyar
92. Sunri
93. Tamariya
94. Tharu
95. Thathera
96. Tiyar
97. Turha, Sao

GUJARAT

1. Adodia
2. Agri
3. Banjara, Vanjara, Charan Banjara, Mathura Banjarah, Maru Banjara, Bagora Banjara, Kangashia Banjara, Bamaina Banjara, Gavaria, Gavalia, Rohidas Banjara
4. Barot, Vahivancha, Charan Gadhvi
5. Burud
6. Bavri or Baori
7. Bhalia
8. Bhamta, Pardeshi Bhamta
9. Bharwad (excluding Nesses of forest of Alech Barada and Gir)
10. Bhoi, Bhoiraj, Dhimar, Zingabhoi, Kevat, Bhoi, Bhanara Bhoi, Machhindra Bhoi, Palewar Bhoi, Kirat Bhoi, Keher Bhoi, Pardesh Bhoi, Shrimali Bhoi
11. Chakrawadya Dasar
12. Chuvalia Koli
13. Chhara, Adodia, Sansi
14. Chunara
15. Dabgar
16. Dekaleru
17. Dhobi
18. Divachakoli
19. Ghantia
20. Hingora
21. Kalbodia
22. Kangasia
23. Kaikadi
24. Khant
25. Kharwa Bhadela
26. Khatik
27. Kotwal or Kotwalia
28. Mahravat, Goti, Hadkashi, Zod, Dhingq, Pelya, Shatbai, Baman
29. Machi, Aaribharatbhara, Bharatbhara, Ghamadia, Chamadia, Chandlia, Dasania, Jansali, Jingar, Myangar, Sonari, Sivania
30. Machhi (Hindu), Bitna, Dhimar, Dhivar, Kahar, Khalas Khalasi, Kharwal, Mangela, Sarang, Tendal
31. Madari, Bharsthari, Nath
32. Me or Meta
33. Mena (Bhil)
34. Mer
35. Nat, Nat-Bajania, Natada, Bajigar
36. Od
37. Padhar
38. Paradhi (excluding Kutch District)
39. Pardhi Advichincher (in the Districts of Amerli, Bhavnagar, Jamnagar, Junagarh, Kutch, Rajkot, Surendra Nagar)
40. Rabari, Sorthia Charalia, Charmata, Luni, Kushar, Tank Muchhal Kadiyakumbhar (excluding the Nesses of the

forests of Alech, Barada and Gir)
41. Rathodia
42. Raval-Ravalia, Jati or Raval Yogi, Rawal Jati, Jagaria, Padat, Ravar Rawalia
43. Rohit
44. Salat
45. Sangheda
46. Sansi
47. Sarania
48. Sargara
49. Shikligar
50. Sumra
51. Talabia
52. Tahkar
53. Targala, Bhaviya, Bhojai, Nayak
54. Thakaroa, Baria, Dharala, Patanwadia, Thakore
55. Vaghri-Gamicho, Vedva Churalia, Jakhudia (excluding Kutch Distt)
56. Vahivancha Charan Gadhvi or Harijan, Vankar and Chamar
57. Vala
58. Valand and Nai (Hindu) Hajjam, Khalipha (Muslims)
59. Vans-foda, Vansfodia or Vanza
60. Wadwa Waghari
61. Waghari, Dataniya, Waghari, Vodu Waghari, Talapada, Waghari, Gamachia, Godalia Waghari, Chibhadia Waghari, Morawad Waghari

HARYANA

1. Aheria, Ahiria, Heri, Aheri, Naik, Thori, Turi
2. Bagaria
3. Banjara, Vanjara, Gwar, Badi
4. Bara, Barra
5. Barma
6. Barwar
7. Battera
8. Beria
9. Beta, Herai or Hesi
10. Bharbhuja, Bharbhunja, Kalanera
11. Churima
12. Dakaut, Dakot, Jyotshi
13. Daoli, Daola
14. Dhanwar
15. Dibbipuria
16. Dhimar, Mallah, Kashyap Rajput
17. Dhobi, Batham, Chauhan-Bhatti, Khurdania, Monson, Rajpar, Tanwar
18. Dhosali, Dosali
19. Gadaria, Baghela, Berela, Biar, Bilria, Hiranwal, Kalanlia, Padnowal, Pal, Shiviya
20. Gaddi
21. Ghasi, Ghasiyara, Ghosi
22. Ghiradh, Ghirath
23. Godri
24. Gorkha
25. Marni
26. Jhimar, Atlas, Bidran, Bire, Bhinwar, Duglan, Dora, Ghitra, Jhewae, Jhinwar, Jimar, Kahar, Kirnal, Lamsar, Malri, Radhav, Tala
27. Kehal
28. Khanghera
29. Labana
30. Lalli
31. Madari
32. Maghya
33. Meena, Mina
34. Mirasi
35. Mochi
36. Naar
37. Noongar, Nungar
38. Rachband

HIMACHAL PRADESH

1. Aheria, Aheri, Heri, Naik, Thori, Turi
2. Ard-Pop
3. Badi, Chinsoras, Meloris, Odmata, Uramamara
4. Bagria
5. Bajigar
6. Bahti
7. Badia

8. Batterha
9. Beda
10. Beta, Hensi, Hosi
11. Bharbhunja, Bharbhuja
12. Bhuhalia
13. Chang, Chahang
14. Changar
15. Chelopa
16. Dhimar, Dhiwar, Dhinwar, Jheevar, Jhinwar, Kahar, Mallah, Kashyap, Rajput
17. Dhosali, Sosal
18. Geddi (excluding the areas where specified as S.T.)
19. Gaderria
20. Ghassi, Ghasiara, Ghosi
21. Godri
22. Gumtian
23. Harni
24. Kahar
25. Kanghera
26. Kehal
27. Kolaga
28. Labana
29. Lalli
30. Madari
31. Muslim Banjara, Muslim Gujar
32. Mehra
33. Mirasi
34. Surera
35. Thawin

JAMMU & KASHMIR

1. Bekewal, Bakkarwal
2. Bedia
3. Bezigar
4. Bhand
5. Bhangi, Khokrob, (Sweepers) (excluding those in S.C.)
6. Barad
7. Banjara Badi Lobana
8. Bangala
9. Bharunja
10. Dheha
11. Dhobi (Washermen)
12. Doom, Dooma Ganai/Qusab (excluding those in S.C.)
13. Dosali
14. Dholwala
15. Fishermen
16. Gaddi
17. Gaudhila
18. Gurjarmar
19. Hangie (Manjhi Boatmen and rowing class excluding house-boat owners)
20. Hilka/Mason
21. Jheewar
22. Kholle
23. Lalli
24. Madari
25. Mahigir
26. Malyar
27. Mir
28. Mirasi
29. Mochi, Saraj
30. Para
31. Pirna
32. Sansi
33. Shypri, Wattal (excluding those in S.C.)
34. Sapera
35. Sikligar
36. Sangtrash
37. Surimar
38. Yashkun
39. Dheha
40. Gurjarmar

KARNATAKA

1. Adiya (excluding Coorg District)
2. Agasa, Madivala, Tsakala, Sakalavadu, Shakala, Vannan, Mannan, Dhobi, Parit, Rajaka, Puthirajvannan, Velluthedan
3. Aghore, Karkarmunda
4. Aranadam
5. Aruthuthiyar
6. Atar
7. Ataari
8. Badaga
9. Bagalu

10. Bagata
11. Baira
12. Bailapatar, Bailaptar, Bikapatar
13. Bajania, Bajonia
14. Bukadra
15. Balasantoshi
16. Bant (excluding Belgaum, Bijapur, Dharwar and North Kanara Distt.)
17. Bantu
18. Barda
19. Barlur
20. Bathai, Battal, Batler, Battar
21. Batahini
22. Battada
23. Bavuri
24. Bawtar
25. Basigar
26. Beda, Bedaru, Bedar, Naik, Bedar Nayaka, Naika Makkalu, Naikwara, Palegar, Talwar, Valmiki, Valmikimakkalu, Boya, Vedan, Berad, Ramoshi
27. Bagari, Byageri
28. Bellara
29. Beria
30. Bestha, Gangamatha, Gangaputra Bhoi, Parivara, Kabbera Kabbaligar, Bariki, Bariker, Mogaverra, Besthar, Bunde, Besthar, Gangamakkalu, Gowri Matha, Ambiga, Ambig, Kharvi, Bhoi Boyi, Thoreya, Harakantra, Kahar, Meenagar, Sunnagar, Koli, Gabit, Daavat, Kanet
31. Bhamta, Bhampta, Paradesi, Bhampata, Takari, Uchillian, Rajput, Bhampta
32. Bhaot, Bhatraj, Bhatraju
33. Bhardi, Bharagi
34. Bhottads, Boto Bhattad, Muria Bhottada, Sano Bhattada
35. Bhumaao-Bhuri, Bhumia Bodo-Bhumia
36. Binapatta
37. Bindili
38. Bingi
39. Bissey, Barangi Jodia, Bennagi, Dadus, Frangi, Bollar, Thoriya, Kollal, Konde, Paranga, Panka Jodia, Sodo and Takora
40. Bagad-Bogadi, Bagodi, Bagadi, Bogodi
41. Budbukhi, Bubdkala, Devari
42. Chakrawadya Dasar
43. Chintala
44. Chitrakathi-Joshi
45. Chitra, Chitrakar
46. Chuhar or Chuhra
47. Chaparband (Muslim)
48. Dandasi
49. Dang-Dasar
50. Dasari, Desari
51. Dhanka including Tadvi, Tataria and Valvi
52. Dher
53. Dhodia
54. Dholi
55. Digwan, Jinger
56. Domba, Dommara, Domba-Audhiya, Domba-Audiniya, Domba-Christian, Domba-Chonal, Domba-Nirgani, Domba-Oriya, Domba-Ponaka, Domba-Telaga, Domba
57. Donga Yerukala
58. Dombidasa
59. Durgamurga, Burburchal
60. Gadaba, Gadababoda, Gadaba-Garilum, Gadaba-Franji, Gadaba Jodia, Gadaba Olaro, Gadaba Pangi
61. Gangani
62. Garudi, Garudiga, Modiga, Modikara, Modikar
63. Gadi
64. Ghadsi, Ghadshi
65. Ghasi, Haddi, Relli, Sachandi, Boda, Ghasia and Sanghasia
66. Ghisadi
67. Ghondali, Gondaliga, Ghondali, Gondahalli
68. Giddibidki, Pingle, Pingale
69. Godagali
70. Godari
71. Gogra

72. Golla, Hawu Golla, Dudi Golla, Adavi Golla, Kishna Golla, Handi Golla
73. Gondu-Bato, Bhirtiya Dubho, Kouria, Bato Jatako and Joria
74. Gondali
75. Goniga
76. Gudigar
77. Halavakki Vakkal, Gramvakkal, Gam-Gowda, Gavada, Karevakkal Attevakkal, Halakkivakkal (North Canara, Distt)
78. Halepaik, Deevar, Namadhari, Billava, Kalal, Kumarpaik
79. Haranshikari, Chigaribetegar, Vaghri, Wagriri, Nirshikaro, Bagri, Baori, Phasa Chard, Vagri
80. Helva, Helava, Helava Mallar, Hevagolla, Handi Helva, Helvaru, Pitchosuntala
81. Honniyar
82. Howgar, Hawagar, Howadiya
83. Jadapu
84. Jaggale
85. Jatgar
86. Javeri, Jawari
87. Jogi, Joger, Sanjogi
88. Kadan
89. Kalloda
90. Kammar, Kumbhar (where they are not S.T.)
91. Kanjar, Kanjari, Kanjir, Khangarbhat
92. Kanisan
93. Kapumari
94. Kari Kudumbi
95. Karimpalan
96. Kashikaffi, Kashi-Kapadi, Tirmali
97. Katabu, Katabar
98. Katipaula
99. Kavadi
100. Kelkari, Khelkari
101. Khilarger, Marathi Dhanagar
102. Kolla, Kollah
103. Kolthats, Kolthating
104. Komakapu
105. Konda Dhora, Kondh Desaya, Kondh Dongria, Kondh Kuttiya, Kond Tikiriya, Nokka Dhora Manna-Dhora, Makka Dhora
106. Konkna Yenity
107. Kunchi Korwar, Kaidadi, Koraggar, Yerkala, Erakala, Kunchi Korva, Koramasetty, Yerukala
108. Kotari, Kottari
109. Kotia-Bartika, Bonth-Oriya, Dhulia, Dulia, Holva Paiko, Putiya, Sanrona and Sidho-Paiko
110. Koyava
111. Kudubi
112. Kurul Kuruboru, Halamath
113. Kudubi Koyi
114. Kurichchan
115. Kurubar, Kurub, Kurab, Kuruba
116. Ladar, Lad, Ladaru, Yelyar
117. Lippara
118. Mahasari
119. Maidhasi
120. Mali, Korchimale, Paikomali and Pedda Mali
121. Maniyani, Muniyani
122. Mitha Dyyalvar
123. Mondiwar, Mondiwaru
124. Monduvar, Muduvan
125. Medu Medar, Buruk
126. Muliya
127. Muria
128. Nat, Natuvan
129. Nalki
130. Nayinda, Nayanaja-Kshatriya, Hajjam, Nhavi, Nadig, Ambattan, Mangala, Kelasi, Kshowrad, Kshowrik, Navaliga, Napitha, Bhandari, Panikkan, Kavathiyan
131. Nelakanvaru
132. Otare
133. Pacha Bhtla, Pacha Botla
134. Padampari
135. Padarti
136. Padia, Padiyar
137. Pagadai
138. Paigarapu
139. Painda
140. Paky
141. Palasi
142. Pamide

143. Pamula
144. Panabas
145. Pannan
146. Panasa, Pansa
147. Panika
148. Patra, Patramela
149. Pentia
150. Pichati
151. Pichari
152. Pichasunta, Pichiguntala, Pichuguntala
153. Pomla
154. Parjas, Bonda, Daruba, Didua, Mundile, Pengu, Pundi and Saliya, Poroja, Bodo-Poroja, Sodia Poroja, Jodia Poroja and Parenga Poroja
155. Powara
156. Pulayan
157. Pullavan
158. Rawal, Ravalia, Paul
159. Rawat, Raya, Rewath
160. Reinudas
161. Relli Orachanji
162. Rona
163. Sadhumatha
164. Sangare
165. Santal
166. Saniyar
167. Sansi
168. Sansia
169. Saara
170. Sare
171. Sarodi, Sarada
172. Sarania
173. Satarkar
174. Savara, Kapusavara, Kuttusavara, Maliya Savara
175. Semman
176. Shingdevor Shingadya
177. Shikkaligar
178. Sholagar
179. Soliga
180. Sunna, Sunnai
181. Surva
182. Tachavira
183. Takankar
184. Talavia
185. Thottia Naik
186. Thotawadu
187. Tilari, Tirate
188. Timali
189. Tiruvalluvan
190. Turi
191. Uppaliga, Uppara, Uppaliyan, Mannu-Upper, Gavandi, Gavandi, Goundi, Veldar, Sagara, Chunar, Lonari, Melusakkare, Agri, Lama
192. Vadi
193. Vaghri
194. Vaidu
195. Valayar
196. Valve
197. Vathiriyan
198. Vitholia
199. Yandi
200. Yeklar, Yeklar, Yekkali, Egalika
201. Yeralu
202. Yerasolawadorthella, Pamalwada
203. Yenadiwad
204. Hondi Golla

KERALA

1. Agasa
2. Alavan
3. Ambalakkaran
4. Arupattun
5. Amblar, Ambathan, Ambithan, Eshavatory, Kalrrikurup, Maruthuvar, Naiken, Pandithar Villakkithalanavi
6. Arayan
7. Arayavathis
8. Aremaharti
9. Badaga
10. Bagata
11. Bendari
12. Bariki
13. Battada
14. Bavuri
15. Bhillava
16. Bhottadas-Bodo-Bhottada, Mùria-Bhottada, and Sano Bhottada

17. Bhumias-Bhumia and Bodo Bhumia
18. Bissoy-Barangi Jodia, Bennangi, Bollar, Daduva, Frangi, Jhoriya Kollai, Konde Pranga, Ponga Jodia, Sodo Jodia and Takora
19. Byagari
20. Chachati
21. Chackaravar
22. Chakkala
23. Chalavadi
24. Chavalakkaran
25. Chenchu
26. Dandesa
27. Dandasi
28. Dheevara
29. Dom, Dombara, Paidi or Pano
30. Dombo
31. Domb-Andhiya Dombs, Audiniya Dombs, Chonel Domb, Christian Dombs, Mirgani Dombs, Oriya Dombs, Ponaka Dombs, Telegaga Dombs and Ummia Dombs
32. Ezhava
33. Eshavathi
34. Eshuthachan
35. Gadabas-Bodo Gadaba, Cellan Gadaba, Franji Gadaba, Jodia Gadaba, Olaro Gadaba, Pangi Gadaba and Pranga Gadaba
36. Gatti
37. Ghasi or Haddi, Relli Sachandi
38. Ghasis-Boda Ghasis and San Ghasis
39. Godari
40. Gond
41. Gondi-Modya Gond and Rajo Gond
42. Khond
43. Kitaran
44. Kodalo
45. Kodu
46. Kond Danoara
47. Konda Dora
48. Kond (Kui)
49. Kondha-Desaya Kondh, Kongria Kondha, Kuttiya Kondh, Tikiria Kondha and Yemity Kondha
50. Kongu Malayan
51. Korachas (or Koravar or Yerukala)
52. Kosalya Goudu, Bosothoriya Goudus, Chitti Goudus, Dangayath Goudus, Doddu Kamariya, Dudu Kamarok, Kadiya Gouds and Pullsoriya Goudus
53. Kotoyar
54. Kotia-Bartika, Beatho Oriya Dhulia or Dulla, Holva Paiko, Putiya, Senrona and Sidho Paiko
55. Koya or Goud, with its subsects Raj or Rasha Koya, Kottu Koyas and Lingadhari Koyas
56. Koyi
57. Krishnanyoka
58. Kudubi
59. Kudumbis
60. Lambodi, Banjara, Sugali
61. Madara
62. Madari
63. Madiga
64. Madivala
65. Magatha, Goddus-Bernia, Goudus Boodo, Magatha, Dongayath Goudus Ladya Goudu, Poana Magatha and Sarna Magatha
66. Mala Dasu
67. Malas or Agency Malas, Valmikies
68. Mala Pantaram
69. Mala Pulayan, Karavali Pulayan, Kurumba Pulayan and Paubu Pulayan
70. Malayekandi
71. Malis, Korchia Malis, Palkomolis and Pedda Malis
72. Malla Malasar
73. Manna Dhora
74. Marakkan
75. Marathi, Marati
76. Medara
77. Magaveera
78. Mukkuven, Mukaya
79. Muliya
80. Muria
81. Muria Bhottada

82. Nadar
83. Naikkans
84. Nattu Malayana
85. Nulayan
86. Onamsica
87. Pagadai
88. Paidi
89. Paigarapu
90. Painda
91. Pahy
92. Palasi
93. Panidi
94. Panniyar
95. Pano
96. Pattariyas
97. Pentias
98. Perunkollans
99. Porja-Boda, Bonda, Daruva, Diduva, Jodia, Kundill Pengll, Phdi and Saliya
100. Poroja
101. Porogas-Bodo Prooja or Sodia, Sano Poraja, Jadia Poroja and Pareng Porja
102. Pulaya
103. Pulluvaw
104. Polli or Sachandi
105. Rona
106. Sakarvar (Kavathi)
107. Saira
108. Sapari
109. Savara
110. Savaras-Kapusavaras, Khotto Savaras and Maliya Devaras
111. Sanai Thalavar (Elavaniar)
112. Sholaga
113. Sholagar
114. Thanta Pulayan
115. Thiyya
116. Tholko Laus
117. Thontaman
118. Thottia Naick
119. Thottian
120. Toda
121. Valmiki
122. Valaan
123. Voluthadathu Nai (Veluthedan and Vannathan)
124. Vilathethal Nair (Vilakkithalavan)
125. Vottakkaran
126. Yadavan (Idayan)
127. Yanudi
128. Yarukula

MADHYA PRADESH

1. Adidharmi
2. Adhori
3. Aheri
4. Asara
5. Athiya
6. Audhic, Avadhi
7. Audhiya
8. Badak
9. Badaka
10. Badi
11. Baghia, Baree, Bawar, Payak, Vaidyanai
12. Bajgar, Bajigar
13. Bahurupi
14. Bairagi
15. Banjara, Banjari, Labana, Banjara, Bamania Banjara, Mathura Banjara
16. Baoria
17. Barasa, Labana, Labhan, Lamame, Mathura, Nayakda
18. Barad
19. Bargi
20. Bari
21. Baria
22. Barhunda
23. Baver
24. Bawaria
25. Bajania, Kannatia
26. Bemariha
27. Beria
28. Ghadi-Waddar, Matti-Waddar, Waddar, Ode, Odiya
29. Bhaduja
30. Bhadre
31. Bhadre
32. Bhaduria
33. Bhamta, Bhamti, Bhanmate, Bhanta, Bhanmate

34. Bhand
35. Bhantu, Sansi
36. Bharari
37. Bharbhuja
38. Bharewa
39. Bharia, Bharihar
40. Bharud
41. Bhoi
42. Bhoyar
43. Bhujwa
44. Bhutia
45. Bhurtiya
46. Bidakia
47. Badia, Sapera
48. Bijoria
49. Choongar
50. Chunkar
51. Dabgar
52. Dafali, Dholi
53. Dahez
54. Dana
55. Dhakad, Bhandari, Nagar, Singhavi, Talaya
56. Dhankia
57. Dhangar, Gadri, Gadaria, Hatgar, Hatkar, Kurmar, Pal Bagala
58. Dhimer, Benua, Banawar, Bhorji, Dhimar, Kewat, Raikar, Raikwar, Saimari
59. Dhirkar
60. Dhirwar, Britia, Navada, Ezingabhui
61. Dhobi (including those in S/C)
62. Dhunkar, Kadore
63. Gadri, Gari
64. Gahamandi
65. Gandia
66. Ghariya
67. Ghati, Ghare
68. Gochaki
69. Godhi
70. Gondhali
71. Gontia
72. Gowtia
73. Habura
74. Hajjam
75. Jhamral
76. Jhari
77. Jingar
78. Jogde
79. Jogi
80. Joginath
81. Kadera, Karnwal
82. Kadore
83. Kahar
84. Kaikari
85. Kalar
86. Kamriya
87. Kandera
88. Kaner
89. Mangar Batwal
90. Kauri, Kori
91. Khamgara
92. Kharol, Telugu-Munar, Beldar, Ghara
93. Kharwar
94. Kirad
95. Krar, Dhakar
96. Kodar
97. Koria
98. Kotil
99. Kulbandhiya
100. Kunjra
101. Kutwar
102. Lonia, Lunia, Nunia, Nonia
103. Mali, Marar
104. Madagi
105. Majhabi
106. Mala
107. Mallah
108. Manga
109. Manjar
110. Maru Sotiya
111. Mauria
112. Mavi
113. Meru
114. Mewati
115. Mhali, Naim, Navi, Nhavi
116. Naik, Nom
117. Naita, Nayata
118. Namsudra
119. Nath
120. Navda
121. Neria
122. Nerali
123. Nilgar

124. Otari
125. Pahar
126. Palhari
127. Panwari
128. Parashar
129. Parthi
130. Patka, Patki
131. Patwa, Pathakar, Sipiya
132. Payak
133. Perki
134. Putligar
135. Rajgir
136. Rajgond
137. Rautia
138. Rawal
139. Rawat, Bedar, Gahira, Rast, Rawar, Thethwar
140. Rhar
141. Rohade, Sujharia
142. Ruch bandhia
143. Saranjia
144. Sarbhangi
145. Sharia
146. Sikligar
147. Singiwala
148. Siyane
149. Sondhiya, Chandel
150. Thami
151. Thoti, Burud
152. Thanwar
153. Thori
154. Thuria
155. Tirgar
156. Tirmale
157. Tirwalli
158. Turha
159. Wanha
160. Yerkilwar, Yerkula

MAHARASHTRA

1. Agri, Agale or Kolan
2. Alitkar
3. Atar
4. Audhiya
5. Bedak
6. Badia
7. Bagalu
8. Bagdi (Gujarati Boori, Marwar Boori, Marwar, Waghri, Salat Waghri)
9. Bajania
10. Baharupi
11. Bajigar
12. Balasanthanam
13. Bandi
14. Banjara, Banjari, Vanjara, Mathura Banjara (A), Goar Banjars, Lambada/Lambara, Lambhani, Charan Banjaras, Labhan, Mathura Labhan, Kuchikiwale, Sanjaras, Laman Banjara, Laman/Lamani, Laban, Dhali/Dhaia, Dhadi/Dhari, Singaris, Navi Banjaras, Jogi Banjaras, Banjari
15. Bantu
16. Baoria
17. Baria, Koli Bari
18. Bathini
19. Bavcha
20. Bagari, Bedar, Borad, Beldar
21. Beldar/OD
22. Baikawadi, Talwar, Walmiki
23. Bastar, Sanchluwaddar
24. Bhadbhunja
25. Bhampta or Ghantichore or Pardesi, Pong, Baser, Uchale
26. Bhand
27. Bhanta
28. Bharadi, Balasantoshi, Kinggriwale, Nathbava, Nath Jogi, Nath Panthi
29. Bhavaiya or Targala
30. Bhina Koya
31. Bhoi, Kharvi, Dhiwar Bhoi, Zinga Bhoi, Pardeshi Bhoi, Raj Bhoi, Bhoi Kahar, Tadia Kahar, Kirat, Machwa, Manzi, Jatia, Kewat, Dhiwar, Dheewar, Dhimar, Paleowa, Mechhendra, Navadi, Malhar, Malhav, Gadhav Bhoi, Khadi Bhoi, Khare Bhoi, Dhevra Dhuria Kahar
32. Bhisti or Pakhali

33. Bhoyar (Pawra)
34. Bhuta, Bhopa
35. Sindli
36. Burbook
37. Burud, Madar
38. Buttal
39. Chadar
40. Chamtha
41. Chandal
42. Chandalagade
43. Chenchu or Chanchwar
44. Chintala
45. Dabgar
46. Dakaleru
47. Dasir Dangdidns
48. Dapala
49. Devari, Gosavi, Nath Panthi
50. Devli
51. Dhangar, Kruba, Kurubar
52. Dhar
53. Dhimar, Dhivar, Gabit, Harkantra, Mangali, Mangale, Page, Sankuri
54. Dhobi, Parit, Watts, Madwal, Rajak
55. Dholi
56. Dommara
57. Gutgudi
58. Gadaba or Godba
59. Gadaria
60. Gadri
61. Gadhavi
62. Ganali or Gandali
63. Gandharap
64. Gangani
65. Garodi,
66. Garpageri
67. Garvdi
68. Gavandi
69. Ghandshi
70. Ghisadi, Ghisadi Lohar, Gadi Lohar, Ghitodi Lohar, Rajput Lohar
71. Gosavi Bava, Dairagi, Bharati, Giri Gosavi, Bharati Gosavi, Saraswati Parbat, Sagar, Ben or Ven
72. Gujarath Baori
73. Habura
74. Hallpaik
75. Helve, Hilav
76. Jatigar
77. Jatiya
78. Jhadi
79. Jingar
80. Jogi, Nath, Nathjogi
81. Jogin
82. Bududki, Damruwale, Kudmude, Madhangi, Sarodo, Sahdev Joshi, Sarvade, Sarode
83. Kenchoro
84. Kadera
85. Kaikadi (or Korach), Dhontle, Korve or Kochi Korva, Makadwale, Padler Korvi, Kuchbauda, Gharo
86. Kandel
87. Kanjar Bhat, Chhera, Kanjar, Nat
88. Kapdi
89. Katabu
90. Katipamul
91. Kharwa or Kharwl
92. Kolhati, Dombari
93. Koraoha or Yerkula or Korva
94. Korchar
95. Korwa including Kodaku
96. Komakapu
97. Kongadi
98. Kuchhria
99. Kurmar
100. Lonari, Chunari
101. Machhi, Tandel
102. Mahali, Mahli
103. Mahil
104. Mirasi
105. Mairal, Dangat, Vir
106. Majhwar
107. Marwar Bouria
108. Masanjogi, Sadgadsiddha, Mapanjogi
109. Mina
110. Mitha
111. Mondiwar, Mondiwaru
112. Munda
113. Namdhari, Paik
114. Navi, Nhavi, Hajam, Kalaseru Navaliga, Kalashi, Nambik, Nai,

Narrbhllish
115. Neeli
116. Nirshikari
117. Nonia
118. Pachabhotla, Pachabotla
119. Padharia
120. Padiar
121. Padampari
122. Pakhali, Bhisti
123. Pal Pardhi
124. Panchama
125. Pangul
126. Panka
127. Parki
128. Phudgi
129. Pachbandhia
130. Rachevar
131. Rachkoya
132. Raikari
133. Raj Pardhi, Gaon, Pardhi, Haran-shikari
134. Rajput Bhamta, Pardeshi Bhamta, Pardeshi Bhamti
135. Ramoshi
136. Raot, Rautia, Rawt
137. Raval, Raval or Raval Yogi
138. Sanjogi
139. Santal
140. Sapera
141. Sarania
142. Sanji
143. Shingdav or Shingadhya
144. Sikkalgar, Katari
145. Singiwala
146. Sore
147. Takankar
148. Talwar Kanade
149. Targala
150. Thelari
151. Thetwar
152. Thotewadu
153. Thoria
154. Timali
155. Vaghri
156. Vaghri, Vaghari, Salat, Salat Vaghri
157. Vaidu
158. Vaiti
159. Valvai
160. Waddar, Wadders (Kalawaders or Patharod)
161. Warthi
162. Yanadi
163. Yenadiwad
164. Yeragolawad of Thella Pamalawade

MANIPUR

1. Bansphor
2. Bhumij
3. Boro, Boro Kachari
4. Dafla
5. Damai (Nepali)
6. Deoria
7. Dugla, Dholi
8. Gara
9. Hajong
10. Hira
11. Jhala, Malo
12. Kaibartta, Jaliya
13. Khasi
14. Khuangsal
15. Kuki
16. Lalbegi
17. Lalung
18. Liamei-Naga
19. Mahara
20. Mali, Bhuimali, Bhuinmali
21. Mech
22. Mehtar, Bhungi
23. Mikir
24. Miri
25. Mishmi
26. Munda
27. Naga
28. Napit, Nai
29. Oraon
30. Rabha
31. Sahte
32. Santal
33. Singpho
34. Synteng
35. Tipera

MEGHALAYA

1. Bhumij
2. Boro-Kachari
3. Choudang
4. Chutiya
5. Dey, Sudra Das
6. Gorkhali
7. Moran, Matak
8. Mukhi
9. Nepali (Damai, Gaine, Gurung, Lama, Limbu Lohar, Newar, Rai, .Sarki, i.e., Cobbler, Thapa)
10. Rabha
11. Saloi
12. Sut
13. Tipara

ORISSA

1. Adi-Dravida
2. Adi-Karnataka
3. Agharia, Agaria, Aghria
4. Ajila
5. Aranedan
6. Arunthuthiyar
7. Asur
8. Badasuda
9. Badaga
10. Balpari
11. Baira
12. Bakuda
13. Banka
14. Bandi
15. Barika, Bhandari, Beja, Napit and Nai
16. Battada
17. Bellara
18. Bentkar
19. Betere or Betra
20. Bhatua
21. Bhogta
22. Bhokta
23. Bhujan
24. Bhuliya
25. Birjhia
26. Bissoy-Barangi Jodia, Bennangi, Daduva, Frangi, Hollar, Jhoriya, Kollai, Konde, Paranga, Pengajodi, Sodo Jodia and Takoara
27. Binedhany
28. Bogada
29. Bolodhia
30. Butakusuda
31. Buruashankar/Barna Sharkar, Beja
32. Chakkiliyan
33. Chalavadi
34. Chero
35. Cheruman
36. Chikbaraik
37. Chik
38. Chitra, Chitrakar
39. Churia
40. Dahalia
41. Damal
42. Dangua
43. Deons
44. Dehuri
45. Dhakkada
46. Dhaner
47. Domb-Andhiya Domb, Audiniya Dombs, Chonel Dombs, Christian Domb, Mirgani Dombs, Oriya Dombs, Ponaka Dombs, Telega Dombs and Ummia Dombs
48. Dumala, Dumal
49. Ghatwar
50. Girigiri
51. Gingra
52. Godda
53. Gondi-Modya Gond and Rajo Gond
54. Gondu-Bato, Bhirthya, Dudho Kouriya, Hato, Jatako and Joria
55. Habra
56. Hansi
57. Hasla
58. Holeya
59. Irula
60. Jadapus
61. Jambuvulu
62. Jaintrapans
63. Jhodia
64. Jogi or Yogi

65. Kadan
66. Kalladi
67. Kalwar
68. Kandarpa
69. Kanjar
70. Kaniyan
71. Kapudia
72. Karhara
73. Karimpalan
74. Karmali
75. Kattunayakan
76. Khaia
77. Khandnals
78. Khanjiman
79. Khatti
80. Khatua
81. Khondal
82. Khodra
83. Kora, Juda
84. Oilar
85. Kolam
86. Komar
87. Kond (Kul)
88. Kondhs-Desaya Kondhs, Dongriya Kondhs, Kuttiya Kondhs, Tikiria Kondhs and Yanity Kondhs
89. Koosa
90. Koraga
91. Kosalya Goudus, Bosothe Riya Goudus, Chiti Goudus, Dangayath Goudus, Doddu Kamariya, Dudu Kamaro, Ladiya Goudus and Pullo Soriya Goudus
92. Kota
93. Koyi
94. Kudiya
95. Kudubi
96. Kudumban
97. Kuli, Koli
98. Kunduma/Kuduma
99. Kundamatia
100. Kulta
101. Kurariar
102. Kuravan
103. Kurichchan
104. Kuruman (Kurumba)
105. Laher
106. Lakhra
107. Lambadi
108. Luhura
109. Machua
110. Maghi or Meghia
111. Magura
112. Mahunta
113. Maila
114. Maladasu
115. Malasar
116. Malis-Korchia Malis, Paido Malis and Pedda Mal
117. Mal Paharia
118. Mangli
119. Matangi
120. Mavilan
121. Minka
122. Moger
123. Mukhadora-Mokka Dhora
124. Muliya
125. Mundala
126. Muria
127. Nat
128. Nayadi
129. Nolia
130. Nuhura, Nuhuraj
131. Nuniya
132. Omeyita
133. Padaria, Pamaria, Pandara
134. Pagadai
135. Paigarapu
136. Paiko
137. Paky
138. Palasi
139. Paliyan
140. Pallan
141. Pulayan
142. Pambada
143. Paniyan
144. Panjira
145. Panniandi
146. Paraiyan
147. Paravan
148. Parhaiya
149. Pathuria
150. Pengua
151. Pita
152. Porjas-Bado, Bonda, Daruva,

Didva, Jodia, Mundil, Sano, Pengu, Pydi, Saliya, Sodia and Pareng
153. Rajwar
154. Raneyar
155. Ronas
156. Routia
157. Sagarpasha
158. Samban
159. Sankhari
160. Savara-Kapu, Savaras, Khutto Savaras, Mallya Savaras
161. Semman
162. Sholagar
163. Sauria Paharia
164. Sinkes
165. Sud
166. Sulia
167. Sundi
168. Tans
169. Thanu
170. Thatari
171. Thoti
172. Thuria
173. Tiyar
174. Toda
175. Tonla Gaul
176. Valluvan
177. Vettuvan
178. Vina Tulavina
179. Yandi
180. Yerna Golta
181. Yerukula

PUNJAB

1. Aheria, Aheri, Heri, Naik, Thori, Turi
2. Bagria, Bagaria
3. Barai, Tarboli, Tamboli
4. Barwar
5. Bateri
6. Beria
7. Barrer
8. Beta, Hensi, Hesi
9. Bharbhunja, Bharbhuja
10. Bhari, Rode
11. Bhuhalia
12. Chahang
13. Daiya
14. Dakaut, Dahkaut
15. Daoli, Daola
16. Daula, Soni-Braderi
17. Dhenwar
18. Dhimar, Dhiwar, Dhinwar, Jheevar, Jhinwar, Kahar, Kashyap, Rajput, Mallah
19. Dhobi, Qasab
20. Dhosali, Dosali
21. Gadderia, Gadaria
22. Gaddi, Guddi
23. Ghasi, Ghasiara, Ghosi
24. Harni
25. Jogi, Nath
26. Kanjar, Kanchan
27. Kehal
28. Kuchband, Kuchband
29. Lobana, Banjara, Vanjara
30. Madari
31. Mirasi
32. Mochi (excluding those in S.C.)
33. Nai, Banvaru, Dhanwal, Dhari, Ghangas, Ghiri, Hajjam, Hazam, Hergun, Jallan, Lekha, Nagi, Naisikh, Palan, Panju, Patara, Raja
34. Shorgir

RAJASTHAN

1. Ager
2. Asada
3. Badera, Baoria
4. Bagdiya, Bawaria
5. Baked, Bant
6. Banchada
7. Banjara, Gamarlia, Kangiwala, Kangi, Baladia, Sirkiwala, Labana, Labhana, Maru Banjara, Bamama Banjara, Bayora, Digora
8. Barahar, Basod
9. Barar
10. Barda, Dhia

11. Bargunda
12. Basor
13. Bhampta, Ghantichor, Pardesi-Bhampt
14. Bhanumati
15. Bharud
16. Chakrawadya-Dasar
17. Chalvadi, Chamnayya
18. Chamana
19. Cheeta
20. Chene-Dasaru
21. Chenna-Dasar, Holaya
22. Chidar
23. Dakot, Garo, Gakudia
24. Dakalaru
25. Damami
26. Dhadi
27. Dhakad, Dhanak, Dhanaka, Dhanuk Gokhi
28. Dhanchi
29. Dhimar
30. Dhobi
31. Dholi
32. Dhodia
33. Dhor, Kakkayya, Kankayya
34. Dubla
35. Gadaria, Chandalia, Gavala, Ghosi, Kabiria
36. Gadolia
37. Gamit, Gamta, Gavit (including Mavchi, Padvi, Vassava, Vasava and Valvi)
38. Gond
39. Halleer
40. Halsar, Haslar, Hulasvar, Halasvar
41. Halalkhor
42. Helar
43. Holar, Valhar
44. Holaya, Holer
45. Kahar, Shoi
46. Kaikadi, Korech
47. Kanders
48. Kanvi
49. Keer
50. Khant
51. Kharol
52. Kirar
53. Kul
54. Koli-Mahadev
55. Korku
56. Malhar
57. Merasi, Miras
58. Mehara
59. Moghia
60. Mogia
61. Mukri
62. Nadia, Hadi
63. Nath, Jogi
64. Naik
65. Nat, Natsansi
66. Mariya
67. Odd
68. Pardhi (including Adwishincher and Phanse-Pardhi)
69. Patwa (Phadal)
70. Pomla
71. Powara
72. Raika
73. Rawat
74. Rebbari
75. Sad-Sausi (Sehar)
76. Sarabara
77. Sakka
78. Sikligar
79. Sirkiwal
80. Sonsi
81. Timali
82. Varli
83. Ved
84. Waghri
85. Zemrol

SIKKIM

1. Bajel
2. Gurung
3. Limboo, Limbu
4. Mongar
5. Rai
6. Suba
7. Sunar
8. Tamang
9. Tsong
10. Yakthungba

TAMILNADU & PONDICHERRY

1. Ampattan
2. Arayan, Arayar (Nulayar)
3. Badaga
4. Badagar
5. Bagata
6. Bariki
7. Battada
8. Bavuri
9. Bestha, Siviar
10. Bharatar
11. Bhatraju (other than Kshatriya Raju)
12. Bhottadas-Bodo Bhettada, Muria Bhottada and Sane Bhottada
13. Bhumias-Bhuri Bhumia and Bodo Bhumia
14. Billava
15. Bissoy-Barangi Jodia, Banagi, Daduva, Frangi, Mollar, Jheriya, Kollai, Konde, Paranga, Panga-Jodia, Sodo Jodia and Takore
16. Bondil
17. Boyar, Oddar
18. Boya
19. Budabukhala
20. Byagari
21. Chanchati
22. Chavalakkaran, Chavalakkarer
23. Chenchu
24. Dasari
25. Dandasi
26. Dhakkada
27. Dhobi, Vannan
28. Domba
29. Domba-Andhiya Dombs, Chonel Domba, Oriya Domba, Poneka Domba, Telaga Domba and Ummia Domba
30. Dommara
31. Donga Vata
32. Dudakula
33. Enadi
34. Eravallar
35. Ezhavathy
36. Ezuthachar
37. Ezhyva
38. Gadabas, Boda Gadaba, Cerllas Gadaba, Olarao Gadaba and Frangi Gadaba, Jodia Gadaba
39. Gangavar
40. Ghagi, Haddi, Relli and Sachandi
41. Godari
42. Gond
43. Goudu, Bato, Bhirithya, Dudhokouria, Hato, Tatake and Jori
44. Hasla
45. Hill Puleya
46. Holve
47. Hovan
48. Jadapue
49. Jambuvanodai
50. Jatapua
51. Jogi
52. Jogula
53. Kabbore
54. Kadan
55. Kadupattar (Malabar)
56. Kakkalan
57. Kaladi
58. Kani or Kanisu or Kaniyar Panikker
59. Kanikaran, Kannikar
60. Kanjar
61. Kannakan, Padanna
62. Kapumarie
63. Katesar or Pattamkatti
64. Kavara
65. Kavathi
66. Kavuthiyar
67. Kerala Muthali
68. Kharvi
69. Khond
70. Kondalo
71. Kodu
72. Kolalar, Davar, Thevar
73. Konda Dhera
74. Kond (Kui)
75. Kondha-Besaya Kondha, Dongria Kondh, Kuttiya Kondha, Tikiria Kondha and Yamity Kondha
76. Kootan, Koodan
77. Koracha Koravar, Yerukale
78. Koselya Goudu, Bosotholya

Goudu, Chith Goudu, Dangayath Goudu, Doddu Kammariya, Dudu Kamaro, Laddiya Goudu and Fullo Soriya Goudu
79. Kote
80. Koteyar
81. Kotia-Bartika, Bantho Oriya, Dhulia or Dulia, Holva, Paiko, Putiya Sanrona and Sindho Paiko
82. Koya or Goud (with its subsects Raj or Resha Koya, Linga Dhari Koya (ordinary) and Kottukoya
83. Koyi
84. Krishnaveka
85. Kubbora, Kukuvan
86. Kudubi
87. Kudumbi
88. Kurumba
89. Kurumbarava
90. Kuravar
91. Lambadi, Banjara, Lambadi Sugali
92. Magatha Goudu, Bernia Goudu, Boodu Magatha, Dongayath Goudu, Ponne Magetha, Sana Magetha and Yadya Goudu
93. Mahandra, Medara
94. Mala Dasu
95. Malapantaram
96. Malapulayan, Kurumbapulayan, Koravalipulayan, Pambupulayan
97. Malayavayan
98. Malayali
99. Male
100. Mali, Korchia Mali, Paiko Mali and Pedda Mali
101. Manne Dhora
102. Mannan, Vannan, Pathiyar
103. Marakkan
104. Maramori, Gramani
105. Marathi
106. Maruthuvar, Navithar
107. Mauna
108. Madara
109. Moniagar
110. Mukkuvan Mukkuvar
111. Mukha Dhora, Nooka Dhora
112. Muliya
113. Muria
114. Gramani, Shanar, Nadar
115. Nakkala
116. Naikar
117. Narikeravar
118. Nokkare
119. Nulayan
120. Paidi
121. Paigarapu
122. Paky
123. Palasi
124. Pamidi
125. Pamulu
126. Panan
127. Panar
128. Panikkan
129. Pano
130. Paravan, Paravar, Kabbora, Parvatharajakulani, Pattanavan
131. Pariyas (Vengur and Vappur)
132. Parkavakulam Suruthinar, Malayamar, Nathamar
133. Pathiyan
134. Patia
135. Poraya
136. Porjas or Poraja-Boda, Bonda, Daruva, Didua, Jodia, Mundili, Parang, Pyadi, Salliya, Sano and Sodia
137. Pulluvan, Pulluvar
138. Pusuale
139. Relli, Sachndi
140. Rona
141. Eakkarauar (Kavathi)
142. Saora
143. Savara-Kopu Savara, Khutto Savara and Maliya Savara
144. Telaga Pamula, Peddati Golla
145. Thandan
146. Thantapulayan
147. Thavar
148. Thiyya
149. Tholuva Naicker and Vetalakara Naickar
150. Thondaman
151. Thoriyar
152. Thottai Naicka
153. Thottiya Naicker (including Gollavar, Silavar, Rajakambalam,

Thockalavar and Tholuva Naicker)
154. Toda
155. Ulladan
156. Ullatan
157. Uppars (Upplillia Segara)
158. Urali Gounders
159. Valan
160. Valaiyar
161. Valmiki
162. Vannan (Mannan, Bathiyan)
163. Vannar, Rajakula Veluthadar (where the community is not a Scheduled Caste Agasa Madivala Mali).
164. Valaiyar
165. Valuthadanayar, Valuthanathwnayar
166. Vedar
167. Vetan
168. Yanady
169. Yanadi
170. Yavana
171. Yarukula.

TRIPURA

1. Agaria, Agariya
2. Asur
3. Badyakar, Dhuli, Nagarchi, Sabdakar
4. Bahelia
5. Baishnab
6. Baiti
7. Banjogi
8. Barui
9. Bedia, Bediya
10. Beldar
11. Berua
12. Bhakta
13. Bhar
14. Bhinhar
15. Bhumij, Bumij
16. Bin
17. Bind
18. Binjhia
19. Birhor
20. Chouhan
21. Dalu
22. Damai
23. Desali
24. Dhemaru
25. Gangin
26. Ganju
27. Gara
28. Gareri
29. Goala
30. Gonda
31. Gonrhi
32. Gorang
33. Gunar
34. Gundi
35. Guri
36. Hadi
37. Halalkhor
38. Hari
39. Ho
40. Khandait
41. Khatik
42. Khemcha
43. Khen
44. Khyang
45. Kichak
46. Koda
47. Koiri
48. Korwa
49. Lalbegi
50. Lohar
51. Maghaiya-Domes
52. Mahar
53. Mahli
54. Mal
55. Mallah
56. Naiya
57. Nat, Nattadas
58. Napit
59. Nayak
60. Nepali (Limbo, Matwali, Rai)
61. Nuniya, Nunia
62. Oraon
63. Paik
64. Paliye
65. Paliye
66. Pan
67. Panki

68. Pasi
69. Pod
70. Rabha
71. Raju
72. Rajwar
73. Rupai
74. Sunri
75. Tiyar
76. Yogi, Jogi, Nath.

UTTAR PRADESH

1. Agri
2. Aheria, Aheriya
3. Arakh
4. Auji
5. Badak
6. Bairi
7. Bajigar
8. Bandi
9. Banjara, Gor, Ladenia, Gamalia, Osaria, Mathura, Labana, Labhana, Dhanakuta Banjora, Brajawasi Banjara, Banjara nut Gwar, Banjara Sikh.
10. Bari
11. Badia
12. Baura
13. Bauriah
14. Bayar
15. Bedia
16. Beriah
17. Bhar
18. Bhathiara
19. Bhil
20. Bhul
21. Bhurji, Bharbhuja, Bharbhunja, Bhunj, Bhunjia, Kandu, Kashodhay
22. Bind
23. Chanal
24. Chik
25. Chunal
26. Chumpa
27. Dalera
28. Dhari
29. Dhobi, Rajak (excluding those in S.C.)
30. Dholi
31. Dhunia, Katheria, Naddaf
32. Faqir
33. Gadaria, Gaddi, Gaderia, Gareria
34. Gadhia
35. Gandharva, Bhatu Sausi
36. Gandhila
37. Gidhiya
38. Giri
39. Gonrh
40. Halalkhor
41. Hankiya
42. Hurkiya
43. Jogi
44. Kahar, Dhiver, Dhuru, Godia, Kashyap
45. Kewat, Bansi, Chai, Jalehar, Kharsa, Majhi, Mallah, Bishad
46. Khairwa
47. Kharot
48. Kingharia
49. Koli
50. Kotwar
51. Kunjra, Rayeen
52. Luniya, Lonia
53. Mewati
54. Mochi (excluding those in S.C.)
55. Muslim Banjara
56. Nadkal
57. Nayak, Naik
58. Nut (excluding those in S.C.)
59. Odhia
60. Orh, Od
61. Pahri
62. Pauri
63. Pawariya
64. Raj
65. Sapera, Kalbelia
66. Saunsi
67. Turi.

WEST BENGAL

1. Adikari
2. Agaria, Agariya
3. Aghore

4. Amant, Amat, Amath
5. Bhar
6. Bag
7. Badia
8. Bagal
9. Bajadar, Bajania, Bedey
10. Banjara
11. Banjogi
12. Banus, Buna, Bunna, Buno
13. Baragiri
14. Barchain, Chai, Chain
15. Baro
16. Bathudi
17. Bentkar
18. Berua
19. Bhangi (excluding those in Scheduled Caste)
20. Bhant
21. Bhar
22. Bhathiara, Basgaqi
23. Bhotia
24. Bhugal
25. Bin
26. Binjhia
27. Binjhawar
28. Binjina
29. Brijia
30. Chaak
31. Chamling
32. Chasadhoba, Haladhar, Halari, Satchasi
33. Chik, Chikwa, Kasai, Kassab
34. Chirimar
35. Chitrakar
36. Churihara, Lakhera, Lahera
37. Dalu
38. Dhaon
39. Dhakaru
40. Dhenuar
41. Dilpali
42. Duraj
43. Gadaba
44. Gain
45. Ganda
46. Garai
47. Ghatwal
48. Ghatwar
49. Ghusuria
50. Godra
51. Gokha
52. Gonda
53. Gora
54. Gudheri
55. Hadi
56. Halalkhor (excluding those in Scheduled Caste)
57. Halwari
58. Hela
59. Irika
60. Juang
61. Kahar
62. Kaira
63. Kalwar
64. Kandh
65. Kapuria
66. Karani
67. Karha
68. Karwalnat
69. Kastha
70. Kala
71. Kharag
72. Kharia
73. Khen
74. Kherwar
75. Khyang
76. Khyara, Ghara
77. Kichak
78. Koda
79. Kol
80. Koli
81. Kolu
82. Kuki
83. Kunjra, Rayeen
84. Lakra
85. Lushei
86. Machhu
87. Maghaiya-Domes
88. Mahadarda
89. Magha Doom
90. Mallah
91. Mangan
92. Mangar
93. Marwari Bauria
94. Matial
95. Mirshikar
96. Mug

97. Hoobhudish
98. Patua
99. Pirali
100. Rakhal
101. Rasali
102. Rohangia, Roshangia
103. Sayar
104. Shagird Pesha
105. Siyal
106. Tamang
107. Tharu
108. Tipara
109. Tippera
110. Tiyar
111. Turha
112. Urao, Bandot, Haro, Karkata, Luidu, Shitheo, Tigga, Tirki
113. Sansi

ANDAMAN & NICOBAR ISLANDS

1. Arundatilu (H)
2. Barar (Umati)
3. Eluvain
4. Dhobi
5. Kharia
6. Munda
7. Namasudra, Adhikari, Sarkar, Dhati, Bala, Hira, Baidal, Maji, Daligbi, Bodoi, Diskas, Poddar, Hindal, Roy, Das, Hadder, Manji, Basi, Manser, Biri, Nag, Bairagi, Bhatra, (Baidya)
8. Nai Thakur

ARUNACHAL PRADESH

1. Diwan
2. Kshatriya
3. Kurmi
4. Maiti
5. Majhiara
6. Nayor

CHANDIGARH

1. Ahir, Yadav
2. Bagaria
3. Barra
4. Barwar
5. Bahari
6. Bajikar
7. Bathi
8. Batterha
9. Beria
10. Beta, Hensi, Hesi
11. Bhand
12. Bharbhunja
13. Bhujru
14. Botehra
15. Charg
16. Chirimar
17. Daiya
18. Dakaut
19. Daoli, Doala
20. Deha, Dhaya, Dhea
21. Dhai
22. Dhenwar
23. Dhimar, Dhinwar, Jhinwar, Kahar, Mallah
24. Dhobi
25. Dhosali
26. Gadaria
27. Gadri
28. Gaddi
29. Ghosi
30. Hadi
31. Hajjam, Nai
32. Hali
33. Harni
34. Jogi, Nath
35. Kanchan
36. Kanghera
37. Kanjar
38. Kehal
39. Kohli
40. Labana, Lobana, Vanzara, Banjara, Banjari
41. Madari
42. Meena, Mina
43. Mewati
44. Mochi

45. Musavar
46. Naar
47. Naik, Heri, Aheri
48. Noongar
49. Rachband
50. Rai-Sikh
51. Rehar, Rehara, Rer, Rihar
52. Shorigir
53. Singhiwala, Singhikaut
54. Thori, Turi.

DADRA AND NAGAR HAVELI

1. Agri
2. Ahir
3. Bharvad
4. Brahmi
5. Dhobi
6. Kahar
7. Kumbhar
8. Kapadi
9. Kolaga (Muslim)
10. Koli
11. Makrana (Muslim)
12. Nai (Valand)

DELHI

1. Abbasi, Bhishti, Sakka
2. Agri Kharwal
3. Bangela, Badia, Perna Sapera
4. Beri
5. Baurla
6. Bazigar, Nat, Kalendar (excluding those in S.C.)
7. Bhubhalia
8. Bhand
9. Bharbhooja
10. Chak
11. Chirimar
12. Daiya Dhaiya, Jallad
13. Dhinwar, Jhinwar, Nishad
14. Dhobi (excluding those in S.C.)
15. Gaderia
16. Gaddi, Garri
17. Gadheri, Ghandila
18. Ghasiara
19. Harni
20. Herbi, Heri
21. Jogi
22. Kahar, Kashyap
23. Karawal
24. Kanjar, Ghair Kuchbanda, Singikat
25. Kewat
26. Khatgune
27. Khatik (excluding those in S.C.)
28. Lalli
29. Machhi, Machhera, Mali, Saini, Southia, Sagarwanshi-Mali, Nayak
30. Masania-Jogi
31. Meo, Mewati
32. Meriasi, Mirasi
33. Mochi (excluding those in S.C.)
34. Nai
35. Nalband
36. Patwa
37. Patharphera, Sangtarash
38. Suriman, Gunjamar
39. Gadilohar
40. Waghri

GOA, DAMAN & DIU

1. Bhandari
2. Banjara, Lambadi, Lamani, Sugali
3. Christian Chamar
4. Christian Mahar
5. Dhangar
6. Dhobi
7. Dhor
8. Gaude
9. Goggi
10. Gosavi
11. Kasar
12. Koli
13. Kunbi
14. Mitna
15. Naidu
16. Nath, Jogi
17. Nhavi, Nai
18. Sagar

MIZORAM

1. Apatani
2. Gurkha
3. Manipuri
4. Paite
5. Relse

PONDICHERRY

1. Achukatlavandlu
2. Agamudiyas (including Thuluva Vellalas)
3. Agaru, Jurakula
4. Agasa
5. Agnikula Kshatriya (Pallekapu, Palloreddi, Vannekapu, Vannereddi)
6. Alwar
7. Ambalakaran
8. Ambika
9. Anandan
10. Andipandaran
11. Anglo Indian
12. Arayan (Nulayan), Araya
13. Archakatalavandu
14. Are Mahrati
15. Arya
16. Aryavathi (Nairuseri)
17. Atagara, Atagora
18. Badaga
19. Balolika
20. Bestha, Beztha (Jalarula Nagavadaity)
21. Bhatraju
22. Bhavassar Kshatriya, Banagarajulu, Rongare, Darji, Simpi
23. Bhottodas-Bodo Bottadu, Muria Bhottada and Sano Bhottada
24. Bhumias, Bado Bhumias and Bhuri Bhumia
25. Bhundari
26. Billava
27. Bissoy
28. Bondili
29. Bonya
30. Boyan
31. Byagari
32. Chakkala
33. Chaptogra
34. Chatadi (Chattada or Srivaishnava)
35. Chavalakaranas
36. Chekkalas whose normal occupation is oil crushing like Cap Vaniyans
37. Chettadara
38. Converts to Christianity from Scheduled Castes
39. Desari
40. Devadiga
41. Dovalkar
42. Devanga, Devangan
43. Dhakkada
44. Dommara
45. Dudubi
46. Dudokula, Pinjari
47. Enadi
48. Eravaliar
49. Exhava (Exhuva, Ezhava Illuvan)
50. Exhuthachan
51. Ezhavathy (Vathi)
52. Ezhuthachans
53. Gaalda, Gaadavars
54. Gaadla Konkani
55. Gandla
56. Gangavars
57. Ganika (including Nagavamasam)
58. Gatti
59. Gazula Balija, Gazulasetti (Gajula)
60. Gavara
61. Gobba
62. Godaba
63. Gondi, Modya Gond and Rajo, Gondo
64. Gound or Gowdi, Machhus, Pal, Paiko Patra or Patara, Sundi or Telli, Tanti, Yeranagollas, Oriya or Veddy Samantho, Oriya Backward Classes Badhai Bhokta, Darji, Gour
65. Goudus Bato, Bhirithya, Dodhokouria, Hato, Jatako and Joria

66. Gowda, Gouda (including Gamalla or Kalali)
67. Grammani, Shanan & Nadar
68. Gudigara
69. Hdiga (including Settibalijas of East and West Godavari Distt.)
70. Hegde
71. Helva
72. Idiga (including Sett Balija)
73. Illuvan (Ezhvan)
74. Irulas
75. Isai Vallalar or Melakarar
76. Jadapus
77. Jakkulas
78. Jalarlu
79. Jambuvandondai
80. Jandara
81. Jangam
82. Jetty
83. Jogi
84. Kabbara
85. Kadaiyan
86. Kadan
87. Kadupattan
88. Koikolan or Koikola (Sengunthar, Sengundar)
89. Kalarikurups (Kairal Panicker)
90. Kalavanthula
91. Kalingi
92. Kallan
93. Kallar
94. Kamalas (Viswakarmala)
95. Kammalana (Kamsalas, Viswav-Brahman and Viswa Karma, Karuvaw)
96. Kandra
97. Kani, Kanian or Kaniyan and Kanisu or Kaniyar Panik kar, Ganka, Kanisy
98. Kavuthiyan
99. Kelasi
100. Kerala Mudali, Kerala Muthali
101. Kharvi
102. Khattis-Khatti, Kammarao and Lohara
103. Kitara
104. Kodu
105. Kohdala
106. Kolarios or Munivanies
107. Kommar
108. Kopplavalamas
109. Koracha
110. Kosalya Goudus, Bosothoriya Goudus, Chitti Goudus, Dangayath Goudus, Doddu, Kamariya, Dudu Komaro, Ladiya Goudus and Pullosoriya Goudus
111. Kosavans, Kuyauar
112. Kotayar (Shoragara Kushatriya)
113. Krishnavaka
114. Kudumbi
115. Kulela, Kulala, Kummari
116. Kumbaran
117. Kummuvar Mannadi
118. Kurumba, Kuruba, Kurubar, Kuruva
119. Kusavan
120. Labbai
121. Lambadi
122. Madugar or Modavar or Vethakkara
123. Nagatha Goudus-Bernia Goudub, Boodo Magatha, Dengoyath Goudo, Ladya Goudu, Ponna Magatha and Sana Magatha
124. Mahaedra, Mahandra, Medara
125. Male
126. Mangala (Nayee-Brahman)
127. Mannus
128. Mappila
129. Marathi
130. Maravar, Maravaw
131. Maruthuvar
132. Mdivla, Madivala
133. Melakudi or Kudiyan
134. Modi Bans
135. Mogaveera
136. Moili, Moli
137. Mondgolla
138. Mongola
139. Moniagar
140. Moundadan
141. Mudava/Muduga
142. Mukhari
143. Mukkuvan or Kukayan, Mogayan,

Logavan (including Bovis)
144. Muria
145. Mutlakampatti
146. Muthuraja
147. Muttiriyan/Muthiriyar
148. Nadar
149. Nagaralu
150. Nagaram
151. Nagavaddily
152. Naidu Gavara
153. Naiker, Vanniya
154. Naikkans, Naicken
155. Nakkala
156. Nalakodaya
157. Namdev, Simpi
158. Naniar
159. Narikoravan
160. Navundian
161. New Buddhists, Nv-Buddhists
162. Nokka
163. Odans, Odde, Voddoo or Vadda or Veddai, Odori (Donga), Odiya
164. Oiulu
165. Omanaito
166. Ottanaickan
167. Padayachi
168. Padmasali
169. Paigarapu
170. Painda
171. Palaekari
172. Palasi
173. Pālli
174. Pamula
175. Pandithar (Anpattan, Pranopkari and Nasivan)
176. Pandi Thattan
177. Pannagadikara
178. Pannan Vettuva Goundor
179. Pannaiyar or Pannayar
180. Paramban
181. Paravan (Christians)
182. Parol Madivala
183. Parrakavakulam (Surithinaman) Malayanan, Nathaman, Moopanar and Nainar
184. Pathukudi
185. Patnulkaran
186. Patrikulam, Patrakulam
187. Patta avam
188. Pattariyas or Pattarias
189. Pattulakaran
190. Pentias
191. Perike, Perike Balija, Piragiri Kshatriya
192. Perumbadlan
193. Perumkollans
194. Peruvannan
195. Picchigunta
196. Pielai
197. Pillava
198. Polinativalma of Srikakulam and Visakhapatanam Distt
199. Pomnala
200. Poraya
201. Praravatharajakulam
202. Pulluvan
203. Pusala, Pusalavaan, Pusalvandlu
204. Rajaka
205. Rajapuri, Raju
206. Rauther
207. Rona
208. Sadan, Dedan
209. Sagalis
210. Saiva vellalan
211. Sakravar (Kavathi)
212. Salian (Pattarayan), Saliyas, Saliyan, Pattusali, Senapathulu, Kamithoktulu, Sale, Jhogata Sali
213. Sanaithalaivar (Senaikudiyan)
214. Senai Thalvivar (Elavabanias)
215. Setti Balija
216. Sistakkaranm
217. Sollar
218. Srisayana
219. Tarakan
220. Tatapux
221. Thandal Vannan
222. Thiya, Elhura, Thiyyas
223. Thogatta Veerakshatriya
224. Tholkollans
225. Tholuva Naicker and Vettalakara Nairko
226. Thondaiman
227. Thoraiyan
228. Thottia Naicken (including Rajakambalam, Gollavar, Sil-

layar, Thokalavar and Tholuva Naikar)

229. Thottiyar
230. Thunnan
231. Thurpur Kapus, Casula Kapus
232. Tigala (Tigla)
233. Tolikula
234. Uppara
235. Urali Goundan
236. Vada Balija, Vadava (Golla or Kondri)
237. Vadra or Vaddara
238. Vadukan, Vadagan Vadugan, Vaduvan
239. Valakatalavan
240. Valans
241. Valmiki
242. Vaniyar
243. Vaniyan or Vaniar (Vanika, Vanika-Vaisya, Vaisyachetty, Vanibaacherry, Ayiravar and Nagarathar)
244. Vannan, Vannar
245. Vanniyakula Kshatriya, including Vanniar or Vanniyar Gounder, Kondar or Vannia Gounder and Vannikandar (other than Vella Gounder belonging to Vanni Vanniyakula Kshatriya Caste)
246. Vathis
247. Veerassiva (Fandaram, Matapathi, Vairagi, Vairavi, Yogiswarar)
248. Velan, Vollan
249. Vellala Pillai, (Nanjinad Vellala)
250. Veluthsdan, Veluthedathu Nair
251. Vettaikaran
252. Vetturan
253. Vettuva Goundar
254. Vettuvan
255. Vikurup
256. Vilakkathala Nairs (Velakkathalavan)
257. Virakadi Veklalar
258. Yadava (Konar, Kolaya, Ayar, Mayar, Muniyan, Eruman)
259. Yorukula
260. Yoggeswaran.

2

NARMADA WATER DISPUTES TRIBUNAL UNDER SECTION 5(3) OF THE INTER-STATE WATER DISPUTES ACT, 1956, 1979 — FURTHER REPORT[1]

Chairman Shri V. Ramaswami
Members Shri A.K. Sinha; Shri M.R.A. Ansari

Appointment

The Narmada Water Disputes Tribunal investigated the matters referred to it under Section 5(1) of the Inter-State Water Disputes Act, 1956 and forwarded its decision and report to the Government of India on 16th August, 1978. The Union of India and the States of Gujarat, Madhya Pradesh, Maharashtra and Rajasthan filed Reference Nos. 1,2,3,4 and 5 of 1978 respectively. Under Section 5(3) of the said Act on 16th November 1978. In each of the references, replies were filled by the respective respondent States on 22nd January, 1979. No reply was filed by the Union of India to Reference Nos. 2 to 5 of 1978 filed by the four States. However in its letter No. F/4/4/78-WD dated 20th January, 1979 the Union of India stated that "It did not consider it necessary to file any replies to References made by the State Governments of Gujarat, Madhya Pradesh, Maharashtra and Rajasthan but it reserved its right to make appropriate oral submission on those References.

Terms of Reference

It is also necessary to say that in Reference No. 1 of 1978, the Union of India did not file a Rejoinder to the replies filed by the four contesting States in that Reference. In Reference No.2 of 1978, Gujarat filed a

1. Delhi, Controller of Publications, 1980, 124 p.

rejoinder on 15th March, 1979. Similarly, in References Nos. 3, 4 and 5 of 1979 Madhya Pradesh, Maharashtra and Rajasthan filed their respective Rejoinders on 15th March, 1979.

Madhya Pradesh filed a separate Rejoinder (CMP No. 8 of 1979) on the scope and ambit of Section 5(3) of the Inter-State Water Disputes Act on 21st February, 1979. Gujarat, Rajasthan and Maharashtra filed Sur-Rejoinders (CMPs 13, 17 and 18 of 1979) to the Rejoinder of Madhya Pradesh on 15th March, 1979. The Union of India did not file a Sur-Rejoinder to the Rejoinder of Madhya Pradesh though it was afforded an opportunity of doing so.

The matter of water disputes regarding the Inter-State River Narmada and the River Valley thereof between–

1. The State of Gujarat
2. The State of Madhya Pradesh
3. The State of Maharashtra
4. The State of Rajasthan

Contents

Scope of the jurisdiction under Section 5(3) of the Inter-State Water Disputes Act (Act 33); Reference No. 1 of 1978 by Union of India; Reference No. 2 of 1978 by the State of Gujarat; Reference No. 3 of 1978 by the State of Madhya Pradesh; Reference No. 4 of 1978 by the State of Maharashtra; Reference No. 5 of 1978 by the State of Rajasthan; Order as to costs and other incidental Matters; Modification in the Report of the Tribunal (except in the Final Order); Final Order of the Tribunal modified as a result of the explanation guidance given by Tribunal under Section 5(3) of the Inter-State Water Dispute Act, 1956; Statements from 1 to 4; Annexure.

Final Order and Decision of the Narmada Water Disputes Tribunal

In Chapters I to VIII of this Further Report Volume I, the Chairman of the Tribunal, Shri V. Ramaswami, and Member, Shri M.R.A. Ansari, have expressed their opinion on all the important points arising in these References. Shri A.K. Sinha, another Member, has expressed on a few points a somewhat different opinion which is reproduced in Volume II of this Further Report. In accordance with the majority opinion, the

Tribunal gives the following modified Decision under Section 5(3) of the Inter-State Water Disputes Act, 1956 read with Section 5(4) of the same Act.

Final Order and Decision of the Tribunal

Clause I. — *Date of Coming into Operation of the Order*

This Order shall come into operation on the date of publication of the Decision of this Tribunal in the Official Gazette under Section 6 of the Inter-State Water Disputes Act, 1956.

Clause II. — *Determination of the Utilisable Quantum of Narmada Waters at Sardar Sarovar Dam Site*

The Tribunal hereby determines that the utilisable quantum of waters of the Narmada at Sardar Sarovar Dam Site on the basis of 75 per cent dependability should be assessed at 28 Million Acre Feet (34,537.44 M.cu.m.).

Clause III. — *Apportionment of the Utilisable Quantum of Narmada Waters*

(1) The Tribunal hereby orders that out of the utilisable quantum of Narmada waters. (a) Madhya Pradesh is entitled to a share of 18.25 Million Acre Feet (22,511.01 M.cu.m.), (b) Gujarat is entitled to a share of 9 Million Acre Feet (11,101.32 M.cu.m), (c) Rajasthan is entitled to a share of 0.5 Million Acre Feet (616.74 M.cu.m.) and (d) Maharashtra is entitled to a share of 0.25 Million Acre Feet (308.37 M.cu.m);

(2) Further, it is clarified that the apportionment relates to actual withdrawals and not consumptive use;

(3) Within its share of water, each party State is free to make such changes in the pattern of water use and in the areas to be benefited within or outside the Narmada basin in is territory as it may consider necessary.

Clause IV. — *Order with Regard to Excess Waters and Sharing of Distress*

(1) The utilisable flow of Narmada in excess of the 28 Million Acre Feet (34,537.44 M.cu.m.) of utilisable flow in any water year, i.e., from Ist of July to 30th of June of next calendar year is appor-

tioned in the following ratios of allocation, i.e., 73 for Madhya Pradesh, 36 for Gujarat, 1 for Maharashtra and 2 for Rajasthan;

(2) In the event of the available utilisable waters for allocation in any water year from 1st of July to 30th June of the next calendar year falling short of 28 Million Acre Feet (34,537.44 M.cu.m.), the shortage should be shared between the various States in the ratio of 73 for Madhya Pradesh, 36 for Gujarat, 1 for Maharashtra and 2 for Rajasthan;

(3) The available utilisable waters in a water year will include the waters carried over from the previous water year as assessed on the Ist of July on the basis of stored waters available on that date;

(4) The available utilisable waters on any date will be inclusive of return flows and exclusive of losses due to evaporation of the various reservoirs;

(5) It may be mentioned that in many years there will be surplus water in the filling period after meeting the storage requirements and withdrawals during the period. This will flow down to sea. Only a portion of it will be utilised for generating power at Sardar Sarovar riverbed power-house, and the rest will go waste. It is desirable that water, which would go waste without even generating power at the last riverbed power-house, should be allowed to be utilised by the party States to the extent they can.

Gujarat is, therefore, directed that whenever water starts going waste to sea without generating power, or based on the information received from upstream gauging stations, it anticipates that water would so go waste, it shall inform the Narmada Control Authority (hereinafter referred to as the Authority) and designated representatives of all the concerned States. Gujarat shall also inform them when such flows cease. During the period of such flows, the party States, whose reservoirs are spilling and the spill water cannot be stored elsewhere, may utilise such flows from the said reservoirs as they like and such utilisation by the party States will not count towards allotment of supplies to them, but use of such water will not establish any prescriptive rights.

Clause V. — *Period of Operation of the Order of Apportionment*

Our Orders with regard to the equitable allocation in Clauses III and IV are made subject to review at any time after a period of 45 years from the date of publication of the Decision of the Tribunal in the Official Gazette.

Clause VI. — *Full Supply Level of the Navagam Canal*

The Tribunal hereby determines that the Full Supply Level of Navagam Canal off taking from Sardar Sarovar should be fixed at 91.44 m., (+300′) at its head regulator with a bed gradient of 1 in 12,000 from head to 290 km. (mile 180), that is, up to the offtake of Saurashtra branch. From that point to Rajasthan border the bed gradient should be 1 in 10,000. These bed gradients may be changed by Gujarat and Rajasthan by mutual agreement. Gujarat and Rajasthan shall be at liberty to decide the canal capacity required by each in the light of water which would be expected to be available within their share.

Clause VII. — *Full Reservoir Level and Maximum Water Level of the Sardar Sarovar Dam*

The Tribunal hereby determines that the height of the Sardar Sarovar Dam should be fixed for Full Reservoir Level +138.68 m., (+455′) and Maximum Water Level at +140.21 m., (+460′). Gujarat shall take up and complete the construction of the dam accordingly.

Clause VIII. — *Sharing of Costs and Benefits*

(1)(i) The Tribunal hereby determines that out of the net power produced at Navagam at canal head and river bed power houses on any day the share of Madhya Pradesh will be 57 per cent; Maharashtra's share will be 27 per cent and Gujarat's share will be 16 per cent.

(ii) The party States shall make available in annual instalments their share of funds required according to approved construction programme and take all the necessary steps to complete the Sardar Sarovar Dam within ten years of the date of publication of the Final Order and Decision of the Tribunal in the Official Gazette.

(2) The Tribunal makes the following further Orders:

(i) The power generated in the River Bed and Canal Power

Houses at Navagam will be integrated in a common switchyard.

(ii) Madhya Pradesh and Maharashtra will be entitled to get 57 per cent and 27 per cent respectively of the power available at bus bar in the switchyard after allowing for station auxiliaries.

(iii) The above entitlement applies both to availability of machine capacity for peak loads and to the total energy produced in any day.

(iv) The entitlement of power and energy for any day can be utilised fully or partly by the concerned States of sold to another participating State under mutual agreement. It cannot, however, be carried forward except under a separate agreement or working arrangement entered into among the effected parties.

(v) Gujarat will construct and maintain the transmission lines needed to supply the allotted quantum of power to Madhya Pradesh and Maharashtra up to Gujarat State border, along an alignment as agreed to between the parties and if there is no agreement, along such alignment as many be decided by the Narmada Control Authority. The transmission lines beyond Gujarat State border shall be constructed and maintained by Madhya Pradesh and Maharashtra in their respective States.

(vi) The power houses and appurtenant works including the machinery and all installations as well as the transmission lines in Gujarat State will be constructed, maintained and operated by Gujarat State or an authority nominated by the State.

(vii) The authority in control of the Power Houses shall follow the direction of the Narmada Control Authority in so far as use of water is concerned.

(viii) The scheme of operation of the Power Houses including the power required and the load to be catered for the different party States during different parts of the day shall be settled between the States at least one week before the commencement of every month and shall not be altered during the month except under agreement among the States or under emergencies.

If and when Sardar Sarovar Power Complex gets linked with the Regional or National Power Grid, the operation of the Sardar Sarovar Power Complex will be governed by such altered system conditions. But in that event the Narmada Control Authority should arrange to take such steps as are necessary to enable the three States of Gujarat, Madhya Pradesh and Maharashtra to get their entitlement of power and energy from the Sardar Sarovar Power Complex according to these orders.

(ix) The capital cost of the power portion of Navagam Complex shall comprise the following:

(a) Full cost of Unit III electrical works and control works pertaining thereto, upto and including the switchyard;
(b) Full cost of transmission lines in Gujarat State constructed for supplying power to Madhya Pradesh and Maharashtra;
(c) 56.1 per cent of the net cost of common facilities such as Dam and Appurtenant Works, i.e., Unit I of Sardar Sarovar Project, after allowing for credits, if any; and
(d) 56.1 per cent of the credit given to Madhya Pradesh for the downstream benefits derived from Narmadasagar Dam.

(x) Madhya Pradesh and Maharashtra shall respectively pay to Gujarat 57 per cent and 27 per cent of the capital cost of the power portion of the Sardar Sarovar headworks worked out vide (ix) above. This amount shall be paid in annual instalments until the capital works are completed. Each instalment will be worked out on the basis of the budgeted figures of the concerned works at the commencement of each financial year and shall be set off and adjusted against actual figures at the end of the financial year.

(xi) In addition to the payments vide (x) above, Madhya Pradesh and Maharashtra shall also pay to Gujarat 57 per cent and 27 respectively of the operation and maintenance costs of the Sardar Sarovar Power Complex each year. These payments are also to be based on budgeted figures at the commencement of each financial year and adjusted against actual cost at the end of the year.

(xii) Notwithstanding the directions contained hereinabove, the party States may, by mutual agreement, after, amend, or modify any of the directions in respect of sharing of power and payment for it.

Clause IX. — *Regulated Releases to be made by Madhya Pradesh for the Requirement of Sardar Sarovar Project*

With regard to the quantum and pattern of regulated releases, the Tribunal makes the following Order:

It has been agreed by the party States and decided by the Tribunal in its Order dated 8th October, 1974, that the utilisable quantity of water of 75 per cent dependability in the Narmada at Sardar Sarovar Dam site should be assessed at 28 MAF (34,537,44 M.cu.m.). The actual inflow of 75 per cent dependability, however, is only 33,316.29 M.cu.m (27.01 MAF) and this is brought up to utilisable quantity of 28 MAF (34,537.44 M.cu.m.) by means of carryover in various reservoirs allowing for evaporation losses and regeneration. Out of 28 MAF (34,537.44 M.cu.m), 11,101.32 M.cu.m. (9 MAF) has to be provided for Gujarat and 0.5 MAF (616.74 M.cu.m.) for Rajasthan at Sardar Sarovar. The requirements at Sardar Sarovar have to be met by releases by Madhya Pradesh and by inflows from the intermediate catchment, surplus to the requirements of Madhya Pradesh below Narmadasagar and Maharashtra. The releases from Maheshwar work out to 10,015.86 M.cu.m. (8.12 MAF). Making uniform monthly releases the amount of water to be released by Madhya Pradesh per month would be 834.65 M.cu.m. (0.677 MAF). The actual inflow in the river system, however, would vary from year to year and, therefore, the releases by Madhya Pradesh would also vary.

The inflow during the filling period, July to October, cannot be predicted at the beginning of the season. It is only in October that it would be fully known whether the particular year is a normal year or the extent to which it is a surplus or deficit year. Normally the releases by Madhya Pradesh during the filling period, therefore, would have to be more or less on the basis of the year yielding 28 MAF (34,537.44 M.cu.m.) utilisable quantity. The month of July and early part of August are crucial for Kharif sowing. It is important that during this period regulatory arrangements should ensure that due share of water is made available to all parties.

Having regard to the facts mentioned in the preceding two paragraphs, we order that detailed rules of regulation and water accounting shall be framed by Narmada Control Authority in accordance with the guidelines given below. These guidelines may, however, be altered, amended or modified by agreement between the States concerned.

(i) The 28 MAF (34,537.44 M.cu.m.) utilisable supplies of 75 per cent dependability in a water year (1st July to 30th June next year) shall be shared by the party States as under:

Madhya Pradesh	18.25 MAF	(22,511.01 M.cu.m.)
Gujarat	9.00 MAF	(11,101.32 M.cu.m.)
Rajasthan	0.50 MAF	(616.74 M.cu.m.)
Maharashtra	0.25 MAF	(308.37 M.cu.m.)
	28.00 MAF	(34,537.44 M.cu.m.)

(ii) Surplus or deficit utilisable supplies in a water year shall be shared to the extent feasible by the party States in the same proportion as their allotted shares in (i) above. The surplus water shall first be utilised for filling up the reservoirs to capacity and surplus water shall be utilised for irrigation and other purposes only after that has been ensured.

(iii) The water available in the live storages of the various reservoirs on 30th June shall be reckoned as an inflow to be shared in the next water year.

(iv) The releases necessary to ensure Gujarat and Rajasthan's share of water in a water year shall be let down by Madhya Pradesh at a reasonably uniform rate, permitting only such variation as the Authority may direct or approve and keeping in view the directions for regulated releases.

(v) The Authority shall ensure by so directing the releases by Madhya Pradesh that there is at all times sufficient utilisable water in Sardar Sarovar to meet the requirements of the next ten days subject to water being available in the storages in Madhya Pradesh after taking into account the proportionate requirements of Madhya Pradesh. For this purpose, Gujarat and Rajasthan would intimate their requirements of the 10 daily period well in advance.

(vi) Utilisation in a water year by each party State shall be figured out on the basis of actual daily discharge at canal head on every major and medium project. For minor works, it shall be on the basis of area irrigated under different crops, the delta for each crop being approved by the Authority. For pumping schemes, drawing directly from the river, its tributaries or servoirs, whether for irrigation, domestic or industrial use, water drawn shall be reckoned on the basis of the rated capacity of pumps and the number of hours they run. For a cross check, the seasonwise and cropwise area irrigated by each pumping scheme shall also be recorded, and if the figures of water drawn as worked out by the two aforesaid methods differ, the decision of the Authority as regards water drawn shall be final.

(vii) Withdrawals from Sardar Sarovar for Navagam Canal for Gujarat and Rajasthan shall be measured at the head of Navagam Canal. The supply to Rajasthan shall be measured at Gujarat-Rajasthan border. The loss in the canal in carrying the supply for Rajasthan shall be determined by the Authority after the canal has been constructed and shall reckon against the share of Rajasthan.

Water let down into the river from Sardar Sarovar through power house turbines shall be measured on the basis of power generated by it and that escaped through the spillway by measurement at the spillway.

Gujarat may let down water from Sardar Sarovar for its downstream use by making specific indent for it and such releases shall reckon against its share. Such releases for downstream use shall be made through the turbines and the power so generated shared between Madhya Pradesh, Maharashtra and Gujarat in the prescribed ratio. Water let down into the river from Sardar Sarovar except at the specific indent of Gujarat shall not reckon against the share of Gujarat.

The water drawn from Sardar Sarovar for use in Madhya Pradesh and Maharashtra, as the case may be, shall reckon against the share of water of that State.

(viii) For major and medium projects, water account shall be kept by 10 daily period. The last 10 daily period of a month may have 11 days, 10 days or less, depending upon the number of days in the month. For minor schemes water accounts shall be kept by crop seasons, kharif (July to October) rabi (November to March) and hot weather (April to June). For pumping schemes and domestic and industrial uses it shall be monthly.

(ix) The water use by minor and pumping schemes in any ten daily period may provisionally be taken to be the same as in the corresponding period in the previous year on the basis of average use during the crop period. For final water account, however, it will be determined as in (vi) above.

(x) Each State shall furnish to the Authority and make available to any party State desiring the same, such data and information as the Authority may require and ask for.

(xi) The Authority shall arrange the review of the ten day releases made by Madhya Pradesh at least once a month and oftener as considered necessary for directing any change in the releases. It may designate a person for doing so.

(xii) The Authority shall direct final adjustment to be made in the following water year of the use in excess of the authorised use, if any, by any State or States during the preceding water year by curtailing the share(s) of the State or States concerned which have used water in excess and make over the same to the State or State which have received short supplies. Water supplied to Rajasthan on any day in excess of 10 per cent over and above its indent shall reckon against use by Gujarat.

(xiii) The Authority shall furnish the annual water account for the water year to the Governments of the party States by the end of August of the next water year. Each State may make any observation on the account and/or point out corrections in it, if any, within one month of its receipt. After making the necessary modifications, the Authority shall furnish to each party State the final annual water account for the water year by 31st October. The Authority shall cause the annual water account to be published each year.

Clause X. — *Payment to be made by Gujarat to Madhya Pradesh for such Regulated Releases*

(1) Madhya Pradesh shall take up and complete the construction of Narmadasagar dam with FRL 262.13 m (860 ft.) concurrently with or earlier than the construction of Sardar Sarovar dam.

(2) The Tribunal further orders that Gujarat should credit to Madhya Pradesh each year 17.63 per cent of the expenditure on account of Narmadasagar dam in the financial year commencing from the year of taking up of the construction of Narmadasagar dam. This will be initially credited on the basis of budget allotment to be adjusted at the end of the year on actual expenditure. The post construction expenditure on maintenance is not to be considered as cost of construction.

Clause XI. — *Directions Regarding Submergence Land Acquisition and Rehabilitation of Displaced Persons*

Sub-Clause I.—*Definitions*

I(1): "Land" The expression "land" shall have the same meaning as defined in the Land Acquisition Act, 1894 (hereinafter referred to as the Act) which states "the expression 'land' includes benefits to arise out of land, and things attached to the earth or permanently fastened to anything attached to the earth."

I(2): "Oustee" An 'oustee' shall mean any person who since at least one year prior to the date of publication of the notification under Section 4 of the Act, has been ordinarily residing or cultivating land or carrying on any trade, occupation, or calling or working for gain in the area likely to be submerged permanently or temporarily.

I(3): "Family" (i) A family shall include husband, wife and minor children and other persons dependent on the head of the family, e.g., widowed mother.

(ii) Every major son will be treated as a separate family.

Sub-Clause II.— *Lands which are to be Compulsorily Acquired*

II(1): Madhya Pradesh and Maharashtra shall acquire for Sardar Sarovar Project under the provisions of the Land Acquisition Act, 1894, all lands of private ownership situated below the FRL+138.68 m (455′) of Sardar Sarovar and all interests therein not belonging to the respective States. If on the basis aforesaid, 75 per cent or more land of a contiguous holding of any person is required to be compulsorily acquired, such person shall have the option to compel compulsory acquisition of the entire contiguous holding.

II(2): Madhya Pradesh and Maharashtra shall also acquire for Sardar Sarovar Project under the provisions of the Land Acquisition Act,

1894, all buildings with their appurtenant land situated between FRL+138.68 m (455′) and MWL+141.21 m (460′) as also those affected by the backwater effect resulting from MWL + 141.21 m (460′).

II(3): The backwater level at the highest flood level in Sardar Sarovar shall be worked out by the Central Water Commission in consultation with Madhya Pradesh and Gujarat.

Sub-Clause III.— *Liability of Gujarat to Pay Compensation for Land Acquisition and Rehabilitation, etc.*

III(1): Gujarat shall pay to Madhya Pradesh and Maharashtra all costs including compensation, charges and expenses incurred by them for or in respect of the compulsory acquisition of lands required to be acquired as aforesaid.

III(2): Gujarat shall pay to Madhya Pradesh and Maharashtra and the Union of India compensation for the respective Government lands and structures on principles similar to those underlying the Land Acquisition Act, 1894. Where any dispute or difference arises between Gujarat, Madhya Pradesh, Maharashtra and the Union of India with respect to the compensation payable as aforesaid any of the three States of Gujarat, Madhya Pradesh and Maharashtra or the Union of India may refer the matter in dispute to arbitration. The State of Gujarat on the one hand and the States of Madhya Pradesh, Maharashtra or the Union of India (as the case may be) on the other hand shall respectively nominate one Arbitrator each. In the event of disagreement between the Arbitrators, such dispute or difference shall be referred to an Umpire who shall be a person appointed in that behalf by the Chief Justice of India from among persons who are, or have been Judges of the Supreme Court. The decision of the Arbitrators, or, as the case may be, of the Umpire shall be final and binding on the parties and shall be given effect to by them.

III(3): Gujarat shall pay to Madhya Pradesh and Maharashtra land revenue in accordance with the respective Land Revenue Codes of Madhya Pradesh and Maharashtra in respect of all lands in their respective territories acquired for Gujarat or conveyed to it.

III(4): Gujarat shall pay to Madhya Pradesh and Maharashtra all costs, charges and expenses incurred by Madhya Pradesh and Maharashtra for the purpose of removal and reinstallation of any ancient or historical monuments, archaeological remains, religious place of worship or idols likely to be affected by submergence under Sardar Sarovar and that in the even of such payment being made, no separate compensation as hereinbefore provided shall be required to be paid in respect of the same having been affected by the submergence.

III(5): Gujarat shall pay to Madhya Pradesh and Maharashtra all costs, charges and expenses required to be incurred by them for rehabilitation of oustees and oustee families in their respective territories in accordance with the directions hereinafter contained.

III(6): Gujarat shall pay to Madhya Pradesh and Maharashtra costs on account of establishment charges for land acquisition and rehabilitation and other departmental staff which Madhya Pradesh and Maharashtra may consider necessary for the purpose of such acquisition and rehabilitation.

Sub-Clause IV. — *Provision for Rehabilitation*

IV(1): According to the present estimates the number of oustee families would be 6147 spread over 158 villages in Madhya Pradesh, 456 families spread over 27 villages in Maharashtra. Gujarat shall establish rehabilitation villages in Gujarat in the irrigation command of the Sardar Sarovar Project on the norms hereinafter mentioned for rehabilitation of the families who are willing to migrate to Gujarat. For oustee families who are unwilling to migrate to Gujarat, Gujarat shall pay to Madhya Pradesh and Maharashtra the cost, charges and expenses for establishment of such villages in their respective territories on the norms as hereinafter provided.

IV(2)(i): According to the present estimates the number of oustee families below RL 106.68 metres (RL 350′) would be 30 spread over 20 villages in Madhya Pradesh and 250 families spread over 20 villages in Maharashtra. Within six months of the publication of the decision of the Tribunal in the Official Gazette, Gujarat, Madhya Pradesh and Maharashtra shall determine by mutual consultation the location of one or two rehabilitation villages in Gujarat to rehabilitate oustees from areas below Rs 106.68 meters (RL 350′). Gujarat shall acquire necessary lands for the rehabilitation villages and make available the same within the two years of the decision of the Tribunal. Within six months of the decision of the location of the rehabilitation villages in Gujarat, Madhya Pradesh and Maharashtra shall intimate to Gujarat the number of oustee families from areas below RL 106.68 metres (RL 350′) willing to migrate to Gujarat. For the remaining oustee families,

Madhya Pradesh and Maharashtra shall arrange to acquire lands for rehabilitation within the respective States.

IV(2)(ii): Madhya Pradesh and Maharashtra shall set up adequate establishments for land acquisition and rehabilitation of oustee families. Gujarat shall deposit within three months of the decision of the Tribunal Rupees ten lakhs each with Madhya Pradesh and Maharashtra in advance towards cost of establishment and rehabilitation in these States to be adjusted after actual costs are determined. Madhya Pradesh and Maharashtra shall start land acquisition proceedings for areas below RL 106.68 metres (RL+350′), within six months of the decision of the Tribunal and convey the lands to Gujarat for project purposes within three years of the decision of the Tribunal. Within 18 months of the decision of the Tribunal Gujarat shall make an advance payment of Rs. 70 lakhs to Madhya Pradesh and Rs. 100 lakhs to Maharashtra towards the compensation of land, to be adjusted after actual costs are determined.

IV(2)(iii): Regarding the oustee families from areas above RL 106.68 metres (RL+350′), Gujarat shall intimate to Madhya Pradesh and Maharashtra within six months of publication of the decision of the Tribunal in the Official Gazette the number and general location of rehabilitation villages proposed to be established by Gujarat in accordance with the decision of the Tribunal. Within one year of the receipt of proposal of Gujarat, both Madhya Pradesh and Maharashtra shall intimate to Gujarat the number of oustee families willing to migrate to Gujarat. The three States by mutual consultation shall determine within two years of the decision of the Tribunal, the number and general location of rehabilitation villages required to be established by Gujarat in its own territory. Madhya Pradesh and Maharashtra shall intimate to Gujarat the number of such villages to be established in Madhya Pradesh and Maharashtra and for which Gujarat would be required to make payments to Madhya Pradesh and Maharashtra respectively.

IV(2)(iv): Gujarat shall acquire and make available a year in advance of the submergence before each successive stage, irrigable lands and house sites for rehabilitation of the oustee families from Madhya Pradesh and Maharashtra who are willing to migrate to Gujarat. Gujarat shall in the first instance offer to rehabilitate the oustees in its own territory.

IV(3): Gujarat shall also provide the following grants and amenities to the oustees:

(a) Resettlement Grants (Rehabilitation Grant)—Gujarat shall pay per family a sum of Rs. 750 inclusive of transportation charges as resettlement grant.

(b) Grant-in-aid.

In addition, Gujarat shall pay per family grant-in-aid in the following scale:

Where total compensation is received	Grant-in-aid
Above Rs. 2000	Nil
Between Rs. 2000 and Rs. 500	Rs. 500 less an amount equal to one-third of the compensation in excess of Rs. 500
Less than Rs. 500	Rs. 500

(c) Civic amenities:

1. One primary school (3 rooms) for 100 families.
2. One Panchayat Ghar for every 500 families.
3. One Dispensary for every 500 families.
4. One seed store for every 500 families.
5. One children's park for every 500 families.
6. One village pond for every 500 families.
7. Drinking water well with through for every 50 families.
8. Each colony should be linked to main road by roads of appropriate standard.
9. One platform for every 50 families.
10. Every oustee family shall be entitled to and allotted a house site, i.e., a plot of land measuring 18.29 x 27.43m. (60′ x 90′) free of cost. In addition, a provision of 30 per cent additional area for roads, Government buildings, open space, etc., shall be made by Gujarat under civic amenities.
11. The State of Gujarat shall make the following provision for rehabilitation in Madhya Pradesh and Maharashtra:

(a) Resettlement	Rs. 750 per family
(b) Grant-in-aid	Rs. 500 per family
(c) Acquisition of land for resettlement of families affected @ 0.40 hectares (one acre) for 6 families	Rs. 1500 per aere

(d) Civic amenities:

1.	One primary school @ 100 families	Rs. 30,000 each
2.	One Community Hall-cum-Panchayat Bhavan @ 500 families	Rs. 20,000 each
3.	One Dispensary @ 500 families	Rs. 25,000 each
4.	One seed store @ 500 families	Rs. 10,000 each
5.	One Children's Park @ 500 families	Rs. 6,000 each
6.	One Well with through @ 50 families	Rs. 10,000 each
7.	One pond @ 500 families	Rs. 20,000 each
8.	One tree platform @ 50 families	Rs. 1,500 each
9.	One religious place of worship @ 100 families	Rs. 1,000 each
10.	Construction of approach roads and link roads for *Abadies* 3 km every new *Abadi*	Rs. 30,000 per km.
11.	Electrical distribution lines and street lights 2 km. per 100 families	Rs. 11,000 per km.
12.	Social amenities for each municipal town going under submergence, viz., water supply and sanitary arrangements layout, levelling of site, etc.	Rs. 5,00,000 each town.

IV(4)(i): Gujarat is directed to provide for rehabilitation and civic amenities as per directions contained hereinabove in sub-clause IV(3) in its estimate for B-Land compensation and rehabilitation.

IV(4)(ii): Notwithstanding the provisions hereinbefore contained, Gujarat shall not be liable to pay any compensation for the loss of public properties, facilities or amenities such as drinking water wells, primary school buildings, internal roads, village sites, approach roads, dispensaries, Panchayat buildings, rural electrification, highway, bridges, telegraph lines, power lines, etc., if corresponding alternative properties, facilities or amenities are to be provided at the cost of the Sardar Sarovar Project. The party owning the facility shall have the option to accept compensation for utilities as existing or ask for their replacement or re-location at the cost of Gujarat.

IV(5): It is made clear that the monetary values in Clause IV(3)(c) are liable to be changed at the time of actual rehabilitation. Where any dispute or difference arises as regards the changed valuation the matter shall be determined by Arbitration in the manner provided in Clause III(2) above and Gujarat's liability shall stand altered accordingly.

IV(6)(i): In the event of Gujarat being unable to resettle the oustees or the oustees being unwilling to occupy the area offered by Gujarat, Madhya Pradesh and Maharashtra shall make such provisions for rehabilitation, civic amenities, etc., on the lines mentioned in Clauses IV(1) to (4) above. Gujarat shall, in that event, be liable to pay all such expenses, costs, etc., arising out of or in connection with rehabilitation and provision of civic amenities for the oustees including the cost of all acquisition proceedings and payment of compensation, etc., as per the Land Acquisition Act, for the land allotted to oustees for cultivation and habitation.

IV(6)(ii): In no event shall any areas in Madhya Pradesh and Maharashtra be submerged under the Sardar Sarovar unless all payment of compensation, expenses and costs as aforesaid is made for acquisition of land and properties and arrangements are made for the rehabilitation of the oustees therefrom in accordance with these directions and intimated to the oustees.

IV(7): *Allotment of Agricultural Lands:* Every displaced family from whom more than 25 per cent of its land holding is acquired shall be entitled to and be allotted irrigable land to the extent of land acquired from it subject to the prescribed ceiling in the State concerned and a minimum of 2 hectares (5 acres) per family, the irrigation facilities being provided by the State in whose territory the allotted land is situated. This land shall be transferred to the oustee family if it agrees to take it. The price charged for it would be as mutually agreed between Gujarat and the concerned State. Of the price to be paid for the land a sum equal to 50 per cent of the compensation payable to the oustee family for the land acquired from it will be set off as an initial instalment of payment. The balance cost of the allotted land shall be recovered from the allottee in 20 yearly instalments free of interest. Where land is allotted in Madhya Pradesh or Maharashtra, Gujarat having paid for it *vide* Clause IV(6)(i) supra, all recoveries for the allotted land shall be credited to Gujarat.

IV(8): Any dispute between the States in respect of Clauses IV(1) to (7) of these directions shall be referred to and determined by arbitration in the manner provided in Clause III(2) of these directions.

Sub-Clause V.— *Programme for Payment to be made by Gujarat to Madhya Pradesh and Maharashtra*

V(1): As soon as practicable after the publication of the decision of the Tribunal in the Official Gazette, Gujarat shall prepare and furnish to the other party States, a fresh estimate of sub-head B-Land for the Sardar Sarovar Project as permitted by the Tribunal including in particular, costs of acquisition of lands in Madhya Pradesh and Maharashtra and of rehabilitation of oustee families in Madhya Pradesh and Maharashtra.

V(2)(i): As soon as practicable after the publication of the decision of the Tribunal in the Official Gazette and in any case before expiry of three months thereafter, both Madhya Pradesh and Maharashtra shall furnish to Gujarat three sets of Majmuli/Taluka maps of all talukas in their respective territories likely to be submerged wholly or partly under Sardar Sarovar. These maps shall indicate village boundaries. Within three months after the receipt of the Majmuli/Taluka maps Gujarat shall mark thereon the boundary of the area situated below the FRL as also that between FRL and MWL including the area affected by back water resulting from MWL and shall return one respective set so marked to Madhya Pradesh and Maharashtra.

V(2)(ii): As soon as practicable after the receipt of one set of the Majmuli/Taluka maps marked as aforesaid and in any case within six months thereof, the Governments of Madhya Pradesh and Maharashtra shall publish notifications under Sub-section (1) of Section 4 of the Act notifying that the lands in their respective territories situated below the FRL and buildings with their appurtenant lands between FRL and MWL, as also those affected by the back water effect resulting from MWL (to be specified in the notifications) are likely to be needed for the Sardar Sarovar Project.

V(2)(iii): As soon as practicable, after publication of the decision of the Tribunal in the Official Gazette as hereinbefore referred to and in any case within one year thereof, Gujarat shall intimate to Madhya Pradesh and Maharashtra yearwise programme of construction of the dam.

V(2)(iv): Objections, if any, received against the proposed acquisition of lands as notified under Section 4 of the Act shall be heard and disposed of and any reports to the State Governments as contemplated by Sub-section (2) of Section 5A of the Act shall be made with utmost expedition. The Governments of Madhya Pradesh and Maharashtra shall issue requisite notifications under Section 6 of the Act with utmost expedition and in any case before the expiry of three years from the dates of publications of the respective notifications under Sub-section (1) of Section 4 of the Act.

V(2)(v): As soon as practicable, after receipt of the yearwise programme of construction of the Sardar Sarovar dam from Gujarat both Madhya Pradesh and Maharashtra in consultation with Gujarat shall finalise their respective yearwise programme of completing the proceedings for compulsory acquisition of lands in their respective territories up to the stages of making awards under Section 11 of the Act and of taking possession of the lands under Section 16 of the Act.

V(3)(i): Gujarat is required to pay to Madhya Pradesh and Maharashtra compensation for compulsory acquisition of lands, market value of Government lands to be conveyed to Gujarat and expenditure to be incurred in connection with the rehabilitation of oustee families to be rehabilitated in Madhya Pradesh and Maharashtra as hereinbefore provided. Madhya Pradesh and Maharashtra shall on or before 30th September of each year intimate to Gujarat the amounts required to be paid by Gujarat to Madhya Pradesh and Maharashtra respectively having regard to (a) the extent of lands in Madhya Pradesh and Maharashtra in respect of which awards are likely to be made under Section 11 of the Act (b) the extent of Government lands likely to be conveyed by Madhya Pradesh and Maharashtra to Gujarat during the next financial year and (c) the expenditure likely to be incurred by Madhya Pradesh and Maharashtra in connection with rehabilitation of oustee families in Madhya Pradesh and Maharashtra during the next financial year. In arriving at these estimates for the next financial year, Madhya Pradesh and Maharashtra shall also take into account the differences, if any, between the payments made by Gujarat in pursuance of this clause for the current financial year and the amount actually payable during the said financial year.

V(3)(ii): On the basis of these estimates, Gujarat shall on or before the 31st May of the following financial year make payments to Madhya Pradesh and Maharashtra of the amounts estimated as provided in Clause V(3)(i) above.

V(3)(iii): Gujarat shall at each successive stage of submergence intimate to Madhya Pradesh and Maharashtra the area coming under submergence at least 18 months in advance. The inhabitants of the area coming under the respective stages of submergence will be entitled to occupy or use their properties without being required to pay anything for such occupation and use till a date to be notified by the State concerned which date shall not be less than six months before submergence. They must vacate the area by the notified date.

V(4)(i): On payment of the amounts to be paid each year by Gujarat as compensation for compulsory acquisition of lands as aforesaid, Madhya Pradesh and Maharashtra shall, as expeditiously as possible, complete the acquisition and transfer such lands to Gujarat so as to vest the lands in Gujarat to be used only for the purpose of submergence and subject to Clauses V(5) to (8) of these directions.

V(4)(ii): On payment of the market value of Government lands by Gujarat as hereinbefore provided Madhya Pradesh and Maharashtra and the Union of India shall convey such lands to Gujarat so as to vest in Gujarat to be used only for the purpose of submergence and subject to Clauses V(5) to (8) of these directions.

V(5): Gujarat shall pay to Madhya Pradesh and Maharashtra in accordance with the respective Land Revenue Codes, the amount of land revenue payable every year for the lands in their respective territories acquired for Gujarat or conveyed to it, at the rates prevailing in Madhya Pradesh and Maharashtra respectively from time to time.

V(6): Madhya Pradesh and Maharashtra, as the case may be, shall remit each year to Gujarat any revenue which they may derive from the cultivation of lands which get periodically exposed in Sardar Sarovar, after deducting collection charges for the same.

V(7): Notwithstanding vesting in Gujarat of the lands coming under submergence, Madhya Pradesh and Maharashtra shall continue to enjoy all rights of sovereignty intact over the submerged area in the respective States.

V(8): Madhya Pradesh and Maharashtra respectively shall be exclusively entitled to all rights of fishing, boating and water transportation over the part of lake over the submerged land within Madhya Pradesh and Maharashtra respectively, provided, however, that such right is not exercised to the prejudice of any utilities of the Sardar Sarovar Project or cause hindrance in the legitimate performance of their duties by the project personnel.

V(9): All residual rights not specifically transferred to Gujarat in respect of the lands coming under submergence shall continue to vest in the Government in whose territory they are situated.

V(10): In the event of the said lands not being used for the purpose of submergence for which it is acquired, the State of Gujarat shall retransfer such land to Madhya Pradesh or Maharashtra as the case may be, subject to the condition that Madhya Pradesh and Maharashtra refund to Gujarat the amount of compensation received from Gujarat in respect of such land.

V(11): In the event of any land acquired for rehabilitation of oustee families is not used for the purpose, it shall be returned to the original owner on payment, where feasible or otherwise disposed off and due credit given to Gujarat.

V(12): All costs incurred by Gujarat on acquisition of land and rehabilitation of oustees in respect of Sardar Sarovar shall be charged to Sardar Sarovar Project estimate, Unit I—Dam and Appurtenant Works.

Sub-clause VI

Nothing contained in Clause XI shall prevent the alteration, amendment and modification of all or any of the foregoing clauses by agreement between all the party States.

Clause XII:— *Allocation of Cost of Sardar Sarovar Project between Irrigation and Power*

We determine that the cost of Unit I—Dam and Appurtenant Works—should be apportioned between Irrigation and Power as follows:

Irrigation — 43.9 per cent
Power — 56.1 per cent

Clause XIII:— *Allocation of Irrigation Component of Cost of Sardar Sarovar Project between Gujarat and Rajasthan*

(a)(i) The irrigation component of the cost of Unit-I of Sardar Sarovar Project (Dam and Appurtenant Works) should be shared by Gujarat and Rajasthan in the ratio of 18 : 1.

(a)(ii) Madhya Pradesh and Maharashtra shall contribute a *pro rata* share to the irrigation component of the cost of Sardar Sarovar Dam as also towards its operation and annual maintenance, for water drawn from Sardar Sarovar for use in their territory. The *pro rata* share shall be in proportion of the quantity of water so drawn to 9.5 MAF. The amount so contributed shall be credited to Gujarat and Rajasthan in the ratio of 18 : 1.

(b) The cost of Navagam Canal with its design approved by Narmada Control Authority shall be shared by the two States as under:

(i) The cost differential in respect of land, earth work and lining for the gradients proposed by Gujarat and that now prescribed, to be borne by Rajasthan in full; and
(ii) The actual cost of the canal less (i) above to be shared on cusec-mile basis.

The actual cost should be shared by Gujarat and Rajasthan on cusec-mile basis in the first instance and on completion of the work the share cost shall be adjusted as indicated above. Rajasthan shall credit its share cost each year initially on the basis of budget allotment. This should then be adjusted at the end of the year to actual expenditure. The post-construction expenditure on maintenance is not to be considered as cost of construction.

Should any difference arise between Rajasthan and Gujarat on figures of cost in respect of Navagam Main Canal for purposes of sharing the cost, the matter shall be referred to the Narmada Control Authority and on such a reference its decision shall be final and binding.

Clause XIV:— *Setting up of Machinery for Implementing the decision of the Tribunal*

We make the following orders with regard to setting up of machinery for implementing the decision of the Tribunal:

Sub-Clause 1:— *Constitution of the Authority*

1(1): An inter-State administrative authority to be called Narmada Control Authority (hereinafter referred to as the 'Authority') shall be established for the purpose of securing compliance with and implementation of the decision and directions of the Narmada Water Disputes Tribunal (herein referred as the 'Orders').

1(2): The Authority shall consist of seven high-ranking Engineer Members, of whom one each shall be of the rank of Engineer-in-Chief, Chief Engineer, or Additional Chief Engineer of the Irrigation Department, Power Department or the State Electricity Board appointed by the Government of each of the States of Madhya Pradesh, Gujarat,

Maharashtra and Rajasthan and three other eminent Engineers of a rank not-less-than that of a Chief Engineer to be appointed by the Central Government in consultation with the party States. One of the three Independent Members shall be nominated by the Central Government, as the Chairman of the Authority with a deliberative vote at meetings where decisions are taken on any matter affecting the interest of more than one State and he will be in a charge of the administrative work of the Authority. The Central or State Government, as the case may be, shall have the power to remove or suspend from the Authority any Member who, in its opinion, is not suitable to continue as Member.

1(3): Each Independent Member shall be a full-time Member and be appointed for a term not exceeding five years. The Members appointed by the State Governments shall be part-time Members. The appointing authority for Independent Member or that for part-time Member, as the case may be, shall determine the terms and conditions of appointment in each case. As far as practicable, the first appointment of the seven members of the Authority shall be made within three months from the date of publication of the decision of the Tribunal in the Official Gazette.

1(4): *Vacancies of Members*—On any vacancy occurring in the offices of the three independent Members, the Central Government shall appoint a person to such vacant office, and on any vacancy occurring in the office of the four Members other than the independent Members, the State Government by whom the Member whose office falls vacant was appointed shall appoint a person to the vacant office.

In case of illness or absence for any cause whatever of a Member, the Central Government or State Government by whom he was appointed (as the case may be) may appoint a person as an acting Member during such illness or absence and such acting Member shall, while so acting, have all the powers and perform all the duties and be entitled to the indemnities of the Member (vide Sub-clause 5) in whose stead he so acts, save and except that the next senior independent Member appointed by the Central Government and not the acting Member shall act as Chairman at business meeting of the Authority or as the Chairman of the Authority in the event of illness or absence of the Chairman of the Authority.

Sub-Clause 2. — *Secretary of the Authority*

The Authority shall employ a Secretary, who shall be an Engineer. He shall not be a Member of the Authority.

Sub-Clause 3. — *Quorum and Voting*

Five members shall be a quorum and the concurrence of the majority shall be necessary for the transaction of the business of the Authority except such business as the Authority may from time to time prescribe as routine. The Authority shall not prescribe as routine any business in which the interests of any two of the States are likely to be in conflict. For the transaction of routine business three Members shall be a quorum and in the absence of the Chairman of the Authority, the Chairman elected at the meeting shall have a deliberative vote and in the event of an equality of votes a casting vote also.

Subject as aforesaid the Members shall have equal powers.

Sub-Clause 4. — *Disposal of Business by the Authority*

4(1): Subject to the provisions of Sub-clause 4(2) below, the Authority may dispose of any matter before it either by circulation or by holding a meeting. However, it will be open to any Members of the Authority to require that a matter shall not be disposed off by circulation but at a meeting.

4(2): On the following matters the Authority shall record its decision by a Resolution at a meeting in which the Chairman and all the Members from the party States are present:

(i) Framing of Rules of Business;
(ii) Delegation of functions to a Member or Secretary or any official of the Authority;
(iii) Categorising any part of the business of the Authority as of a formal of the routine nature; and
(iv) Any other matter which any of the four party States require that it shall be decided at a meeting where all the members from the party States are present.

However, if any particular item under this Sub-clause cannot be disposed of at two successive meetings owning to the absence of one or more Members from the party States, it shall be disposed off under Sub-clause 3 of Clause XIV.

4(3): Subject to the foregoing provisions, the Authority shall frame its own Rules for the conduct of its business.

4(4): The Authority shall cause proper minutes or records of all its proceedings to be kept as a permanent record.

Sub-Clause 5. — *Indemnity of Members*

No Member, officer or employee of the Authority shall be liable for loss, injury or damages resulting from (a) action taken by such Member, officer or employee in good faith and without malice under the apparent authority of the Orders, even though such action is later determined to be unauthorised, or (b) the negligent or wrongful act of omission of any other person, employed by the Authority and serving under such Member, officer or employee unless such Member, officer or employee failed to exercise due care in the appointment of such other person or the supervision of his work.

Sub-Clause 6. — *Officers and Servants of the Authority*

The Authority may from time to time appoint or employ such and so many officers and servants as it thinks fit and remove or dismiss them, under the rules and regulations applicable to the appointment, removal and a dismissal of the Central Government officers and servants. All such officers and servants shall as such be subject to the sole control of the Authority. The scales of pay and other service conditions shall be as applicable to Central Government employees.

Persons employed in the services of the four States may be appointed or employed by the Authority in such proportions as the Authority may deem fit. The Authority shall arrange with the State Governments to spare the services of the persons employed in the State Governments for whole-time employment with the Authority, or for the performance of any work or services for the Authority. The Authority may also make direct recruitment of any personnel or obtain the same from the Centre or other source as considered appropriate.

Sub-Clause 7. — *Administrative and Field Organisation Costs*

(1): All expenses of the Authority (including the salary and expenses of the independent Members) shall be borne by the State Governments of Madhya Pradesh, Gujarat, Maharashtra and Rajasthan in equal shares. The expenses pertaining to a Members representing a State shall be borne by thc State concerned. The cost of maintaining, operating and controlling the gauging and other hydrological stations in each State and the telecommunication systems for communicating the data shall be borne by the State concerned.

(2): The costs of construction of the storages, power installations, diversion works, headworks and canal networks shall be borne wholly by the State Government in whose territory the work is located except for works whose cost has been ordered by the Tribunal to be shared between two or more party States. Where the capital cost is thus shared, the operation and maintenance cost shall also be shared in the same proportion.

Sub-Clause 8. — *Powers, Functions and Duties of the Authority*

8(1): The role of the Authority will mainly comprise co-ordination and direction. Normally all bilateral matters should be dealt with mutually by the States concerned and referred to the Authority only if there is a dispute.

8(2): The Authority shall be charged with the power and shall be under a duty to do any or all things necessary, sufficient and expedient for the implementation of the Orders with respect to:

(i) the storage, apportionment, regulation and control of the Narmada waters;
(ii) sharing of power benefits from Sardar Sarovar Project;
(iii) regulated releases by Madhya Pradesh;
(iv) acquisition by the concerned State for Sardar Sarovar Project of lands and properties likely to be submerged under Sardar Sarovar;
(v) compensation and rehabilitation and settlement of oustees; and
(vi) sharing of costs.

8(3): In particular and without prejudice to the generality of the foregoing functions, the Authority shall perform *inter alia* the following functions:

(i) Madhya Pradesh or Gujarat, as the case may be, shall submit to the Authority the Sardar Sarovar Project Report, the Narmadasagar Project Report, the Omkareshwar Project Report and the Maheshwar Project Report. The Authority shall point out to the States concerned, the Central Water Commission, the Central Electricity Authority and Planning Commission any features of these projects which may conflict with the implementation of the Orders of the Tribunal. Any subsequent changes in the salient features or substantial increase in cost in respect of dams, power houses and canal headworks shall be reported to the Authority for taking appropriate action in the matter.

(ii) The Authority shall decide the phasing and shall co-ordinate construction programmes of the Narmadasagar Project and Sardar Sarovar Unit II— Canals with view to obtaining expeditiously optimum benefits during and after the completion of the construction of the projects, having due regard to the availability of funds.

(iii) The Authority shall obtain from the concerned States periodical progress reports both as to works and expenditure, and shall on receipt of such reports review the progress of construction of different units of the projects and whenever necessary advise the State concerned on the steps to be taken to expedite the work, except in respect of Unit I—Dam and Appurtenant Works and Unit III—Power Complex of Sardar Sarovar Project. The States shall submit, in respect of projects in Sub-clause 8(3)(i), completion reports to the Authority.

(iv) The Authority shall issue appropriate directions whenever necessary for timely and full compliance by the concerned States with the Orders of the Tribunal in the matter of acquisition for and making available to Gujarat lands and properties likely to be submerged under the Sardar Sarovar Project and in the matter of compensation and rehabilitation of oustees thereunder.

(v) The Authority shall cause to be established, maintained, and operated by the State Governments, concerned or any one or more of them, such stream and other gauging stations, equipped with automatic recorders where necessary, discharge, silt and evaporation observation stations and measuring devices as may be necessary from time to time for securing the records required for carrying out the provisions of the Orders. If deemed necessary, the Authority may require the installation, maintenance, and operation by the State concerned of measuring devices of approved type at the head of main canals as also at the offtake of the canal for Rajasthan for measuring amount of water diverted from Narmada river system.

(vi) Concurrent records shall be kept of the flow of the Narmada at all stations considered necessary by the Authority and the records correlated.

(vii) The Authority shall frame rules of regulation and water accounting as per guidelines given in Clause IX. It shall determine the share of water of each State for every ten-day period for purposes of regulation and water accounting.

(viii) The Authority shall ensure implementation of the Orders of the Tribunal in respect of: (a) quantum and pattern of regulated releases by Madhya Pradesh; and (b) payment for such regulated releases/sharing of costs.

(ix) The Authority shall collect from the State concerned data of the areas irrigated by Narmada waters in each season, of power generated at each hydro-electric power station at and downstream of Narmadasagar, of withdrawals for domestic, municipal and industrial or any other purposes and of waters going down the river from Sardar Sarovar Project.

(x) The Authority shall determine the volume of water flowing in the river Narmada and its tributaries in a water year (1st July to 30th June next year).

(xi) The Authority shall determine from time to time the volume of water stored by each State in reservoirs and other storages and may for that purpose adopt any device or method.

(xii) The Authority shall determine at appropriate periodic intervals the use of Narmada waters made by the States, or such of them as necessary, at any place or in any area at any time and for that purpose it may take note of all diversions or obstructions, whether natural or artificial or partly natural and partly artificial, from the river Narmada and its Tributaries and measure such use by any method as it deems fit.

(xiii) The Authority or any of its duly authorised representative shall have power to enter upon any land and property upon which any project or development of any project, or any work of gauging evaporation or other hydrological station or measuring device has been or is being constructed, operated or maintained by any State for the use of Narmada water. Each State through its appropriate departments shall render all co-operation and assistance to the Authority and its authorised representatives in this behalf.

(xiv) The Authority shall meet as often as necessary and decide on a proper management of waters including in particular the manner and details of withdrawals of waters from the storages on the Narmada river system in accordance with the Orders. In particular, the Authority shall meet at the end of filling season, and review the availability of waters in the storages on the Narmada river system and decide upon the pattern of their regulation for the next irrigation season, taking into account the carryover storages.

(xv) The Authority shall give directions for a phased programme of construction for generation and transmission of power in fulfilment of the shares of power allocated to the three States of Madhya Pradesh, Maharashtra and Gujarat from Sardar Sarovar and for payments therefor in accordance with the Orders of the Tribunal. The Authority shall also ensure that generation and transmission of power from Sardar Sarovar complex are in accordance with the Orders.

(xvi) The Authority shall issue appropriate directions for the establishment, maintenance and operation of an effective system of flood forecasting and flood control, including reporting of heavy precipitation, and telecommunication systems. The safety of a structure shall primarily be the responsibility of the Chief Engineer incharge of the structure and no decision or order shall be binding on him if in his opinion the safety of the structure will be endangered thereby. The Authority shall publish annually and make available to party States the data regarding operation of reservoirs during floods.

8(4): In the light of its experience, the Authority may modify or add to the functions enumerated hereinabove in Sub-clauses 8(3)(i) to (xvi) by a resolution.

8(5): All the concerned States shall submit to the Authority all the relevant information called for by the Authority in connection with the Narmada Valley Development expeditiously.

Sub-Clause 9. — *Annual Report of the Authority*

The Authority shall prepare and transmit to each of the four States as early as possible and in any case before the end of the current Water Year (1st July to 30th June) an Annual Report covering the activities of the Authority for the preceding year and to make available to each State on its request any information within it possession any time and always provide access to its record to the States and their representatives.

Sub-Clause 10. — *Records of the Authority and their Location*

The Authority shall keep a record of all meetings and proceedings, maintain regular accounts, and have a suitable office where documents, records, accounts and gauging data shall be kept open for inspection by the four States for their representatives at such times and under such regulations as the Authority may determine.

The location of the Central, Regional and Sub-regional offices of the Narmada Control Authority shall be determined by the Authority.

The headquarters of the Authority shall be at New Delhi till such time as it decides on its permanent location.

Sub-Clause 11. — *Contracts and Agreements*

The Authority shall enter into such contracts and agreements as may be necessary and essential for the full and proper performance of the functions and duties conferred or imposed on it.

Sub-Clause 12. — *Financial Provisions*

(1) All the capital and revenue expenditure required to be incurred by the Authority shall be borne by the four States of Madhya Pradesh, Gujarat, Maharashtra and Rajasthan equally. The Governments of the four States shall provide the necessary funds to the Authority to meet all capital and revenue expenditure required to be incurred by the Authority for the discharge of its functions.

(2) On the constitution of the Authority each of the Government of the four States shall contribute Rs. 5,00,000 (Rupees five lakhs) to the fund of the Authority in the first instance.

(3) The Authority shall in the month of September of each year prepare detailed estimate of the amounts of money required during the twelve months from the first day of April of the ensuring year, showing the manner in which it is proposed to expend such money. The Authority shall on or before the fifteenth of October forward a copy of such detailed estimate to the concerned Chief Engineers of the four States and indicate the amount required to be contributed by each State for the ensuring financial year. Each of the State Governments shall pay to the Authority its contribution as indicated by the Authority on or before the 30th day or April of the ensuing year.

(4) The Authority shall maintain detailed and accurate accounts of all receipts and disbursements and shall after the close of each financial year prepare an Annual Statement of Accounts and send copies thereof to the Accountants General as well as the concerned Chief Engineers of the four States. The form of the Annual Statement of Accounts shall be such as may be prescribed by rules. The Accounts maintained by the Authority shall be open for inspection at all reasonable times by the four States through their duly authorised representative or representatives.

(5) Disbursement shall be made from the fund of the Authority only in such manner as may be prescribed by the Authority. The Authority may incur such expenditure as it may think fit to meet any emergency in the discharge of its functions.

(6) The accounts maintained by the Authority shall be audited by the Comptroller & Auditor General of India or his nominee, who shall certify subject to such observations as he may wish to make on the annual accounts of the Authority. The Authority shall forward to the Accountants General and the concerned Chief Engineers of the four States copies of the Report of the Comptroller & Auditor General of India and shall include the same in its Annual Report.

Sub-Clause 13. — *Decision of the Authority*

The decision of the Authority on all matters covered under Sub-clause 8 shall be final and binding on the four party States. However, there shall be a Review Committee which may *suo motu* or on the application of any party State review any decision of the Authority. In urgent cases the Chairman of the Review Committee may, on the application of the party State, grant stay of any order of the Authority pending final decision on review.

Sub-Clause 14. — *Review Committee*

14(1): The Review Committee shall consists of five members including a Chairman as under:

(i)	Union Minister for Irrigation as the	—*Chairman*
(ii)	Chief Minister of Madhya Pradesh	—*Member*
(iii)	Chief Minister of Gujarat	—*Member*
(iv)	Chief Minister of Maharashtra	—*Member*
(v)	Chief Minister of Rajasthan	—*Member*

The Secretary of the Union Ministry of Agriculture and Irrigation, Department of Irrigation, shall be the Convener of the Review Committee but shall not have any voting right.

In case there is President's rule in any of the States, the Governor of that State or his authorised representative will act as Member of the Review Committee.

14(2): The Chief Minister of the four States may nominate the respective Irrigation Ministers either generally or specially as the alternate Member with full powers of voting, taking decisions, etc.

14(3): The Review Committee may review the decision of the Authority at a meeting at which the Chairman and all the Members of the Review Committee are present. It is expected that the decisions of the Review Committee will be by consensus. Failing consensus it shall be by majority of votes of Members including the Chairman.

14(4): Advance notice of the proposed meeting of the Review Committee, its agenda and agenda notes will be forwarded by the Convener to the party States.

14(5): The decision of the Review Committee shall be recorded in writing and shall be final and binding on all the States.

Sub-Clause 15. — *Construction Out-side Jurisdiction of the Authority*

The planning and construction of the projects will be carried out by each State through its own agencies, save and except to the extent prescribed in Sub-clause 16 of Clause XIV.

Sub-Clause 16. — *Supervisory Function of the Authority Over Construction of Sardar Sarovar Project*

(1) The four party States have financial commitment in respect of

Unit I—Dam and Appurtenant Works of the Sardar Sarovar Project and three of them, namely, Gujarat, Maharashtra and Madhya Pradesh have such commitment in respect of Unit III—Power Complex of the Project. With a view to ensuring efficient, economical and early execution of these Units of the Project, and taking into account the financial commitments of the party States, it is desirable and necessary that a Construction Advisory Committee should be constituted for the purpose. We, therefore, order that such an Advisory Committee to be called Sardar Sarovar Construction Advisory Committee should be set up within three months from the date of a publication of the Decision of the Tribunal in the Official Gazette.

(2) The Construction Advisory Committee shall have a whole-time Secretary of the rank of Chief Engineer to be appointed by Union of India and such other staff as may be necessary.

(3) The Committee shall comprise:

(i) The Secretary to the Government of India, in charge of Irrigation—Chairman;

(ii) Chairman, Central Water Commission (CWC), or a Member of the CWC representing him in case the Chairman is unable to attend a meeting;

(iii) Chairman, Central Electricity Authority (CEA), or a Member of the CEA representing him in cases the Chairman is unable to attend a meeting;

(iv) Chairman, Narmada Control Authority (NCA) or an Independent Member of NCA representing him in case the Chairman is unable to attend a meeting;

(v) Joint Secretary (Financial Adviser) in the Union Ministry of Agriculture & Irrigation (Department of Irrigation);

(vi) Secretaries in charge of Finance Department of Governments of Madhya Pradesh, Gujarat, Maharashtra and Rajasthan;

(vii) Secretaries in charge of Irrigation Department of Governments of Gujarat and Rajasthan;

(viii) Secretaries in charge of Power Department of Madhya Pradesh, Maharashtra and Gujarat;

(ix) Secretaries in charge of Revenue Department or any other Department concerned with land acquisition of Madhya Pradesh, Maharashtra and Gujarat;

(x) General Manger or Chief Engineers of Gujarat in charge of the project and Chief Engineers of Madhya Pradesh,

Maharashtra and Rajasthan concerned with the Project;

(xi) Chairman, State Electricity Boards of Madhya Pradesh, Maharashtra and Gujarat;

(xii) Financial Adviser, Sardar Sarovar Project; and

The Chairman may co-opt any other Member for any particular meeting.

(4) The Sardar Sarovar Construction Advisory Committee shall:

(i) Scrutinise the project estimates prepared for these works, advise necessary modifications and recommend the estimates for the administrative approval of the concerned Governments;

(ii) Examine and make recommendations on all proposals pertaining to technical features and designs as may be referred to it by any of the party States and where necessary consult experts for the purpose;

(iii) Examine and make recommendation on the programme of construction of different parts of the project in a co-ordinated manner, keeping in a view the funds available, the economics of the project and the desirability of obtaining quick results;

(iv) Examine the requirement of funds for the construction of works and other purposes according to the approved programme and make necessary recommendations;

(v) Examine and recommend, from time to time, the delegation of such powers, both technical and financial, as it may deem necessary for the efficient execution of the project, to the General Manager/Chief Engineer, Superintending Engineers, Executive Engineers and Sub-Divisional Officers engaged in the execution of the project;

(vi) Examine and, where necessary, recommend specifications for various classes of work;

(vii) Examine and make recommendation on all sub-estimates and contracts, the cost of which exceeds the powers of sanction of the General Manager/Chief Engineers; and

(viii) Review progress reports, both for works and expenditure from the General Manager/Chief Engineers and recommend, where necessary, steps to be taken to expedite the work.

(5) The headquarters of the Construction Advisory Committee will be fixed by the Committee.

(6) The Construction Advisory Committee will frame rules regarding procedure and delegation of power for the purpose of carrying out its business.

(7) The recommendations of the Construction Advisory Committee shall be conveyed to the Governments concerned by the Committee and copies sent to the Review Committee and Narmada Control Authority for information.

(8) The recommendations of the Construction Advisory Committee shall normally be accepted by the State Governments concerned. In the event of any disagreement, the matter shall be referred to the Review Committee and the decision of the Review Committee shall be final and binding on all the concerned States.

In all matters relating to the construction of the Sardar Sarovar Dam and appurtenant works (Unit-I), Power House and generating machinery (Unit-III) and Transmission lines to feed power to Madhya Pradesh, Maharashtra and Gujarat up to the next sub-station in each case, the Narmada Control Authority will carry out only such functions as do not specifically devolve upon the Construction Advisory Committee set up under Sub-Clause 16, Clause XIV.

(9) The Construction Advisory Committee will be dissolved after three years of the completion of construction of Units I and III of the Sardar Sarovar Project. The post-construction management of Units-I and III will be by Gujarat under the supervision of the Narmada Control Authority.

(10) The expenditure of the Construction Advisory Committee will be borne by the four States of Madhya Pradesh, Gujarat, Maharashtra and Rajasthan equally.

Sub-clause 17

Nothing contained in this Order shall prevent the alteration amendment or modification of all or any of the foregoing clauses by agreement between all the States concerned.

Sub-clause 18

The Union of India has consented to participate in the Machinery to be established by the Order of the Tribunal, if so directed and to do its best to implement the decision of the Tribunal.

Accordingly, we direct the Union of India to participate in the

Machinery set up by the Order of the Tribunal to implement the directions of the Tribunal specially under Clause 1(2), 4, 12(6), 13, 14 and generally to implement all the other directions so far as the Union of India is concerned.

Clause XV. — *Order as to Costs of Proceedings*

(i) The States of Gujarat, Madhya Pradesh, Maharashtra and Rajasthan shall bear their own costs of appearing before the Tribunal. The expenses of the Tribunal shall be borne and paid by the aforesaid four States in equal shares. These directions relate to the references under Section 5(1) of the Inter-State Water Disputes Act, 1956.

(ii) The States of Gujarat, Madhya Pradesh, Maharashtra and Rajasthan shall bear their own costs of appearing before the Tribunal in the references under Section 5(3) of the said Act. The expenses of the Tribunal in respect of the aforesaid references shall be borne and paid by the States of Gujarat, Madhya Pradesh, Maharashtra and Rajasthan in equal shares.

Clause XVI. — *Period of Operation of Certain Clauses of the Final Order*

In addition to Clauses III and IV (mentioned in Clause V), our Orders in Clause VII with regard to Full Reservoir Level and Maximum Water Level of the Sardar Sarovar Dam, Clause VIII with regard to Sharing of Costs and Benefits, Clause IX with regard to Regulated Releases to be made by Madhya Pradesh for the Requirement of Sardar Sarovar Project, Clause X with regard to Payment to be made by Gujarat to Madhya Pradesh for such Regulated Releases, Clause XII with regard to Allocation of Costs of Sardar Sarovar Project between Irrigation and Power, Clause XIII with regard to Allocation of Irrigation Component of Cost of Sardar Sarovar Project between Gujarat and Rajasthan and Clause XIV as regards Machinery are all made subject to review at any time after a period of 45 years from the date of publication of the Decision of the Tribunal in the Official Gazette.

RAILWAY ACCIDENT INVESTIGATION REPORT ON COLLISION BETWEEN PASSENGER BUS NO. ASU 7663 WITH NO. 10 DOWN ARUNACHAL FAST PASSENGER AT 'C' CLASS MANNED LEVEL CROSSING NO. RM/I IN RANGIYA STATION YARD ON ALIPURDUAR DIVISION OF NORTHEAST FRONTIER RAILWAY ON JANUARY 28, 1979 — REPORT[1]

One Man Commission Shri Suresh Chandra

Appointment

The Commission was constituted under the Ministry of Tourism and Civil Aviation (Commission of Railway Safety) in accordance with Rule 4 of the Statutory Investigation into Railway Accidents Rules 1973 Vide Notification No. RS. 13-T(8)/71 dated April 19, 1973 on January 28, 1979.

Terms of Reference

To enquire into the collision between Passenger Bus No. ASU-7663 with 10 Down Arunachal Fast Passenger at 'C' Class manned level crossing No. RM/I in Rangiya Station Yard on Alipurduar Division of Northeast Frontier Railway on January 28, 1979.

Contents

Summary; Inspection and Inquiry; Relief; Measures; Composition of Train and Damage; Local Features; Summary of Evidence; Observa-

---

1. Delhi, Controller of Publications, 1980, 11 p.

tions and Tests; Discussion; Conclusions; Remarks and Recommendations; Annexure; Railway Boards Comments on Various Paras of the Report.

Conclusions

Cause of the Accident

On full consideration of the factual, material and circumstantial evidence, I have come to the conclusion that the collision between the passenger bus No. ASU 7663 with 10 Dn. Arunachal Fast Passenger at 'C' class manned level crossing No. RM/I at Km 1/6-5 on the approach to Rangiya Junction Station Yard on Alipurduar Division of the Northeast Frontier Railway on 28-1-1979, was the result of the passenger bus having been driven into the level crossing which was closed against road traffic, when the train was already passing over the level crossing.

Responsibility

The responsibility for the accident was that of the Driver of the passenger bus No. ASU 7663 who entered the level crossing in closed condition and dashed against the train. The bus driver is, therefore, responsible for rash and negligent driving leading to the accident.

Relief Measures

I am satisfied that the medical aid was prompt and relief measures were satisfactory.

Recommendations

37. The level crossing is situated on a regular P.W.D. road between the Distant and Home Signals of the Rangiya Junction Station Yard. Provision of the chain and lock arrangement at such an important level crossing is not considered satisfactory since the chain would not be easily visible from a distance to a road vehicle. In the present arrangement, there is no provision for displaying a red lamp to warn the road vehicles if the gate is closed at night. Similar position was noticed at several other places also on the Northeast Frontier Railway. It is,

recommended that the level crossings on important roads should be provided with lifting barriers or gate leaves with lighting arrangements for the night.

38. No traffic census at the level crossing had been carried out for the last 10 years since the Division was formed and the position prior to that also was not known. With the general development in the country and consequent increase in rail and road traffic, it is essential that periodic traffic census is carried out in accordance with Railway Board's orders issued vide their letter No. 64/WI/LX/39 dated 9/3/1971. Immediate action is necessary to carry out the traffic census at the level crossings on the Railway to consider manning/upgrading of level crossings where justified.

39. Due to the large number of structures alongside the road on either side of the level crossing, the view of the road vehicle driver and that of any train approaching from Rangapara side is obstructed. It is necessary to remove the structures with the Railway limits except those essentially required for operation of the level crossing, to improve the visibility.

40. The present arrangement does not provide for interlocking of the gate with the signals although the level crossing is situated between the down Distant and Home Signals. There is also no exchange of private numbers between the East Cabin and the Gateman. Since the level crossing is situated on an important P.W.D. road, it is recommended that the gate should be interlocked with the signals and provision should be made for the exchange of private numbers between the A.S.M. of the East Cabin and the Gateman at the level crossing whenever the gate is to be closed for the reception or departure of a train.

41. The gate was last overhauled on 6-11-77 and was due overhauling. This may be arranged early. The Gateman who had attained the age of 45 years in July 1978, is now required to undergo medical examination at yearly intervals. He should be sent for medical examination immediately.

42. The train No. 10 Down had only one Fire Extinguisher against two specified. The required number should be provided in all trains. It also appeared from the evidence of the Guard that he considered that he was required to render First-aid only to the train passengers. After a train accident, first-aid should be rendered to all those who are injured, whether they are train or bus passengers. This should be clarified to remove any doubt among the Railway staff.

Railway Board's Comments on Various Paras of the Report

Para 37: The recommendations for providing lifting barriers or gate leaves and lighting arrangements at night at level crossing on important roads has been accepted by the railway administration. It has been decided to interlock the level crossing where the accident took place, and also provide it with lifting barriers.

Provision of gate lamps at all manned level crossings is under consideration.

Para 38: The traffic census at this level crossing has been carried out by the Railway, and it has been proposed to upgrade the level crossing to 'A' Class. As for responsibility for not taking the census earlier, necessary action is being taken by the railway administration.

Para 39: Necessary action has been initiated by the railway administration. The Railway is being asked to keep a close watch on the progress of the implementation of the recommendation.

Para 40: As already indicated against para 37, the railway has decided to interlock the level crossing gate with signals. As regards exchange of private numbers between ASM and the Gateman, Railways have been advised that in case of manned traffic level crossing gates provided with telephonic communication, no separate private number may be exchanged specially for closing and opening of level crossing gates in case the gate working instructions also incorporated in Station Working Rules require the closure of level crossing gates being ensured for all trains and shunting movements.

Para 41: The work of overhauling of the level crossing has been taken in hand by the Railway. As regards the Periodical examination of the Gateman, he would be sent for this purpose by due date.

Para 42: According to the evidence of the Guard, he could not render first aid to the injured bus Passengers because of the big crowd that had collected. Nevertheless, instructions have been reiterated by the railway that first aid should be rendered to all the victims of the accident, irrespective of whether they are train passengers, railway staff or others. Instructions have also been issued by the railway to supply two fire extinguishers in the brakevans of passenger carrying trains.

4

RAILWAY ACCIDENT INVESTIGATION REPORT ON DERAILMENT OF NO. 380 UP "QUILON-KOTTAYAM PASSENGER" TRAIN BETWEEN QUILON AND PERINAD STATIONS OF SOUTHERN RAILWAY ON FEBRUARY 2, 1979—REPORT[1]

One Man Commission Shri B.P. Sastry

Appointment

The Commission was constituted under Ministry of Tourism and Civil Aviation (Commission of Railway Safety) in accordance with Rule 4 of the Statutory Investigation into Railway Accidents Rules 1973 Vide Notification No. RS. 13-T(8)/71 dated April 19, 1973 on February 2, 1979.

Terms of Reference

To enquire into the Derailment of No. 380 Up "Quilon-Kottayam Passenger" train between Quilon and Perinad Stations of Southern Railway on February 2, 1979.

Contents

Summary; Inspection and Inquiry; Relief Measures; The Train; Local

---

1. Delhi, Controller of Publications, 1983, 18 p.

Features; Summary of Evidence; Observations and Tests; Discussion; Conclusions; Remarks and Recommendations; Annexure; Railway Board's Comments on Various Paras of the Report.

Conclusions

Cause of the Accident

On full consideration of the factual material and circumstantial evidence at my disposal. I have come to the conclusion that the derailment of No. 380 UP "Quilon-Kottayam Passenger" at km 150/1-2 between Quilon and Perinad stations at about 17-48 hours on the 2nd February, 1979 was due to excessive side bearer clearances of the leading bogie of the locomotive tender and excessive variations in axle loads coupled with alignment irregularities in the 2° curve on which the accident took place.

Responsibility

The staff of Perambur Locomotive Workshop in charge of the periodical overhaul of the locomotive in November 1978 were responsible for poor workmanship which resulted in serious defects developing in a period of less than 3 months.

Permanent Way Supervisory Staff in charge of maintenance of the curve in question were responsible for poor maintenance of the curve on which the accident took place.

Relief Measures

I am generally satisfied with the relief arrangements.

Recommendations

51. For reasons brought out in para 44, I recommend that Railway Board may consider ordering trials in respect of side bearer clearances on the bogies of locomotive tenders and fix their upper service limits *vis-a-vis* acceptable service tolerances of alignment and cross levels on track. It would also be necessary to stipulate schedules for checking and correcting the clearances when they tend to go beyond the upper or lower limits.

52. Quilon—Ernakulam section is an important Broad Gauge section with several long distance Express trains. Maintenance of curves in the section appears to deserve greater attention than at present. While checking of curves at stipulated intervals was being done rectification of defects appeared to be suffering. Evaluation of the quality of the curved alignment by the use of cumulative frequently diagrams which is rational method was still to be introduced in the section. It is recommended that early steps may be taken to introduce that practice in this and other similarly placed sections of the Railway.

53. Records maintained in Perambur Loco Workshops in respect of major repairs undertaken or parts changed during POH of locomotives was far from satisfactory. Cannibalisation of locomotive tenders which appeared to be indiscriminately in vogue in the Workshop is another highly undesirable practice which should be avoided. It is necessary that tenders attached to locomotives bear the same numbers as the locomotives so that they undergo the maintenance schedules together as one entity. These aspects may receive due attention of Southern Railway Administration.

54. In the course of my inquiry it came to light that although a telephone connection was available between the level crossing at km. 151/5-6 and Quilon North Cabin, the procedure of exchange of Private Numbers between the Gateman and the Station Master when trains are scheduled to enter the Block section was not in vogue. It is recommended that this accepted and safe practice should immediately be introduced at this and other similarly placed crossings in the interest of safety of rail and road traffic.

Railway Board's Comments on Various Paras of the Report

Para 51: The RDSO have already been asked to undertake the work of laying down 'service' tolerances for track with reference to speed and riding comfort and make recommendations. It is also proposed to lay down the maximum permissible variation of versines on curves between two adjacent stations 10 m apart with reference to the maximum permissible speed of operation, in the revised version of the Indian Railways Way & Works Manual.

The RDSO have also been asked to go into the question of laying down tolerances for side bearer clearance.

Para 52: The Railway Administration had accepted the Commissioner of Railway Safety's recommendation for implementation. The provision for realignment of curves on the basis of the cumulative frequency of versine variation over the curve is also proposed to be included in the revised version of the Indian Railways Way & Works Manual.

Para 53: This has been accepted by the Railway who is being asked to ensure that the prescribed procedure for POH is followed in Perambur Loco Workshop.

Para 54: The Railway administration are being asked to investigate as to why action was not taken earlier to comply with the Board's directive with regard to the exchange of Private Numbers between the station staff and the Gateman posted at level crossing provided with telephonic communications, and take up with the staff at fault.

5

COMMITTEE ON CHILD LABOUR, 1979 — REPORT[1]

Chairman	M. S. Gurupadaswamy
Members	S. W. Dhabe; Margaret Alva; Kamala Bahuguna; M. Khandekar; Musafir Singh; Ram K. Vepa; M. M. Rajendran; G.L. Bailur; V.S. Bhashyam; R. Thamarajakshi; K. Srinivasan; P.A. Bhatt; Saran Prasad; Madav Sinha
M. Secy.	V.P. Sawhney
Alterations	Shri M.S. Gurupadaswamy, resigned as Chairman of the Committee on 28-11-79. Prior to his resignation, he had approved of the contents and substance of the draft report and recommendations; Mrs. Kamala Bahuguna, did not attend any meeting of the Committee nor participated in its other deliberations; Mr. V.S. Bhashyam: After his superannuation on 30-11-79, he ceased to be a member of the Committee. He, however, continued thereafter to assist the Committee as a consultant; Dr. (Mrs.) R. Thamarajakshi was nominated as a member of the Committee after the superannuation of Shri M.V.S. Rao on 30-9-79; Shri M.V.S. Rao was earlier representing Planning Commission on before his superannuation.

Appointment

The United Nations General Assembly adopted on the 21st December, 1976, the Resolution 31/169 proclaiming the year 1979 as the International Year of the Child. The general objective in doing so was to create world-wide consciousness towards promoting the well being of children, drawing attention to their special needs and encouraging

1. Ministry of Labour, Government of India, New Delhi, 1979, ii + 106 p.

national action on behalf of children, particularly for the least privileged and those who were at work.

India is one of the countries where the problems of child labour are quite openly manifest. The Government of India had, for sometime, been viewing with concern the wide-spread existence of child labour in the country, both in the organised, and unorganised sectors. Keeping in view the total background of the question and the context of the International Year of the Child, it felt the need for a thorough stock-taking of the situation, and the Ministry of Labour, Government of India, through its Resolution No. S-27025/6/78-FAC, dated the 6/7th February, 1979 set up a sixteen-Member Committee comprising of some members of Parliament, representatives from institutions dealing with problems of children, and representatives of concerned Departments of the Central Government as also of few State Governments, to look into in detail the causes leading to and the problems arising out of the employment of children and also laid down its detailed terms of reference.

Terms of Reference

The following terms of reference of the Committee were set out in the above Resolution:

(i) Examine existing laws, their adequacy and implementation, and suggest corrective action to be taken to improve implementation and to remedy defects;

(ii) Examine the dimensions of child labour, the occupations in which children are employed, etc., and suggest new areas where laws abolishing/regulating the employment of children can be introduced; and

(iii) Suggest welfare measures, training and other facilities which would be introduced to benefit children in employment.

The Committee was also requested to submit its Report within a period of six months.

Contents

Chapter I—Introduction: Background; Terms of Reference; Questionnaire; Task Force; Studies and Surveys; Working Group and Spot Inspections, Acknowledgements; *Chapter II*—Child Labour in India: Nature of the Problems; Causes of Child Labour; Migration to Urban Areas; Child Population; Extent of Child Labour; Working Children and their Occupations; Conclusions; *Chapter III*—Legislative Framework in India for Child Labour: Historical Perspective; Enactments Dealing with Employment of Children; Points of Difference in Various Enactments; Need for Single Model Legislation; Definition of Child; Adolescents; Inadequate Enforcement, Advisory Boards; *Chapter IV*—Supportive Measures for Child Labour, Removal of Poverty and Unemployment, Ensuring Minimum Wages, Meaningful Education Policy, Medical and Health Support, Nutrition, Housing Facilities, Recreation and Cultural Activities, Family Planning, Apprenticeship and Vocational Facilities, Health Hazards, Role of Media; *Chapter V*—Summary of Recommendations: Note of Dissent–Dr. Ram K. Vepa; *Annexures:* I to VII; Statements 1 to 12.

Recommendations

5.1 The Committee would wish to underline that all future action in respect of child labour would depend very much on how intensively occupations in which child are employed, studied and remedial action determined thereafter. Accordingly it recommends more studies to be sponsored in this regard together information and data about working children and their working conditions. This task should be spearheaded by the Ministry of Labour which should have an appropriate cell to sponsor such studies in consultation with the Department of Social Welfare, and other concerned Ministries, and to coordinate further action (Paras 1, 21, 1.22 and 2.7).

5.2 The Committee recognises that multiple policy approach is necessary in dealing with the problems of working children. They have to be seen distinctly in the categories of wage earning employment; as paid family workers; as apprentices in traditional to crafts and as working and schooling. Each specific category has its own peculiar problems which need to be attended to comprehensively (Para 2.16).

5.3 The Committee recommends constitution of Advisory Boards both at the Central and at State levels to keep a constant surveillance on the problems of working children. These Boards should have representatives of Government as well as those of voluntary organisations and trade unions. The Boards should have the powers and resources to undertake investigative studies and surveys to locate the specific areas where regulation of child labour is called for. It should also review periodically the results of the implementation of the existing legislation and a report on the working of the advisory boards should be placed on the Table of the House of Parliament or Assembly, as the case may be (Para 3.163).

5.4 The Committee is of the view that the minimum age should be prescribed for the children for entering any employment. It accordingly recommends that the minimum age for entry into any employment should be 15 years and that be existing laws which prescribe an age lower than this should be suitably amended. Correspondingly, the age for adolescents should be specified as between 15 and 18 years (Paras 3.156 and 3.157).

5.5 The Committee is strongly of the view that there is a paramount need for an urgent action on the part of the Government to bring into a proper focus the laws relating to employment of children. To avoid any ambiguity in respect of the basic objectives, the Committee recommends that the existing laws relating to prohibition and regulation of employment of children should be consolidated into a single comprehensive one. The new legislation should adopt uniform definitions of the expressions of 'Child' and 'adolescent' and prescribe the 'hours' of 'work', 'conditions of work', etc. The new law should also have flexibility of extending gradually the provisions contained therein to other occupations, such as, mechanised agriculture, horticulture, forestry, fisheries, etc. (Para 4.149).

5.6 The Committee recommends that concerted steps be taken within five years to achieve the objective of providing minimum educational qualification, say eight standard or equivalent for entry into any regulated employment (Para 3.154 and 4.1).

5.7 The Committee strongly urges that serious attention be given towards strengthening the existing machinery for enforcement of legislation relating to employment of children and that due recognition should also be given in this regard to the role of voluntary agencies and trade union (Para 3.159).

5.8 The Committee recommends to the Government to initiate dialogue with the trade unions at an early date so that some institutional framework could be evolved for ensuring collective bargaining in respect of the needs of working children. (Para 3.160)

5.9 The Committee recommends that the penalty provided in the existing laws for violation of provisions relating to child labour should be made more deterrent. The punishment for the first offence should be imprisonment which may extend to one year or fine extending to Rs. 2,000, or both. In the case of second or continuing offence, the penalty should be only imprisonment and that, too up to two years (Para 3.161).

5.10 The Committee recommends to the Planning Commission to work out the feasibility of taking away all children below the age of 15 years from the labour market in order to find employment for the unemployed able-bodied persons between the age group of 15 and 59 in the country, and to work out a cost benefit analysis of this proposition (Para 4.2).

5.11 While accelerated efforts are necessary in national planning to improve the earnings of adult workers, the Committee feels that stricter enforcement of the Minimum Wages Act needs to be ensured. In this regard greater participation should be sought of the entire administrative machinery (Para 4.4).

5.12 The Committee feels that a more meaningful and effective educational policy is called for to take into account the following:

(a) change of curriculum and integration of educational requirements with local crafts;
(b) greater involvement of voluntary agencies; and
(c) changes and adjustments in the schedule of vacations and holidays to coincide with environmental requirements (Paras 4.5 and 4.6).

5.13 The Committee would also underline more comprehensive statutory provisions for providing educational facilities for child workers and to include education as a part of labour welfare measures to be adopted by employers. It recommends arrangements for non-formal education in areas where there is concentration of working children (Paras 4.9 and 4.8).

5.14 The Committee recommends that in rural areas, creches/child-care centres should be established at the school premises, or at the community centres, so as to encourage girls who have to take care of young siblings in the family to attend schools. This arrangement would also be of great help to working parents (Para 4.7).

5.15 The Committee underlines the needs for periodical medical check-ups to be linked with national health scheme in respect of child workers (Para 4.10).

5.16 The Committee feels that constant attention needs to be paid to keep the working environmental hygienically free especially in places where children are employed (Para 4.11).

5.17 Supplementary nutrition is to be provided to working children by the employers who could be given suitable subsidy for this programme. The possibility of imposing a cess, or alternatively to allow concessions in taxes, etc., to employers who undertake to implement the schemes as envisaged above, and other welfare schemes, needs to be considered seriously (Paras 4.12 and 4.9).

5.18 Greater emphasis is needed on housing schemes and provisions of basic amenities in areas in which large number of children are working (Para 4.13).

5.19 More library and reading facilities linked with special teaching classes for working children need to be established in selective areas (Para 4.14).

5.20 Arrangements for recreational and cultural activities should be provided in areas in which there are large number of working children (Para 4.15).

5.21 The Committee recommends effective enforcement of the Apprentices Act and the setting up of separate vocational guidance clinics and employment bureaus for children (Para 4.17).

5.22 The Committee also underlines the need for a more systematic effort for identification of hazardous occupations, and for detecting occupational diseases and their treatment. There are several areas, both in the organised and unorganised sectors where children are exposed to serious hazards, but no efforts have so far been made to regulate their employment (Paras 3.162 and 4.20).

5.23 The Committee recommends a more purposeful effort on the part of the media to create greater social consciousness in respect of evils of child labour (Para 4.21).

6

TRIBUNALS FOR NON-JOURNALIST NEWSPAPER EMPLOYEES OF NEWSPAPER ESTABLISHMENTS OTHER THAN NEWS AGENCIES, 1979 — REPORT[1]

One Man Tribunal Shri D.G. Palekar

Appointment

The Government of India by Notification No. S.O. 81(E) dated the 9th February, 1979, of the Ministry of Labour, constituted a Tribunal under Section 13 DD (1) of the Working Journalists and Other Newspaper Employees (Conditions of Service) and Miscellaneous Provisions Act, 1955, for the purpose of fixing and revising rates of wages in respect of Non-Journalist Newspaper Employees, on the ground that the Wage Board constituted on 11th June, 1975 under Section 13 C of the said Act had not been able to function effectively.

Terms of Reference

The Tribunal was constituted for the purpose of fixing and revising rates of wages in respect of Non-Journalist Newspaper Employees of Newspaper establishments.

Contents

Part—I (Recommendations with regard to Non-Journalist Newspaper Employees other than of News Agencies.), Introductory, Recommendations; Part—II (Recommendations with regard to Working Journalists other than of News Agencies), Introductory, Recommendations;

1. Controller of Publications, Delhi, 1980, iii + 156 p., Bound in *Recommendations of the Tribunals for working Journalist and Non-Journalist Newspaper Employees.*

Part—III (Recommendations with regard to Newspaper Employees of News Agencies), Introductory, Recommendations; Part—IV (Report); Wage Determination in Newspaper Establishments; The State of Newspaper Industry; Classification and Gross Revenue; Revision of Pay Scales and Wages; News Agencies; Additional Financial Burden; Miscellaneous; Part—V Annexures I to VII; Appendices I to VIII.

Recommendations

SECTION—I

Preliminary

1. *Definitions*

The expressions 'Newspaper Establishment', 'Working of Journalist' and 'Non-Journalist Newspaper Employee', shall have the same meaning as assigned to them in the Working Journalists and Other Newspaper Employees, (Conditions of Service) and Miscellaneous Provisions Act, 1955, hereinafter called the 'Act'. For the purpose of the recommendations in this Part, 'Newspaper Establishment' shall not include a News Agency.

'Accounting Year' used with reference to a particular year, shall, in the case of a newspaper establishment whose accounting year is a calendar year, mean that calendar year and shall, in the case of a newspaper establishment whose accounting year is different from the calendar year, mean that accounting year of the establishment of which more than half falls in the particular year.

Example—If the accounting year of a newspaper establishment starts from April 1st, reference to the accounting year 1977 in the succeeding paragraphs shall be construed as reference to the accounting year 1977-78 of such establishment. On the other hand, if the accounting year of a newspaper establishment starts from 1st October, reference to the accounting year 1977 in these paragraphs will be construed as reference to the accounting year 1976-77 of that establishment.

In the case of a newspaper establishment where the accounting year starts from 1st July, the accounting year would be the year in which the first six months fall.

'Category' means any of the kind of employees mentioned under the groups set out in paragraph 14.

'Gross Revenue' of a newspaper establishment means revenue derived by the establishment from all sources of its newspaper business, including circulation of and advertisements in its newspaper or newspapers, and also includes income from the assets acquired and investments made by it out of funds earned in the newspaper business.

Revenue in respect of circulation and advertisement shall be taken to be the amount arrived at after deducting the commission actually allowed to the extent of which the amount of commission allowed is reasonable. Reasonable commission is one which is finally accepted by the Income Tax authorities in the case of a particular newspaper establishment. In cases where no such final decision of the Income Tax authorities is available, the circulation commission shall be 28 per cent and the advertisement commission shall be 15 per cent of the respective revenues.

SECTION—II

Classification of Newspaper Establishments

2. For the purpose of fixation of wages of the Non-Journalist Newspaper Employees, newspaper establishments shall be classified in the manner herein after provided.

3. Classification of newspaper establishments should be based on the average gross revenue of 3 accounting years, 1977, 1978 and 1979.

4. In the case of a newspaper establishment completing two out of the aforesaid 3 accounting years, its classification should be determined on the basis of its average gross revenue for these 2 years.

5. In the case of a newspaper establishment which has completed only one year of the said accounting years, its classification should be determined on the basis of its gross revenue for that year.

6. A new newspaper establishment, i.e., a newspaper establishment to which the provisions of paras 3, 4 and 5 do not, in terms apply, is liable to be classified after the completion of its first accounting year on the basis of its gross revenue for that year.

7. Notwithstanding anything said in paras 4 to 6 above, a newspaper establishment which is classified on the basis of 2 accounting years shall be placed one class lower than the class in which it is liable to be placed and a newspaper establishment which is classified

on the basis of one accounting year, two classes lower. In either case, it shall not be lower than class VII.

8. Where a classified newspaper establishment starts one of its old newspaper from a new centre where it has no other newspaper publication, it shall, so far as the new centre is concerned, be placed for the first 2 accounting years one class below the class in which it would be liable to be placed on the basis of its total gross revenue; and a classified newspaper establishment which starts a new newspaper from a centre where it has not other newspaper publication, shall be similarly liable to be placed in a lower class for 3 accounting years at the new centre. In either case, it shall not be placed lower than class VII, so far as the new centre is concerned.

9. The classification determined in accordance with the provisions of paragraphs 3 to 8 shall continue until the newspaper establishment is reclassified in accordance with the provisions of paragraph 13.

10. If the ownership of the newspaper establishment is transferred by one person to another, the provisions of paragraphs 2 to 9 shall apply to such newspaper establishment as if the gross revenue of the newspaper establishment for the relevant accounting years under the previous owner were its revenue for those years under the new owner.

11. Newspaper establishments shall be classified under the following 9 classes on the basis of their gross revenue:

Class	Gross Revenue
IB	Rs. 25 Crores and above.
IA	Rs. 10 Crores and above and less than Rs. 25 Crores
I	Rs. 4 Crores and above and less than Rs. 10 Crores.
II	Rs. 2 Crores and above and less than Rs. 4 Crores.
III	Rs. 1 Crore and above and less than Rs. 2 Crores.
IV	Rs. 50 lakhs and above and less than Rs. 1 Crore.
V	Rs. 25 lakhs and above and less than Rs. 50 lakhs.
VI	Rs. 10 lakhs and above and less than Rs. 25 lakhs.
VII	Less than Rs. 10 lakhs.

12. If the advertisement revenue derived by a newspaper establishment other than one falling in class VII, is less than 40 per cent of its gross revenue reduced by advertisement revenue, it should be placed in the class next below that in which it would fall on the basis of

its gross revenue.

Reclassification

13. It shall be open either to the Employer or to the Employees to seek a reclassification of a newspaper establishment at any time after the accounting year 1982 on the basis of the average gross revenue of the 3 immediately preceding accounting years, provided that such reclassification should not be sought more than once in any period of 3 consecutive accounting years.

SECTION—III

14. *Grouping of Non-Journalist Newspaper Employees*

I. *Administrative Staff:*

(a) For Newspaper Establishments other than classes, V, VI and VII.

Group 1: General Manager, Manager and Secretary

Group 2: Departmental Managers (those who are in-charge of Circulation, Advertisement Departments, Personnel, etc.) Chief Accountant (Accountant), P.R.Os. (classes IB, IA, I and II newspaper establishments).

Group 2A: Liaison Officers, Accounts Officers, Chief Internal Auditor, Assistant Advertisement Managers, Assistant Circulation Managers and Personnel Officers.

Group 3: Sectional Heads (supervising work of 5 clerks), Business Canvassers, Sales Representatives, Head Clerks, Personal Assistants (Steno-Secretaries), Assistant Accountant, Advertisement Representative.

Note: The recommendations in this Part shall not apply to employees other than Non-Journalist Newspaper Employees as defined in the Act though included in the above 4 Groups.

Group 4: Stenographers, Assistants, Accounts Clerks, Watch and Ward Inspectors, Advertisement Translators, Senior Clerks, (i.e., those whose work involved special skills). Operators of Accounting machines/Calculating machines and Teleprinters, Field Organisers and those doing audit bureau of circulation, Advertisement Proof Readers, Artists (Commercial and Process).

Group 5: Junior Clerks (i.e., those doing normal clerical work including acceptance of advertisements and sale of publications, Time Keepers, Typists, Telephone Operators, Addressographers, Receptionists, Franking Machine Operators, Canteen Supervisors, Junior Artists (Commercial and Process).

Group 6: Bill Collectors, Daftry or those doing semi-clerical work, Watchmen and Delivery Peons.

Group 7: Peon, Sweeper, Bearer, Cleaner, Call-boy, Canteen-boy, Water-boy, Mali, Tailor, Orderly, Durwan, Masalchi.

(b) For newspaper establishments classes, V, VI and VII.

Group 1: General Manager, Manager and Secretary.

Group 2: Departmental Managers (those who are in-charge of Circulation, Advertisement Departments, Personnel, etc.) Chief Accountant (Accountant).

Group 3: Sectional Heads (supervising work of 5 clerks), Business Canvassers, Sales Representatives, Head Clerks, Personal Assistants (steno-secretaries), Assistant Accountant, Advertisement Representative.

Note: The recommendations in this Part shall not apply to employees other than Non-Journalist Newspaper Employees as defined in the Act though included in the above 3 Groups.

Group 4: Stenographers, Assistant, Accounts Clerks, Watch and Ward Inspectors, Cashiers, Circulation Inspectors, Advertisement Translators, Senior Clerks (i.e., those whose work involves special skills.) Operators of accounting machines/Calculating machines and teleprinters, Field Organisers and those doing audit bureau of circulation advertisement Proof Readers, Artists (Commercial and Process).

Group 5: Junior Clerks (i.e., those doing normal clerical work including acceptance of advertisements and sale of publications), Time Keepers, Typists, Telephone Operators, Addressographers, Receptionists, Franking Machine Operators, Sanitary Inspectors, Canteen Supervisors, Junior Artists (Commercial and Process).

Group 6: Bill Collectors, Daftary or those doing semi-clerical work, Watchmen and Delivery Peons.

Group 7: Peons, Sweeper, Bearer, Cleaner, Call-boy, Canteen-boy, Waterboy, Mali, Tailor, Orderly, Darwan, Masalchi.

. *Factory Staff for all Newspaper Establishments*

Group 1: A & B Grade Supervisor, Air Condition Plant Mechanic, Armature Winder, Chief Press Advertising Assistant, Colour-etcher, Film Impositor, Lino Mechanic, Lino Operator, Microfilm Technician, Microfilm Unit Assistant, Mono-Mechanic, Mono-Operator, Motor Mechanic, Offset Machineman, Off-set Mechanic, Off-set Printer, Off-set Retoucher, Photographer (Process) Press Advertising Assistant, Printer (Foreman Composing Supervisor), Reprophotographer, Rotary Mechanic, Senior Paster, Senior Printer, Supervisor, Supervisor (composing, weekly job and other sections.) T.T.S. Operator, Cameraman (Off-set), Senior Mechanic.

Group 2: Departmental Managers (those who are Assistant Layout-man) Assistant Foreman, Assistant Printer, Block-room Assistant, Block-room Man, Camera Operator, Colour Printer, Contact Operator, Conveyor Striket Machineman, Corrector, Deputy Foreman (Gullotine), Engraver, Enlarger Operator, Filing Assistant Flongman, Graining Machineman, Halftone etcher, Headingman, Imposer, Joiner, Junior Lino Mechanic, Junior Printer, Fudlow Operator, Make-up man, Pageman, Metal Printer, Operator Colour (Highly skilled), Photogravure Machineman, Photo Lettering Machine Operator, Process Assistant, Process Printer,

Proofing Machineman (off-set), Reelstar Machineman, Rotarymachine Headman, Rotary Machineman (General), Rotary Machineman, Sarang, Stereo Blockman, Stereo Caster, Stereo Castingman, Stereo Casting Headman, Stereo Fireman, Stereo Mouldingman, Stonehand, Junior Mechanic.

Group 3: Air Condition Plant Cleaner, Assistant Mukadam, Assistant Printing Machineman (all categories), Caster, Carpenter, Charge Hand (Palatia), Chipper or Router, Colour work Proofing Pressman, Copyholder, Cutter, Cycle Mistry, Dark room Assistant, Driver, El-Rod Operator, Electrician, Fitter Hammerman, Hand Compositor, Hand Pressman, Caster, Machineman (except Rotary Machineman), Machineman (other than printing), Mangleman, Mason, Metal Caster, Mistry, Mono-Caster, Moulder, News Daftary, Off-Inkman, Operator (Black & White), Painter, Plate Maker (Black & White), Plumber, Roller-maker, Rotary Mukadam, Ruling Machineman, Senior Chargehand, Sign writer, Store Mukadam, Turner, Wireman, Welder, Stereoman.

Group 4: Assistant Machineman, Assistant Fitter, Assistant Welder, Assistant Electrician, Assistant Turner, (all with 5 years service) Blacksmith, Cook, Cutting Machineman, Distributor, Treadleman, Line-etcher.

Group 5: Baller Mukadam, Barman, Binder, Case Room Cleaner, Colour-work Examiner, Counter, Daftary, Dhobi, Feeder, Flyboy, Gally Pressman, Ravildar, Headpeon, Interlay Cutter, Jamadar, Knife Sharpner, Lead Melter, Liftman, Lino Cleaner, Lock-up man, Mounter, Mono-cleaner, Numberer, Packer, Paperman, Plate Grinder, Proof Puller, Reel Minder, Rollerman, Semi-skilled Baller, Store-paper counter, Stitcher, Wheeler, (Rotary Cleaner), All other semi- skilled attendants, Cleaners, and helpers by whatever name they are called.

Group 6: Baller, Binding boy, Mazdoor, Reel Loader and Unloader, Trolleyman.

15. The categories mentioned above are those which are generally

found in newspaper establishments. Some newspaper establishments have created other categories which are peculiar to the establishments and not generally considered to be essential by other establishments. Where in an establishment any individual category is already fixed in a higher group, it shall not be placed in a lower group.

16. It is not obligatory for a newspaper establishment to employ any or all of the categories mentioned in the groups above. Functions of some categories may be combined, in which case the employee shall be deemed to belong to the highest category of which functions are normally performed by him. In other cases, the principal duties performed by an employee should determine the category of the employee, neither designation nor casual or occasional work should be taken into account for such categorisation.

SECTION-IV

Remuneration

17. *Wages, Scales and Grades*

Non-Journalist Newspaper Employees of different groups employees in different classes of newspaper establishments should be paid basic pay per mensem in accordance with the scales as shown in Table I attached hereto.

Dearness Allowance

18. The existing fixed Dearness Allowance, variable Dearness Allowance and Basic Wage including interim relief granted by Government by order dated 1-4-1977 are pegged, as the case may be, at the All India Average Consumer Price Index Number 400 (1949=100) which is the basis for the payment of variable Dearness Allowance for the year commencing 1-1-1979 and in Index Number 425 (1949=100) which is the basis for the payment of variable Dearness Allowance for the year commencing 1-1-1980. The relevant date for the application of revised scales of Pay and Dearness Allowance is 1-10-1979 in the case of employees of Newspaper Establishments placed in classes, IB, IA, I, II and III, and the relevant date for employees of other establishments is 1-10-1980. The new variable Dearness Allowance will be substituted for the old one on these two dates for the respective

employees of other establishments is 1-10-1980. The Allowance, however, the old series with base 1949=100 will be discontinued and the series with base 1960=100 will be followed. The new variable Dearness Allowance will vary with every rise or fall of 6 points in the Consumer Price Index Number of the series 1960=100. It will be revised half-yearly on 1st April and 1st October at the rate of Rs. 5 for every variation of 6 points. The Dearness Allowance will also vary with wage slabs as illustrated in Table II attached to the recommendations.

SECTION-V

Other Allowances

19. (a) *House Rent Allowance*

House Rent Allowance as indicted in Table III attached herewith will also be paid by Newspaper Establishments mentioned there-in to their employees posted in the respective zones. Provided that:

(i) Where an employee is provided residential accommodation by a Newspaper Establishment, no House Rent Allowance will be payable;

(ii) If an employee is being paid House Rent Allowance, the same will be adjusted against the amount of House Rent Allowance payable under this provision; and

(iii) Where a newspaper establishment contributes on behalf of an employee any amount towards a fund to enable the employee to own his residential accommodation, such amount shall be adjusted against House Rent Allowance payable under this provision.

(b) *Night Shift Allowance*

Night Shift Allowance will be paid to an employee at the rates as shown in Table IV attached herewith by newspaper establishments mentioned therein, provided that where an employee is already in receipt of Night Shift Allowance either in cash or kind or both, the same or the money value thereof shall be adjusted against the amount payable under this provision.

SECTION-VI

20. *Fitment Rules*

(1) For the purpose of fitment rules an "employee" means a "Non-Journalist Newspaper Employee."

(2) The "Present Emoluments" of an employee shall mean his Basic Pay, Fixed Dearness Allowance, variable Dearness Allowance at the Consumer Price Index Number 400 and 425 as the case may be, (base 1949=100) and Interim Relief (by way of *Ad hoc* payment) applicable individually, granted in pursuance of the Notification dated 1st April, 1977, issued by the Government of India, Ministry of Labour, in respect of Non-Journalist Newspaper Employees.

(3) (a) The "Additional Emoluments" of an employee shall mean emoluments other than the "Present Emoluments" referred to in rule (2) granted by Newspaper Establishments, as a result of collective bargaining, agreement or award, as increase in Basic wage, Dearness Allowance of Interim Relief.

(b) The "Additional Allowances" of an employee shall mean any monthly payments, by whatever name called, not related to a specific purpose nor agreed to be adjusted against any revision of pay or Dearness Allowance.

(4) The "Revised Pay Scale" shall mean the pay scale applicable to an employee as per these recommendations.

(5) The revised scales of Pay and Dearness Allowance shall come into force with effect from 1st October, 1979, in respect of classes IB, IA, I, II and III. With regard to classes IV, V, VI and VII, the revised scales of Pay and Dearness Allowance shall come into force with effect from 1st October, 1980. These dates will be referred to hereinafter as the "relevant dates."

(6) Every employee with his "Present Emoluments" will be brought on to the revised pay scale with effect from the relevant date and fitted into that pay scale at the appropriate stage, either at the initial new minimum or higher than the initial in the pay scale, as the case may be.

(7) In case the present emoluments of an employee are higher than the minimum of the revised pay scale, but not at the level with any stage in the revised pay scale, he will be stepped up to the immediate next level.

(8) In addition, every employee shall be given one increment in

the revised pay scale for completion of every five years' service in the pay scale prior to the relevant date. The total number of increments shall not be more than two.

Provided that

(i) no employee shall get more than the maximum of the revised pay scale; and

(ii) in no case should the total of the present emoluments be reduced as a result of fitment or operation of the provisions contained in these recommendations; the balance, if any, may be treated as Personal Pay to be absorbed in future increments.

(9) (a) These recommendations will not affect the terms and conditions on which 'Additional Emoluments' referred to in Rule (3)(a) were granted.

(b) 'Additional Allowances' referred to in Rule (3) (b) shall be treated as Personal Pay to be absorbed in future increments of the revised pay scales.

(10) Within six months from the date of publication of Government Notification enforcing these recommendations every employee shall exercise his option either to retain his existing pay scale and "Present Emoluments" or to come on the revised pay scale with effect from the relevant date.

(11) The "Present Emoluments" together with Variable Dearness Allowance as per the last Wage Board will continue to be paid till such time as the option is exercised by an employee under rule (10).

(12) When a newspaper establishment is reclassified under Para 13 above, the employee should be fitted into the revised pay scale appropriate to that class. When the basic pay does not coincide with a stage in the revised pay scale of that class the employee should be fitted at the next higher stage when the classification goes up and at the next lower stage, when the classification goes down. In the latter case, the higher existing basic pay should be protected and the difference between the existing basic pay and the pay to which he is so fitted may be treated as personal pay or it may be absorbed in future increments.

(13) Where an employee is fitted into a scale in accordance with the provisions of these rules as on the relevant dates, he should be entitled to count increments in the appropriate scale as from that date.

21. A Non-Journalist Newspaper Employee, during his appren-

ticeship period shall be paid a stipend of 60 per cent of the Basic pay and Dearness allowance applicable to the post for which he is being trained.

22. Subject to the provisions of the standing orders applicable to a particular newspaper establishment, a Non-Journalist Newspaper Employee may be employed as a probationer for a period not exceeding one year during which, he shall be paid basic pay of not less than the minimum of the scale applicable to the class of establishment and group in which he is a probationer alongwith the allowances attached to the post. In the case of a Non-Journalist Newspaper employee acting as a probationer in a higher post if he is drawing more than the minimum pay of the higher post, then, he should get 10 per cent of the minimum pay of the higher post in addition to his salary of the lower post during the probationary period.

Date of Operation

23. (1) Recommendations with regard to revised scales of pay and Dearness Allowance shall be operative in respect of the respective newspaper establishment from the relevant dates applicable to it in accordance with Para 20(5).

(2) The rest of the recommendations shall come into force from the date of the order of the Central Government under Section 12 giving effect to the recommendations.

Payment of Arrears

24. The arrears payable, if any, as a result of retrospective operation provided in Para 20(5) should be paid in not more than two instalments, not later than nine months from the date of the publication of the order of the Central Government under Section 12 of the Act.

TABLE I: Non-Journalists : Administrative Staff

Class of establishment	Group of employees	Scales	Years
IB	1	No Scales.	
(Rs. 25 crores and above)	2	Rs. 1140-50-1340-75-1640-90-1910-110-2240 (4) (4) (3) (3)	14

(Contd.)

Class of establishment	Group of employees	Scales	Years
	2A	Rs. 990-45-1170-60-1410-70-1620-85-1875 (4) (4) (3) (3)	14
	3	Rs. 810-40-970-45-1150-50-1350-55-1570 (4) (4) (4) (4)	16
	4	Rs. 770-35-910-40-1070-50-1270-55-1490 (4) (4) (4) (4)	16
	5	Rs. 670-27-778-30-898-33-1030-35-1170 (4) (4) (4) (4)	16
	6	Rs. 610-14-680-15-755-16-819-17-887 (5) (5) (4) (4)	18
	7	Rs. 550-13-615-14-685-15-745-16-809 (5) (5) (4) (4)	18
IA (Rs. 10 crores and above and less than Rs. 25 crores)	1	No. Scale.	
	2	Rs. 1090-50-1290-70-1570-85-1825-100-2125 (4) (4) (3) (3)	14
	2A	Rs. 940-45-1120-55-1340-65-1535-80-1775 (4) (4) (3) (3)	14
	3	Rs. 770-35-910-40-1070-50-1270-55-1490 (4) (4) (4) (4)	16
	4	Rs. 735-35-875-40-1035-50-1235-55-1455 (4) (4) (4) (4)	16
	5	Rs. 640-25-740-27-848-30-968-33-1100 (4) (4) (4) (4)	16
	6	Rs. 580-13-645-14-715-15-775-16-839 (5) (5) (4) (4)	18
	7	Rs. 525-12-585-13-650-14-706-15-766 (5) (5) (4) (4)	18
I (Rs. 4 crores and above and less than Rs. 10 crores).	1	No Scale.	
	2	Rs. 1035-50-1235-65-1495-80-1735-95-2020 (4) (4) (3) (3)	14
	2A	Rs. 900-35-1040-50-1240-60-1420-75-1645 (4) (4) (3) (3)	14
	3	Rs. 735-35-875-40-1035-50-1235-55-1455 (4) (4) (4) (4)	16
	4	Rs. 700-30-820-35-960-50-1160-55-1380 (4) (4) (4) (4)	16
	5	Rs. 610-23-702-25-802-27-910-30-1030 (4) (4) (4) (4)	16

(Contd.)

Class of establishment	Group of employees	Scales	Years
	6	Rs. 555-12-615-13-680-14-736-15-796 (5) (5) (4) (4)	18
	7	Rs. 500-11-555-12-615-13-667-14-723 (5) (5) (4) (4)	18
II	1	Not less than Rs. 1700	
(Rs. 2 crores and above less than Rs. 4 crores).	2	Rs. 840-40-1000-45-1180-55-1345-65-1540 (4) (4) (3) (3)	14
	2A	Rs. 770-35-910-30-1070-50-1220-60-1400 (4) (4) (3) (3)	14
	3	Rs. 685-30-805-35-945-45-1125-50-1325 (4) (4) (4) (4)	16
	4	Rs. 665-30-785-35-925-45-1105-50-1305 (4) (40 (4) (4)	16
	5	Rs. 590-21-674-23-766-25-866-27-974 (4) (4) (4) (4)	16
	6	Rs. 530-11-585-12-645-13-697-14-753 (5) (5) (4) (4)	18
	7	Rs. 475-10-525-11-580-12-628-13-680 (5) (5) (4) (4)	18
III	1	Not less than Rs. 1,500	
(Rs. 1 crore and above and less than Rs. 2 crores)	2	Rs. 770-35-910-40-1070-50-1220-55-1385 (4) (4) (3) (3)	14
	2A	Rs. 735-35-875-40-1035-45-1170-50-1320 (4) (4) (3) (3)	14
	3	Rs. 665-30-785-35-925-40-1085-45-1265 (4) (4) (4) (4)	16
	4	Rs. 630-30-750-35-890-40-1050-45-1230 (4) (4) (4) (4)	16
	5	Rs. 555-19-631-21-715-23-807-25-907 (4) (4) (4) (4)	16
	6	Rs. 500-10-550-11-605-12-653-13-705 (5) (5) (4) (4)	18
	7	Rs. 450-9-495-10-545-11-589-12-637 (5) (5) (4) (4)	18
IV	1	Not less than Rs. 1,000	
(Rs. 50 lakhs and above and less than Rs. 1 crore)	2	Rs. 700-30-820-35-960-45-1095-50-1245 (4) (4) (3) (3)	14

(Contd.)

Class of establishment	Group of employees	Scales	Years
	2A	Rs. 675-30-795-35-935-40-1055-45-1190 (4) (4) (3) (3)	14
	3	Rs. 600-25-700-30-820-35-960-40-1120 (4) (4) (4) (4)	16
	4	Rs. 560-25-660-30-780-35-920-40-1080 (4) (4) (4) (4)	16
	5	Rs. 505-17-573-19-649-21-733-23-825 (4) (4) (4) (4)	16
	6	Rs. 465-9-510-10-560-11-604-12-652 (5) (5) (4) (4)	18
	7	Rs. 425-8-465-9-510-10-550-11-594 (5) (5) (4) (4)	18
V	1	Not less than Rs. 1,300	
(Rs. 25 lakhs and above less than Rs. 50 lakhs)	2	Rs. 660-30-780-35-920-40-1040-45-1175 (4) (4) (3) (3)	14
	3	Rs. 600-25-700-30-820-35-960-40-1120 (4) (4) (4) (4)	16
	4	Rs. 540-25-640-30-760-35-900-40-1060 (4) (4) (4) (4)	16
	5	Rs. 460-15-520-17-588-19-664-21-748 (4) (4) (4) (4)	16
	6	Rs. 400-9-445-10-495-11-539-12-587 (5) (5) (4) (4)	18
	7	Rs. 350-7-385-8-425-9-461-10-501 (5) (5) (4) (4)	18
VI	1	Not less than Rs. 1200	
(Rs. 10 lakhs and above and less than Rs. 25 lakhs)	2	Rs. 630-30-750-35-890-40-1010-45-1145 (4) (4) (3) (3)	14
	3	Rs. 575-25-675-30-795-35-935-40-1095 (4) (4) (4) (4)	16
	4	Rs. 500-20-580-25-680-30-800-35-940 (4) (4) (4) (4)	16
	5	Rs. 420-13-472-15-532-17-600-19-676 (4) (4) (4) (4)	16
	6	Rs. 375-8-415-9-460-10-500-11-544 (5) (5) (4) (4)	18
	7	Rs. 325-6-355-7-390-8-422-9-458 (5) (5) (4) (4)	18

(Contd.)

Class of establishment	Group of employees	Scales	Years
VII (Less than Rs. 10 lakhs)	1	Not less than Rs. 1,150	
	2	Rs. 605-30-725-35-865-40-985-45-1120 (4) (4) (3) (3)	14
	3	Rs. 540-25-640-30-760-35-900-40-1060 (4) (4) (4) (4)	16
	4	Rs. 480-20-560-25-660-30-780-35-920 (4) (4) (4) (4)	16
	5	Rs. 410-11-454-13-506-15-566-17-634 (4) (4) (4) (4)	16
	6	Rs. 355-7-390-8-430-9-466-10-506 (5) (5) (4) (4)	18
	7	Rs. 300-5-325-6-355-7-383-8-415 (5) (4) (4) (4)	18

Non-Journalists : Factory Employees

Class of establishment	Group of employees	Scales	Years
IB (Rs. 25 crores and above)	1	Rs. 770-35-910-50-1110-60-1350-70-1560 (4) (4) (4) (3)	15
	2	Rs. 700-30-820-40-980-50-1180-60-1420 (4) (4) (4) (4)	16
	3	Rs. 675-30-795-35-935-45-1115-50-1315 (4) (4) (4) (4)	16
	4	Rs. 650-30-770-35-910-40-1070-45-1250 (4) (4) (4) (4)	16
	5	Rs. 600-25-725-27-860-29-976-31-1100 (5) (5) (4) (4)	18
	6	Rs. 550-13-615-14-685-15-745-16-809 (5) (5) (4) (4)	18
IA (Rs. 10 crores and above and less than Rs. 25 crores)	1	Rs. 735-35-875-45-1055-55-1275-65-1470 (4) (4) (4) (3)	15
	2	Rs. 670-30-790-34-930-45-1110-55-1330 (4) (4) (4) (4)	16
	3	Rs. 645-30-765-35-905-40-1065-45-1245 (4) (4) (4) (4)	16
	4	Rs. 620-30-740-35-880-40-1040-45-1220 (4) (4) (4) (4)	16
	5	Rs. 570-23-685-25-810-27-918-29-1034 (5) (5) (4) (4)	18
	6	Rs. 525-12-585-13-650-14-706-15-766 (5) (5) (4) (4)	18

(Contd.)

Class of establishment	Group of employees	Scales	Years
I	1	Rs. 700-30-820-40-980-50-1180-60-1360	15
(Rs. 4 crores and		(4) (4) (4) (3)	
less than Rs. 10 crores)	2	Rs. 640-30-760-35-900-40-1060-45-1240	16
		(4) (4) (4) (4)	
	3	Rs. 615-30-735-35-875-40-1035-45-1215	16
		(4) (4) (4) (4)	
	4	Rs. 590-25-690-30-810-35-950-40-1110	16
		(4) (4) (4) (4)	
	5	Rs. 540-21-645-23-760-25-860-27-968	18
		(5) (5) (4) (4)	
	6	Rs. 500-11-555-12-615-13-667-14-723	18
		(5) (5) (4) (4)	
II	1	Rs. 665-30-785-35-925-45-1105-55-1270	15
		(4) (4) (4) (3)	
(Rs. 2 crores and	2	Rs. 630-30-750-35-890-40-1050-45-1230	16
above and less than		(4) (4) (4) (4)	
Rs. 4 crores)	3	Rs. 595-25-695-30-815-35-955-40-1115	16
		(4) (4) (4) (4)	
	4	Rs. 570-25-670-30-790-35-930-40-1090	16
		(4) (4) (4) (4)	
	5	Rs. 520-19-615-21-720-23-812-25-912	18
		(5) (5) (4) (4)	
	6	Rs. 475-10-525-11-580-12-628-13-680	18
		(5) (5) (4) (4)	
III	1	Rs. 630-30-750-35-890-40-1050-50-1200	15
(Rs. 1 crore and above		(4) (4) (4) (3)	
and less than Rs.	2	Rs. 595-25-695-30-815-35-955-40-1115	16
2 crores)		(4) (4) (4) (4)	
	3	Rs. 570-25-670-30-790-35-930-40-1090	16
		(4) (4) (4) (4)	
	4	Rs. 550-25-650-30-770-35-910-40-1070	16
		(4) (4) (4) (4)	
	5	Rs. 500-17-585-19-680-21-764-23-856	18
		(5) (5) (4) (4)	
	6	Rs. 450-9-495-10-545-11-589-12-637	18
		(5) (5) (4) (4)	
IV	1	Rs. 575-25-675-30-795-35-935-50-1085	15
(Rs. 50 lakhs and above		(4) (4) (4) (3)	
and less than Rs.	2	Rs. 540-25-640-30-760-35-900-40-1060	16
1 crore)		(4) (4) (4) (4)	

Class of establishment	Group of employees	Scales	Years
	3	Rs. 520-25-620-30-740-35-880-40-1040 (4) (4) (4) (4)	16
	4	Rs. 500-20-580-25-680-30-800-35-940 (4) (4) (4) (4)	16
	5	Rs. 460-15-535-17-620-19-696-21-780 (5) (5) (4) (4)	18
	6	Rs. 425-8-465-9-510-10-550-11-594 (5) (5) (4) (4)	18
V (Rs. 25 lakhs and above and less than Rs. 50 lakhs)	1	Rs. 490-25-590-30-710-35-850-45-985 (4) (4) (4) (3)	15
	2	Rs. 460-25-560-30-680-35-820-40-980 (4) (4) (4) (4)	16
	3	Rs. 440-20-520-25-620-30-740-35-880 (4) (4) (4) (4)	16
	4	Rs. 420-20-500-25-600-30-720-35-860 (4) (4) (4) (4)	16
	5	Rs. 380-13-445-15-520-17-588-19-664 (5) (5) (4) (4)	18
	6	Rs. 350-7-385-8-425-9-461-10-501 (5) (5) (4) (4)	18
VI (Rs. 10 lakhs and above and less than Rs. 25 lakhs)	1	Rs. 470-25-570-30-690-35-830-40-950 (4) (4) (4) (3)	15
	2	Rs. 445-20-525-25-625-30-30-745-35-885 (4) (4) (4) (4)	16
	3	Rs. 425-20-505-25-605-30-725-35-865 (4) (4) (4) (4)	16
	4	Rs. 400-20-480-25-580-30-700-35-840 (4) (4) (4) (4)	16
	5	Rs. 360-11-415-13-480-15-540-17-608 (5) (5) (4) (4)	18
	6	Rs. 325-6-355-7-390-8-422-9-458 (5) (5) (4) (4)	18
VII (Less than Rs. 10 lakhs)	1	Rs. 445-25-545-30-665-35-805-40-925 (4) (4) (4) (3)	15
	2	Rs. 415-20-495-25-595-30-715-35-855 (4) (4) (4) (4)	16
	3	Rs. 390-15-450-20-530-25-630-30-750 (4) (4) (4) (4)	16
	4	Rs. 365-15-425-20-505-25-605-30-725 (4) (4) (4) (4)	16
	5	Rs. 330-9-375-11-430-13-482-15-542 (5) (5) (4) (4)	18
	6	Rs. 300-5-325-6-355-7-383-8-415 (5) (5) (4) (4)	18

TABLE II : Rates of Dearness Allowance

Basic Pay Slabs	Amounts to be paid for every rise of six points over the index of 363 (1960=100) on 1st April and 1st October every year.
Upto Rs. 300	Rs. 5.00
Rs. 301 to 350	Rs. 5.25
Rs. 351 to 400	Rs. 5.50
Rs. 401 to 450	Rs. 6.00
Rs. 451 to 500	Rs. 6.50
Rs. 501 to 550	Rs. 7.00
Rs. 551 to 700	Rs. 8.00
Rs. 701 to 1000	Rs. 9.00
Rs. 1001 to 1150	Rs. 9.50
Rs. 1151 to 1300	Rs. 10.00
Rs. 1301 to 1600	Rs. 11.00
Rs. 1601 and above	Rs. 11.00

TABLE III: Rates of House Rent Allowance

Zone	Pay Rs.	Class IB	Class IA	Class I	Class II
(1)	(2)	(3)	(4)	(5)	(6)
'A' (Cities/Towns with a population of 20 lakhs and above as per census of 1971).	Rs. 300 to Rs.1600 Rs. 1601 and above	8% of pay. Maximum Rs. 128 Rs. 128	7% of pay. Maximum Rs. 112 Rs. 112	6% of pay. Maximum Rs. 96 Rs. 96	5% of pay. Maximum Rs. 80 Rs. 80
'B' (Cities/Towns with a population of 10 lakhs and above but less than 20 lakhs as per census of 1971).	Rs. 300 to Rs. 1600 Rs. 1601 and above	7% of pay. Maximum Rs. 112 Rs. 112	6% of pay. Maximum Rs. 96 Rs. 96	5% of pay. Maximum Rs. 80 Rs. 80	4% of pay. Maximum Rs. 64 Rs. 64
'C' (Cities/Towns with a population of less than 10 lakhs as per census of 1971).	Rs. 300 to Rs. 1600 Rs. 1601 and above	6% of pay. Maximum Rs. 96 Rs. 96	5% of pay. Maximum Rs. 80 Rs. 80	4% of pay. Maximum Rs. 64 Rs. 64	3% of pay. Maximum Rs. 48 Rs. 48

TABLE IV: Rates of Night Shift Allowance

Night Shift allowance will be paid as follows:

Newspaper Establishment

Classes IB and IA	Rs. 4—per night.
Classes I and II	Rs. 3—per night.
Class III	Rs. 2—per night.

7

TECHNICAL ADVISORY COMMITTEE PLANNING COMMISSION PROGRAMME EVALUATION ORGANISATION — REPORT[1]

Chairman Dr. S.M. Shah, Adviser, Planning Commission

Members Prof. S. Sachchidananda; Shri G. Kameshwar Rao; Dr. R.C. Saxena; Shri P.S. Krishnan; Shri Habeeb Mohamed; Shri Y.N. Amble; Shri A.V.R. Char; Dr. Ram Pandey; Secretary, Labour Department, Government of Karnataka; Labour Commissioner, Government of Tamil Nadu, Madras; Director (Evaluation), Government of Uttar Pradesh, Lucknow

M. Secy. Shri P.L. Aware

Appointment

The Government of India passed the Bonded Labour System (Abolition) Act in 1976. Efforts were thereafter initiated for identification, release and rehabilitation of bonded labour in different States. A Centrally Sponsored Scheme for rehabilitation of the freed bonded labourers was started in 1978-79. The scheme provided for matching grant assistance from the centre to the extent of 50 per cent of the total cost which was fixed at Rs. 4000 per bonded labourer.

The main objective of the Bonded Labour Scheme as stated earlier, was to identify, release and rehabilitate the bonded labour both under the Centrally Sponsored Scheme as well as under the ongoing schemes of the State Governments.

The State Governments were asked to prepare rehabilitation schemes for the bonded labour, broadly in conformity with the guidelines issued in this connection. These schemes were then

1. Programme Evaluation Organisation, Planning Commission, Government of India, New Delhi 1984, vi + 106 p.

scrutinised for approval by Screening Committee consisting of representatives of Ministry of Labour, Department of Rural Development and Planning Commission, set up at the Centre. For each of the Schemes, as per the guidelines of the Labour Ministry, the State Governments were required to indicate the district agency responsible for its execution.

The programmes for economic upliftment and rehabilitation of bonded labour needed systematically to be followed up so as to ensure that there was no relapse into bondage in due course. In its 5th meeting held on 9th January, 1979, the Screening Committee recommended that the working of the Centrally Sponsored Scheme for rehabilitation of bonded labour should be evaluated so that corrective measures, if required, could be identified and applied in the formulation of the suitable future policy for the scheme. The Ministry of Labour, therefore, requested the Programme Evaluation Organisation of the Planning Commission to conduct, urgently such an evaluation study.

Terms of Reference

The Main objective of the evaluation study was to find out the extent to which aims of the scheme to identity, free and rehabilitate the bonded labour have been fulfilled with particular reference to:

(a) The administrative arrangements made at various levels for the implementation of the schemes to identify, release and rehabilitate the freed bonded labour;
(b) The detailed contents of the various schemes and the extent to which they have been implemented;
(c) The impact of the various schemes towards the rehabilitation of the bonded labourers in terms of employment and income generated to the released persons;
(d) The administrative support being given and the follow up methods adopted to prevent the lapsing back of the bonded labourers into bondage;
(e) To study the impact of the programmes in bringing about any social change in the life and living conditions of the beneficiaries and the village community; and
(f) Extent of integration of the released labour in the mainstream of the village community.

Contents

Introduction; The Evaluation Study; Administration and Organisation for Implementation of the Programme, Vigilance Committees – Statutory Registers; Bondage; Identification; Procedure for Release; Rehabilitation Programmes; Rehabilitation Schemes – Their Suitability; Credit Facilities; Impact on the Target Groups; Summary of Findings, Suggestions and Action Plans; Appendices.

Recommendations

Summary of Findings, Suggestions and Action Plans

Perspective

1. The problem of bonded labour was being felt in the country even before independence. Some concerted efforts were made to prohibit the use of forced in the thirties in accordance with the ILO Convention of 1930. But a serious view was taken only after independence by making special provision in the constitution vide article 23.

2. The practice of bonded labour has been made a socio-economic offence under the Bonded Labour Abolition Act, 1976. The basic ingredients of the offence are: (a) Denial of freedom to participate in the labour market, (b) Denial of freedom of movement to any part of country, and (c) Exploitation of the innocent labourers and its family members under customary and debt conditions. The main source of the estimates of bonded labour are: (a) Identifications made by State Government, (b) surveys undertaken by the NSSO and (c) Survey by Gandhi Peace Foundation and National Labour Institute. The estimates prepared by these agencies are 1.5 lakhs by State Governments, 4.5 lakhs by NSSO, in 15 States and 26.17 lakhs by Gandhi Peace Foundation in 10 States. The estimates of bonded labour as discussed above vary significantly due to difference in coverage, concepts and methodology vide details given in Appendix 1.2. In view of the different estimates there is a need to have a fresh survey in all the States including those who have not declared bonded labour but have bonded labour according to the NSSO. (Paras 1.2 and 1.3) (Action State Govts. concerned, Ministry of Labour and NSSO).

The PEO Evaluation Study, Scope and Objectives

3. The main objective of the Bonded Labour Scheme, was to identify, release and rehabilitate the bonded labour both under the Centrally Sponsored Scheme as well as under the ongoing schemes of the State Governments. In its 5th meeting held on 9th January, 1979, the Screening Committee recommended that the working of the Centrally Sponsored Scheme for rehabilitation on bonded labour should be evaluated so that corrective measures, if required, could be identified and applied in the formulation of the suitable future policy for the scheme. The Ministry of Labour, therefore, requested the Programme Evaluation Organisation of the Planning Commission to conduct urgently such an evaluation study. (Paras 2.1 and 2.3)

Objectives

4. The main objective of the evaluation study was to find out the extent to which the aims of the scheme to identify, free and rehabilitate the bonded labour have been fulfilled with particular reference to:

(a) the administrative arrangements made at various levels for the implementation of the schemes to identify, release and rehabilitate the freed bonded labour;
(b) the detailed contents of the various schemes and the extent to which they have been implemented;
(c) the impact of the various schemes towards the rehabilitation of the bonded labourers in terms of employment and income generated to the released persons;
(d) the administrative support being given and the follow up methods adopted to prevent the lapsing back of the bonded labourers into bondage;
(e) to study the impact of the programmes in bringing about any social change in the life and living conditions of the beneficiaries and the village community; and
(f) extent of integration of the released labour in the mainstream of the village community. (Para 24)

5. The study was conducted in 8 States, 18 districts (in which the Centrally Sponsored Scheme was being implemented), 38 blocks, 112 villages and 782 beneficiaries were selected for detailed canvassing. (Para 2.5)

6. The main instruments of observation followed were (i) State/District level guide-points-cum-questionnaire, (ii) Village Level Schedule, and (iii) Beneficiary Schedule. (Para 2.12)

Summary of Findings

Administration

7. (i) The officials of the Revenue Department who were equipped with judicial and administrative powers, were more effective in identification and release of bonded labour. It is, therefore, recommended that for effective implementation of the programme, the identification and release of bonded labour should be dealt with in the Revenue Department and rehabilitation aspect under various schemes in the special welfare department, as far as possible. (Para 3.3) (Action all State Governments and Ministry of Labour).

(ii) At district level the District Collectors or Deputy Commissioners were dealing with the subject. At lower levels namely, taluka sub-division of block the BDO, SDO, Tehsildar or labour Inspector look after the rehabilitation programme of bonded labour. It was, however, observed that the staff of the labour department in Bihar was not effective in dealing with this problem. (Para 3.4) (Action Government of Bihar).

(iii) The Vigilance Committees have played an important role in the implementation of the programme. These committees should be constituted in all the districts and divisions wherever they have not been constituted so far. Efforts should also be made to see that the meetings of the Vigilance Committees are held regularly for reviewing the pace of rehabilitation schemes. It was also observed that in on district of Orissa the non-official members did not take interest in the working of the Vigilance Committees. The reasons for their indifferent attitude should be found out and remedial measures taken. It is also recommended that attempt should also be made to nominate only active and committed members to serve on the Vigilance Committees. (Paras 3.7, 3.9 and 3.10) (Action State Governments).

(iv) In regard to the Statutory registers giving details of the bonded labour, it was observed that these were not maintained in some districts and wherever they were maintained, they were not maintained satisfactorily. Discrepancies were also found in records. Since these registers contain vital and basic information about the bonded labour, these should be kept upto date and maintained systematically. (Para 3.12) (Action State Governments).

Bondage

8. It is difficult to trace the origin of bonded labour as the system is continuing from generations in India. However, on the basis of available information collected during the study its origin and perpetuation could be traced to mainly (a) economic compulsions, coupled with social customs and traditions, (b) customary and traditional bondage, and (c) contractual bondage. The money-lenders took full advantage of the economic conditions and social obligations of the poor peasants and advanced small loans from time to time. As these labourers could never free themselves from the vicious circle of poverty they had a perpetuate the bondage. The indebtedness became an economic inevitability and bondage a way of life to majority of them. (Para 4.1)

9. It was observed that Scheduled Castes and Scheduled Tribes together formed 83.2 per cent of the total selected beneficiaries. The rest belong to backward and other classes. The percentage of female selected beneficiaries was meagre 4.2 per cent. It was also observed that the States of Andhra Pradesh, Bihar, Karnataka and U.P. had the highest number of Scheduled Castes bonded labour. Their respective percentage being 80.5, 70.8, 80.5 and 91.7. On the other hand there was concentration of Scheduled Tribes beneficiaries in the remaining States of Madhya Pradesh, Orissa, Rajasthan and Tamil Nadu. Their percentage being 71, 65.8, 86.7 and 45 respectively in these States. It is recommended that the State concerned should integrate the rehabilitation programme with the special component plan and Tribal Sub-plan, so that scope of rehabilitation assistance is enlarged (Para 4.14). (Action all States, Ministries of Labour, Home and Planning).

10. Prior to bondage 68.79 per cent beneficiaries were labourers, 11.65 per cent cultivators 4.19 per cent having animal husbandry as occupation, 1.86 as artisans and 13.3 per cent as others. During bondage the percentage of beneficiaries working as labourers went upto 90.92 per cent followed by 1.66 in animal husbandry and 7.03 per cent in other occupations like hiring of bullocks and grazing of cattle. It will be observed that there was considerable shift in occupation in terms of increase in the percentage of beneficiaries working as labourers during bondage. There was, however, some impact of rehabilitation after the beneficiaries were released and rehabilitated.

Thus presently 67.39 per cent beneficiaries were working as labourers followed by 16.24 per cent as cultivators, 5.24 per cent in animal husbandry, 2.43 per cent in traditional village services such as Barber, washermen, sweepers, etc., while 7.93 per cent were working in occupation as hiring of bullocks and grazing of cattles. (Paras 4.22 and 4.24)

11. It was observed that 43 per cent of the selected beneficiaries were bonded when they were less than 15 years of age. So much so that more than 8 per cent of them were of less than 10 years of age. There were 38 per cent of beneficiaries who were bonded between age of 15 and 25 years and the remaining 19 per cent between 25 to 55. It will thus be seen that the masters preferred young persons as bonded labourers as they could work harder and longer. (Para 4.30)

12. The longivity of the period and bondage could be an indicator of the depth to which the system of bondage was rooted. It was thus observed that about 72 per cent of the selected beneficiaries had remained in bondage for 5 years and above while about 25 per cent remained in bondage for 20 years and above. Statewise it was observed that quite a high percentage of beneficiaries had come out of the clutches of bondage after 20 years and more in the States like Bihar and U.P. This may lead to the conclusion that the system of bonded labour may be oldest in these States. On the contrary the system is comparatively of recent origin in the States of Orissa and Andhra Pradesh as about 90 per cent and 46 per cent of the selected beneficiaries respectively remained in bondage for less than 5 years in these two States. There is, however, a need for further research to determine the causes for varying durations. (Paras 4.32 and 4.33) (Action Ministry of Labour, Planning and Home).

13. As regards the cause of bondage it was revealed that about 98 per cent of the beneficiaries were bonded due to indebtedness while there were about 2 per cent who were bonded due to customary or social obligations, because of belonging to a certain caste. The social and customary bondage was found only in the States of Bihar, Karnataka, Orissa and Rajasthan. This indicates that the social customs and norms seems to be rigid in these States and the weaker sections like SC/ST suffered from such social and customary bondage. The State Directorates of Social Welfare, Tribal Development and researchers should undertake further in-depth studies of these aspects to facilitate social reforms and social development. (Para 4.35) (Action all States and particularly Bihar, Karnataka, Orissa and Rajasthan, Research *Organisation*).

14. Out of the total number of 782 beneficiaries 310 (39.64 per cent) reported that an agreement was signed for entering into bondage but no copy of the agreement was given to them. While 60 per cent of the beneficiaries reported that no such agreement was signed and everything was verbal. (Paras 4.43 and 4.44)

Identification

15. It was observed during the course of the evaluation study that there was some confusion in the minds of various functionaries about the proper definition of bonded labour as distinguished from attached labour, contract labour, migrant labour, etc. It is, therefore, recommended that the State Governments may hold training workshop to explain the various sections of the Bonded Labour Act including correct definition so that the implementing officials are clear about the proper application of the definition. (Para 5.12)

16. In most of the cases the identification was done only at one point of time and perhaps hurriedly as well as half-heartedly in some States and as such the process of identification itself seems to have remained incomplete in almost all the States. It is also recommended that fresh efforts should be made to identify the remaining bonded labourers by adopting some of the following methods:

(a) Most of the State Governments are conducting household surveys to locate the poorest of the poor families for giving assistance under various rural development programmes. Opportunity may be taken during such surveys to locate bonded labour on a systematic basis;
(b) Some of the States might be proposing to undertake surveys to locate the landless, siteless and houseless persons under the rural housing programme. Such surveys also could be utilised for identification of the bonded labour;
(c) NSSO had earlier conducted the survey of Bonded Labourers alongwith their employment and unemployment survey during the 36th round and have also conducted similar survey during their 38th round (July 1983 – June 1984). That agency may be requested to undertake a more detailed survey of the bonded labour in collaboration with the State Governments. Since this is one of the important items of 20-Point Programme, the NSSO might be asked to undertake a special survey on bonded labour

in due course in collaboration with States;

(d) The Central Statistical Organisation which is another National Level Statistical Organisation like the NSSO is undertaking economic census every 5 years in collaboration with the State Statistical Organisation. The next census is due in 1985. Since C.S.O., N.S.S.O. and the State Statistical Bureaus undertake house listing, both in rural and urban areas, the identification of the bonded labour could also be considered during the economic census; and

(e) The Labour Bureau under the Ministry of Labour also undertakes periodic surveys including Rural Labour Enquiry, etc. The Labour Bureau, therefore, as a specialised agency could also be entrusted with this work including coordination of such surveys.

The Ministry of Labour should consider the above suggestions for identification of the bonded labour so that the process of identification is complete. (Paras 5.16 and 5.17) (Action Ministry of Labour and Employment and Planning, Department of Statistics).

17. It was observed that in all the States no preparatory work was done before launching the process of identification. Instructions were, however, issued to the district collectors to take the necessary steps in accordance with the provisions of the Act. These instructions could be of routine nature. It was only in Karnataka that wide publicity was given about the Bonded Labour Abolition Act, 1976. (Para 5.13)

18. No voluntary agency as such was duly involved in the identification of bonded labour. In Andhra Pradesh some social workers in their individual capacity were reported to have brought some cases of bonded labour to the notice of authorities for necessary action. It is desirable for State Governments to encourage reputed organisations and social welfare organisations and social welfare associations to undertake the work of identification and rehabilitation of bonded labour. The State Governments should also involve an organisation of bonded labour themselves. The university students associations such as NSS, young people from the weaker sections like Dalit Panthers should their energies are utilised for social good. (Para 5.14) (Action all States, Ministry of Labour and Education and Universities).

19. Majority of the selected beneficiaries were identified with little or no time lag and as many as 88 per cent or so within 3 months of the first contact. The only State which reported 34 beneficiaries having identified between one to two years of the first contact was Bihar and

the beneficiaries belong to the districts of Bhagalpur and Santhal Parganas. (Para 5.19).

Release

20. The Bonded Labour Abolition Act, 1976 stipulates preparation of the list of released bonded labourers and its maintenance in a special statutory register prescribed for the purpose. It was observed that such registers were not maintained in some of the districts and wherever they were maintained they were not maintained properly. (Para 6.1)

21. In majority of the districts of the 8 States the landlords released bonded labourers voluntarily without making any hue and cry for fear of legal proceedings. However, in Orissa out of 1123 identified bonded labourers upto June 1981 only 329 were reported to be released. This was mainly because in Orissa prosecution was regarded as inevitable in each and every case. This fear of inevitable prosecution compelled the landlords to produce evidence against the complaint to keeping bonded labour. Only recently some flexible approach has been adopted by the Government under which the masters have been persuaded to release bonded labour voluntarily. In case of Bihar, proceedings were prolonged because many a time landlords managed to get adjournment or forced the labourers to leave station for avoiding prosecution. This also showed the lack of protection from the State Officials. (Para 6.2)

22. Out of eight State evaluated only the States of Bihar and Orissa reported some problem created by the landlords. In these two States it was reported that landlords forcibly prevented the bonded labourers from appearing in the courts. They also forced the bonded labourers to leave the States and even went to the extent of implicating them in criminal cases. Some of the reasons for the delay in release related to procedure, court proceedings and indifferent attitude of the officials. (Para 6.5)

23. There were 739 beneficiaries out of 782 who reported that they were really released while seven reported that they were partly released and 36 reported that they were not at all released. About 36 beneficiaries in Bihar reported that they were not released at all and continued to work with the same master. This shows not only lack of physical monitoring and follow up on the part of the State officials who did not verify whether all the bonded labourers were really released but also lack of administrative will and non-concern to the implementation of this important item of 20-Point Programme. (Paras

6.13 and 6.15) (Action Government of Bihar/Ministry of Labour).

24. Majority of respondents reported that the condition had improved after release. (Para 6.16) (Action Government of Bihar).

25. About 76 per cent of the beneficiaries had reported that their masters were angry as a result of their release. They were unhappy because either they will lose a cheap source of labour or face problem of labour in peak season or may not get a person who could be at their back and call or the loan will be written off. The voluntary social development organisations, Directorates of Social Welfare, Tribal Development, Researchers, Sociologists and Anthropologists from the States should undertake in-depth studies and make suggestions for reorienting the better off sections of the rural areas so that conducive atmosphere is created for rapid socio-economic change and upliftment of the rural poor. (Para 6.18) (Action Ministries of Labour, Home and Planning).

26. It was found that more than 97 per cent of the beneficiaries were happy after their release. However, there were also categories of the beneficiaries who were either indifferent or not happy. The number of such beneficiaries was seven. Out of seven, three beneficiaries from Monghyr, Jabalpur and Kolar had felt that they will lose permanent source of employment after release. Three of the beneficiaries from Monghyr (2) and Tehri Garhwal (1) had mentioned that they had fear from the ex-masters even after release and hence they were not happy. It appears that in these States there was lack of follow up action in this direction. It is, therefore, suggested to entrust their problems to committed officials, (Paras 6.24 and 6.33) (Action all State and particularly Bihar and U.P.)

Rehabilitation Programmes

27. By and large it was found that at the time of formulation of the programme no norms as such were prescribed by the Government of India or State Governments for allotment of various items of rehabilitation. It was thus, observed that for allotment of land in Andhra Pradesh the size of the allotted land varied between 0.4 to 0.56 acres. While in Orissa and Madhya Pradesh it was 2.5 acres per bonded labour. In regard to supply of inputs Rs. 200 were provided in district Ganjam and Rs. 170 each in districts of Kalahandi, Koraput and Phulbani of Orissa. In Tehri Garhwal of U.P. the required inputs were however, provided free of cost. *No norms were, however, fixed in the remaining*

districts in respect of supply of inputs. In regards to development and reclamation of land, a sum of Rs. 750 was prescribed in the district of Ganjam and Rs. 600 in the districts of Kalahandi, Koraput and Phulbani of Orissa. In Tehri Garhwal of U.P. cash grant upto Rs. 2000 was allotted. *No norms had been fixed in the remaining districts for this programme.* In regard to supply of milch cattle, etc., under non-land based scheme it was observed that no fixed norms were prescribed in various districts and the number of animals or birds varied from 1 to 2 in case of cattle and 3 to 4 in regard to goats and 4 to 5 in regard to pigs. (Para 7.8)

28. It is clear from the above that no proper planning was made in prescribing any economic size of the various units which could provide suitable income to the beneficiaries.

29. It was observed that out of 18 districts 8 districts reported that some sort of selection was made on the basis of aptitude and experience of the beneficiaries while giving schemes to them. In the remaining 10 districts schemes were generally chosen by the implementing agencies themselves and no choice was allowed to the beneficiaries. (Para 7.9)

30. The main source of financial assistance for the rehabilitation programme was the 100 per cent rehabilitation grant from the Central and State Governments on 50:50 basis. It was, however, observed that in the district of Periyar (Tamil Nadu) in addition to the rehabilitation assistance the State Bank of India and the Indian Overseas Bank also gave assistance to the beneficiaries for purchase of bullocks, buffaloes and iron ploughs. It was further noted that majority of the district authorities did not find much difficulty in utilising the meagre financial assistance. Six district authorities however, reported some difficulty in providing benefits, such as delay in identification of schemes, obtaining sanctions at block and district levels, non-availability of required staff and non-acceptance of schemes by the beneficiaries. (Para 7.10)

31. Since in most of the districts the single agency like Collector at the district level and BDO/Tehsildar at the block level were responsible for coordination not much difficulty was faced in coordinating the programmes. (Para 7.11)

32. In majority of the cases no raw material was required to be provided. As regards marketing facilities it was disappointing to note that there were no arrangements for marketing of milk and other products in 17 out of 18 districts studied. It was only in Kolar district of Karnataka that marketing arrangements were reported to have been

made through milk producers cooperative societies and sheep producers association for marketing of milk and livestock respectively. This shows the lack of Planning and Foresight in the 17 districts. (Para 7.13)

33. The implementing agencies made three main suggestions for improving the programme namely (a) integration of the programme with other beneficiary oriented programme, (b) provision of adequate staff, and (c) arrangements for providing technical knowhow. These suggestions need to be seriously considered at higher levels. (Para 7.15) (Action all States).

34. The progress of rehabilitation of released bonded labour was reported very low. Only 9493 bonded labourers were covered under various schemes in all the 18 districts studied as against the number of 22458 released bonded labourers. More than 50 per cent of the released bonded labourers were yet to be rehabilitated at the time of study. The plight of the 58 per cent of the released bonded labourers was, however, reported to be very pathetic. One of the reasons attributed to such state of affairs related to lack of urgency on the part of the officials at various levels in dealing with the problem of the released bonded labourers. Besides, there were several avoidable administrative problems like lapsing of funds, delays in the allotments of funds, frequent references between the State Governments and the Ministry of Labour for clarification, etc. (Para 7.17)

35. Out of 18 districts, no money was spent in three districts for welfare and rehabilitation of the bonded labourers. In Raigarh district of Madhya Pradesh the funds remained unutilised because there was no bonded labour on whom the money could be spent. Similar was the situation in Ganjam district of Orissa were only 5.7 per cent of the funds could be utilised. In Kota districts of Rajasthan 700 bonded labourers were given only paper benefits in terms of share certificates of Rs. 4000 each in the name of bonded labour industrial cooperative society and the whole of the amount of Rs. 28 lakhs was reported to have been deposited in the bank. (Para 7.23)

36. In all districts except one no efforts were reported to have been made to integrate the rehabilitation of bonded labour schemes with other on-going beneficiary oriented programmes such as Food for Work, IRDP, PWD works, etc. In Kolar district of Karnataka efforts were made to employ the beneficiaries under Food for Work Programme, Janta housing scheme and employment under PWD works. (Para 7.25)

37. Over 60 per cent of the selected beneficiaries were rehabilitated any where between 2 to 4 years. It was further observed that 100 per cent of beneficiaries were rehabilitated after 3 to 4 years in Kolar of Karnataka, Jabalpur of Madhya Pradesh after 2 to 3 years in Raigarh of Madhya Pradesh and Ganjam of Orissa and after 1 to 2 years in district Nalanda of Bihar. It was further observed that 75 per cent of selected beneficiaries from Rangareddy (Andhra Pradesh), Kalahandi (Orissa), Kota (Rajasthan) were rehabilitated after 2 to 3 years of their release. In district Periyar of Tamil Nadu 85 per cent of beneficiaries were rehabilitated after 4 to 5 years of release. This is a very disappointing situation. Some of the reasons furnished for such an undue delay related to procedure, slackness on the part of officials, delay in release of funds, non-availability of funds and shortage of staff. Overall it was observed that only 41.2 per cent of the released bonded labourers were rehabilitated in 9 States at the time of the study during 1981. This is a very disappointing situation. If a bonded labour is not rehabilitated soon after release he is likely to be exploited by the ex-master causing his relapse into bandage. (Paras 7.27, 7.28, 7.30, 7.31 and 7.32) (Action all States, Ministry of Labour).

38. Only 317 (48 per cent) beneficiaries out of a total of 782 reported that they were provided some benefit of subsistence allowance. There were about 59 beneficiaries who had not received any subsistence allowance and it is not known as to how these released bonded labourers had survived in the absence of any immediate relief. This indicates absence or failure of proper follow-up action (Paras 7.39 and 7.41)

39. Out of 782 beneficiaries 725 (93 per cent) had reported time lag between release and rehabilitation. Out of these 725, 381 (52.55 per cent) stated that their income during the intervening period was not sufficient to support their families. They gave various reasons for this such as non-availability of work, no subsistence allowance, etc. To tie over the difficulty of insufficiency of income most of them namely, 139 or 36 per cent resorted to missing a meal whereas 19 per cent of them were just starving to cope with the situation. Others adopted some other means to overcome these difficulties. It was further observed that about 74 beneficiaries in 8 districts out of the 381 who reported time lag between release and rehabilitation were just starving and struggling hard for existence during this period. Of these 51 were Scheduled Castes, 13 Scheduled Tribes, 9 backward classes and 1 others. (Paras 7.46 and 7.51)

40. This indicates the failure of the concerned State-district authorities in not providing sufficient subsistence allowance during the intervening period of release and rehabilitation thereby exposing most of the beneficiaries to the danger of re-lapse into bondage. The main reasons put forward by the beneficiaries for insufficiency of income related to "work not available or no subsistence allowance given". (Paras 7.48 and 7.49)

41. Out of 782 beneficiaries 326 (42 per cent) reported that the schemes were thrust upon them while 426 (58 per cent) reported that they had the choice of the scheme. All the selected beneficiaries from Tamil Nadu had no choice of the scheme which were thrust upon them. In Orissa, Madhya Pradesh and Rajasthan more than 95 per cent of the selected beneficiaries reported that the schemes were thrust upon them. It was only from the States of Karnataka, U.P. and Bihar that the majority of the beneficiaries had the choice of the scheme. It is evident that no steps were taken by the concerned authorities to assess the choice of the beneficiaries in the matter of rehabilitation schemes. (Paras 8.2 and 8.4)

42. Out of the 782 selected beneficiaries 205 reported that benefits were adequate while 262 (33.50 per cent) reported that they were partially adequate whereas remaining 315 (40.28 per cent) reported that the benefits were not adequate and gave suggestions for improvement. Thus the majority of the beneficiaries amounting to about 73.78 per cent reported the inadequacy of the rehabilitation assistance. To overcome this inadequacy the beneficiaries made certain suggestions. These related to increase in the size of the scheme, payment of subsistence allowance or regular basic till rehabilitation, allotment of more and good quality of land for cultivation, financial assistance for agricultural inputs and irrigation facilities. Some of the beneficiaries also suggested provision of regular wage employment, provision of grazing land, provision of feed and fodder and provision of houses/house-sites. (Paras 8.32, 8.33 and 8.34)

43. The State Governments should consider these suggestions for rehabilitation in future. It is also recommended that the concerned State authorities should carry out the studies about the economic benefits to the ex-bonded labourers according to size of land allotted to them so that more land could be allotted whenever necessary. It was also recorded that the State/district authorities in many cases had failed to provide the required inputs to the ex-bonded labourers resulting in non-utilisation of allotted land. It is suggested that the concerned

authorities at the Centre and in the States should review the situation urgently. (Para 8.34) (Action Ministry of Labour, State Govts.)

44. Out of 782 selected beneficiaries 310 (about 40 per cent) had availed rehabilitation facilities. Out of these about 92 beneficiaries had faced certain difficulties in availing these facilities. Majority of them had said that the disbursement of assistance was irregular and/or procedure involved was cumbersome and time consuming. Some of them even reported that the officials were not helpful. (Para 8.57) (Action all States).

45. It was noted that only 79 beneficiaries forming a meagre percentage of 10 per cent out of 782 beneficiaries received financial assistance/loan. The assistance/loan was received in three years, i.e., 1979, 1980 and 1981. Some of the beneficiaries reported that the assistance was not sufficient and suggested that the quantum of assistance should be increased. (Para 8.61)

46. The analysis regarding rehabilitation schemes, their norms, selection criterion, etc., indicates that in majority of cases enough efforts were not made to identify viable schemes/programmes for the rehabilitation of the released bonded labourers. In majority of cases, where land was allotted, it was reported to be not of good quality and was located generally far away from the houses of the bonded labourers. Except in few districts like Medak and Ranga Reddy (Andhra Pradesh), no irrigation facilities were made available to the beneficiaries as a result of which they were unable to utilise allotted land. Similarly, in a good number of cases where milch animals were provided, the breed was of improved variety which required clean surroundings, to avoid extremes of temperature and good feeding arrangements besides, veterinary facilities. The absence of these requirements had resulted into not only affecting adversely the improved breed milch animals but also the economic conditions of the beneficiaries. It could have been better if local breeds of animals were supplied to the released bonded labourers so that they could stand the local climate, rough handing and ordinary feeds. In few cases, it was also observed that the officers and beneficiaries were not clear about the nature of benefits as to whether it was a loan or a grant. (Para 8.68)

47. The amount of Rs. 4,000 fixed by the Government of India was not found enough for proper rehabilitation of the bonded labour. The study of the models in Andhra Pradesh and Karnataka indicate that an amount between Rs. 10,000 to Rs. 15,000 should be provided for proper rehabilitation of these bonded labourers on the long-term basis.

In the case of the bonded labourers who were in possession of some 'Inami' land or were provided some piece of land would require an assistance of Rs. 10,000 for an irrigation well besides the additional amount of Rs. 5,000 for pumpsets and other agricultural implements. Likewise, for non-land based schemes like small-scale industries, industrial estates, etc., similar amount would be necessary. These resources could be better utilised if an approach of group rehabilitation is adopted. It is, therefore, recommended that the Ministry of Labour may advise the State Governments to provide rehabilitation on group basis. The Ministry may also examine raising the amount of rehabilitation assistance from Rs. 4,000 to Rs. 10,000 to Rs. 15,000 depending upon the nature of rehabilitation. (Para 8.69)

48. Out of the total of 782 beneficiaries only 174 beneficiaries became members of the various cooperative societies such as agricultural cooperative, multi-purpose cooperatives, milk cooperatives and industrial cooperatives. It was also noted that not a single beneficiary became member of the marketing cooperative, poultry cooperative and consumer cooperative. This may be due to lack of dissemination, guidance and assistance from the concerned agencies. No social worker or voluntary agency had been responsible for inducing the beneficiaries in becoming members or involving them in the cooperative efforts and by and large they were induced mostly by government agencies followed by fellow villagers, another bonded labour, etc. (Paras 9.2, 9.3, 9.8, and 9.9)

49. Out of the 174 members of the various cooperative societies majority of 115 beneficiaries reported certain difficulties such as non-availablity of loan, cumbersome procedure, higher rate of interest, low price for their produce, some of them also reported that the societies were also not functioning properly. By and large the cooperative credit societies have not been able to do much in assisting proper rehabilitation of the erstwhile bonded labourers. (Paras 9.19)

50. Out of 782 beneficiaries 291 (37 per cent) reported full satisfaction, 232 (30 per cent) reported partial satisfaction and 259 (33 per cent) reported full dissatisfaction with the rehabilitation programmes. Majority of the beneficiaries amounting to about 63 per cent had not felt positive impact of the programmes and they were not satisfied with the rehabilitation assistance. Among the district studied beneficiaries from 8 districts, viz., Raigarh (MP), Ganjam (Orissa), Periyar (Tamil Nadu), Kota (Rajasthan), Ranga Reddy (A.P.), Nalanda (Bihar), Phulbani and Kalahandi (Orissa) reported a very high degree

of dissatisfaction. (Para 10.1)

51. Among the reasons put forward by the beneficiaries for dissatisfaction, the most important one related to insufficiency of the scheme, assistance for their needs. This was followed by the drawbacks such as bad quality of land, poor animals, inadequate yield of milk, schemes not suitable to their background and schemes not suited to their areas, etc. It could be seen that rehabilitation assistance besides not being sufficient was not planned according to the background and aptitude of the individuals and also of the area and surrounding which they lived. (Paras 10.4 and 10.6)

52. The study had revealed that there were some labourers though reported to be released and rehabilitated but were still working with the old master. The NSSO survey has also brought out that there were much more bonded labourers than what the nine states have identified and rehabilitated. Besides this there were other states who failed to identify bonded labour but the NSSO has found bonded labour in such states like Gujarat, Maharashtra, etc. The efforts made so far are therefore inadequate. It is, therefore, recommend that the Government of India should direct the States of resort to identification and rehabilitation of bonded labour on a continuing basis till this system becomes a thing of the past. (Para 10.11) (Action Ministry of Labour, State Government).

53. About 92 per cent of the selected beneficiaries reported that they were leading an honourable life after release and rehabilitation because they could now breathe in fresh air, earn more and as human being could think about the future. Eight per cent of the beneficiaries which came from the States of Bihar, Karnataka, Madhya Pradesh reported that they were not leading an honourable life because either their earnings from the scheme were not sufficient, earlier master was exerting pressure or had to depend on the ex-master for the petty things and employment was not sufficient 49 of the beneficiaries also reported the fear of going back into bondage for the reasons stated above. This again indicates the failure of the rehabilitation schemes and lack of follow up action on the part of the authorities particularly from the States of Bihar, Karnataka, Madhya Pradesh and Tamil Nadu.

54. The majority of beneficiaries reported that they were able to spend money on several new items such as education of children, social functions, visit to religious places and relatives, entertainment, medical care, etc. Thus it will be seen that majority of the beneficiaries have started a new and better life in terms of the socio-cultural ac-

tivities mentioned above. They had also freedom of movement and mobility in terms of domestic tourism, e.g., visits to religious places, etc. *There was only district namely, Nalanda in Bihar from where all the selected beneficiaries reported that they were not able to spend any money on any of the above mentioned items.* (Paras 10.16, 10.17 and 10.18).

55. Out of the 782 beneficiaries only 46 per cent reported that their earnings were sufficient to meet their day to day requirements of their family. The remaining 54 per cent beneficiaries who reported insufficient income indicated that their source of supplementing the income as borrowing from landlords or money-lenders, borrowing from friends and relatives. It was further revealed that 121 beneficiaries resorted to going without meals and two of them resorted to begging for lack of sufficient income. The concerned State Governments should take prompt follow up action to see that borrowing by the released bonded labourers do not relapse into bondage. It is also desirable to see that sufficient income is generated to the beneficiaries who were going without meals or resorting to begging. The districts from when the beneficiaries reported to be starving or begging were Bhagalpur, Monghyr and Nalanda of Bihar, Chittradurga and Kolar of Karnataka and Koraput of Orissa where the percentage of beneficiaries resorting to such means was also quite high. (Paras 10.19, 10.20 and 10.22) (Action State Governments)

56. About 30 per cent of the selected beneficiaries were indebted prior to rehabilitation. After rehabilitation it was found (on the date of the field study) that only 17.3 per cent had loan outstanding with them. The source of borrowing were money-lenders, landlords, friends and relatives, cooperatives, Government agencies, etc. After rehabilitation however, the dependence on borrowing from moneylender had come down to 8.7 per cent from 18.2 per cent after rehabilitation. It is, however, desirable that the dependence of these ex-bonded labourers on the landlords and moneylenders should be totally eliminated in the interest of abolition of the bonded labour system. (Para 10.24) (Action all States).

57. The released and rehabilitated bonded labourers had obviously a good opinion and feeling about the rehabilitation programme. However, in order to find out how the rural society felt about the released and rehabilitated ex-bonded labourers they (the bonded labour) were asked to give their reactions in this regard. About 50 per cent of the beneficiaries reported that the well off and influential vil-

lagers did not like the programme of release and rehabilitation. This feeling could be due to the setback they might have suffered in not setting easily available cheap labour from the bonded labour. Among the districts high degree of negative reaction of the village community was reported from six districts of Mehboobnagar, Ranga Reddy, Nalanda, Chittradurga, Santhal Parganas and Koraput. (Paras 10.26 and 10.27).

58. About 230 or 29 per cent of the beneficiaries reported the social prejudices due to low caste, lower economic status, untouchability and being an ex-bonded labour. It was encouraging to note that in three districts namely, Raigarh (MP), Kalahandi and Phulbani (Orissa) there was no selected beneficiary who reported any disability. The highest percentage of disabilities was, however, reported from the three districts of Orissa and Bihar, namely, Ganjam, Nalanda and Santhal Parganas. It was reported that 64 per cent of the beneficiaries out of 230 reported that they were handicapped and looked down upon by the society because they belong to Scheduled Caste. This reason was most prominent in seven districts, viz., Bhagalpur, Monghyr, Nalanda, Chittradurga, Kolar, Jabalpur and Periyar. Besides suffering as a bonded labour these persons also suffered from the disabilities attached to untouchability and caste system. A majority of the bonded labour belong to Scheduled Caste who suffer from the disability of untouchability. It is, therefore, recommended that the Civil Rights Act may be enforced strictly and reputed voluntary organisation may be encouraged for undertaking social movement, social reform, etc. (Paras 10.28 and 10.29)

59. The ex-bonded labourers were asked to make suggestions to overcome the social disabilities and handicaps suffered by them from the society. 230 beneficiaries made several suggestions which included: (a) people who discriminate should be punished, (b) social education programme should be speeded up, (c) all caste and communities should meet at one place, (d) voluntary organisations should be encouraged to deal with social reforms, and (e) help of religious heads/groups should be enlisted to enlighten people, etc.

60. The State Governments and the social welfare organisations in different States should seriously consider the suggestions for educating people to overcome the age old social handicaps and prejudices so that there is rapid social change in the rural areas. (Paras 10.30 and 10.31) (Action all State Governments, Ministries of Home, Education, Planning and I & B).

61. Forty-eight beneficiaries out of 782 reported that they were under pressure from the ex-masters to return to them as bonded labourers.

These beneficiaries belong to six districts namely, all the four districts of Bihar, and one each from Karnataka and Rajasthan. It was further disappointing to note that all the beneficiaries from Bihar reported that they had no protection from official agencies like police, BDO, revenue department or department of labour incharge of bonded labour for saving them from the pressure of the ex-masters. The beneficiaries also reported the reasons for unhelpful attitude as: (a) people at the helm of affairs were not serious in the problem of bonded labour and of people belonging to lower castes, and (b) higher caste people were more influential, etc. The State Governments of Bihar, Karnataka and Rajasthan need to take urgent steps to see that the harassed bonded labourers are given necessary protection. (Para 10.33 and 10.35) (Action all States).

62. By and large it was observed that there was no specific staff or specific arrangement for follow up action in regard to: (a) watching the progress of the rehabilitation programme for the ex-bonded labourers or (b) to protect them from relapsing into bondage. It is felt that absence of machinery for follow up action and for providing necessary protection from relapsing into bondage will defeat the very purpose of the Centrally Sponsored Scheme for rehabilitation of bonded labour. It is, therefore, recommended that specific arrangements in this regard should be made by the respective State Governments and the Ministry of Labour. (Para 10.37) (Action all State Governments and Ministry of Labour).

63. There is hardly any impact of modern facilities such as irrigation, development infrastructure, literacy, etc., on the reduction of bonded labour system. On the country it was revealed that ownership of amenity like tubewells was also associated with keeping of bonded labourers by household from Bihar. At the same time in the State like Andhra Pradesh absence of irrigation and other facilities were also associated with the existence of bonded labour. There may be other factors like particular social system or the power and property structure in the villages or the mental attitude of the society in the various areas for this system. This needs to be investigated in detail.

RAILWAY ACCIDENT INVESTIGATION REPORT ON COLLISION BETWEEN 49 UP HOWRAH-AMRITSAR EXPRESS AND FOOD GRAIN SPECIAL AT JANDIALA STATIONS ON FEROZEPUR DIVISION OF NORTHERN RAILWAY AT ABOUT 15.10 HOURS ON MARCH 9, 1979 — REPORT[1]

One Man Commission Shri Suresh Chandra

Appointment

The Commission was constituted under Ministry of Tourism and Civil Aviation (Commission of Railway Safety) in accordance with Rule 4 of the Statutory Investigation into Railway Accidents Rules 1973 Vide Notification No. RS. 13-8(T)/71 dated April 19, 1973 on March 9, 1979.

Terms of Reference

To enquire into the Collision between 49 Up Howrah-Amritsar Express and Food Grain special at Jandiala Stations on Ferozepur Division of Northern Railway at about 15.10 hours on March 9, 1979.

Contents

Summary; Inspection and Inquiry; Relief Measures; Composition of Trains and Damages; Local Features; Summary of Evidence; Observation and Tests; Discussion; Conclusions; Remarks and Recommendations; Railway Board's Comments on Various Paras of the Report.

1. Delhi, Controller of Publications, 1983, 13 p.

Conclusions

Cause

On full consideration of the factual, material and circumstantial evidence, the cause of the collision of 49 Up Howrah-Amritsar Express with the Foodgrain Special load in the goods sidings of Jandiala station on Ludhiana-Amritsar Section of the Northern Railway on 9-3-1979 was due to the Express train being driven past the reception signals at danger.

Responsibility

*(a) Shri Gobind Singh, Driver of 49 Up is held responsible for passing the reception signals of Jandiala station at danger.

[Shri Gobind Singh joined service as a Cleaner in 1941 and was promoted as a Fireman, Shunter and Driver in 1944, 1955 and 1958 respectively. During his service, he has been punished on 16 occasions for various offences. His accident index on the date of accident was 325. He last attended the Diesel Refresher course in October 1979 and the safety camp in September 1976.]

*(b) Shri Ram Lubhya, Assistant Driver of 49 Up is held responsible for not assisting his driver in correctly observing the signals.

[Shri Ram Lubhya, Assistant Driver of 49 Up joined service as a Cleaner in 1958 and was promoted as a Fireman in 1966. He has been working as a Diesel Assistant since 16-12-1977. During his service, he has been punished on 8 occasions for various irregularities. His accident index on the date of accident was 1657. He has not attend any refresher course. He attended the safety camp in August 1977.]

Relief Measures

I am satisfied that the medical arrangements were prompt and the relief measures satisfactory.

---

* Since qcquitted.

Recommendations

The first coach behind the engine of 49 Up was a Second Class sleeper coach instead of a SLR, as required under the instructions for marshalling issued by the Railway Board. It is essential that the Safety Marshalling Instructions issued by the Railway Board are strictly observed.

The speed recording chart on the locomotive of 49 Up was the same as provided when the same loco worked 50 Dn. Express from Amritsar to Lucknow on 7-3-1979. Apparently, the chart was not replaced at Lucknow when the locomotive was booked to work 49 Up on 8-3-1979 ex-Lucknow. It is essential that the Speed Recording Graph should be replaced to avoid overlapping recordings.

Railway Board's comments on various paras of the Report

Para 43: The matter has been brought to the notice of the Eastern Railway. Instructions have also been reiterated to the Railways, vide Board's letter No. 78 Chg. II/14/8 dated 24-4-1979, emphasising, *inter alia,* that since the position of availability of SLRs on the Railways is quite satisfactory, it should be ensured that Mail/Express trains run with 2 SLRs one in front and the other in rear. Copies of the said circular have also been endorsed to Chief Commissioner of Railway Safety.

Para 44: This has been accepted by the Railway Administration who have issued instructions to all concerned to ensure:

(a) Availability of graph-rolls and their regular recoupment;
(b) Pin-pointing the staff responsible for changing graph-rolls at the nominated station; and
(c) Random checks whether these staff are actually changing the graph-rolls or not.

The observations of Commissioner of Railway Safety have been brought to the notice of the Railways vide letter No. 79M(M&P) 7/2/N-3 dated 11-12-1979. It has been emphasized that officials visiting the loco sheds should examine the working of Speed Recorder Section and see that the staff are alert and follow the extant instructions.

CYCLONE REVIEW COMMITTEE, 1979 — REPORT[1]

Chairman Prof. A.K. Saha

Members Shri S.K. Das; Dr. P.K. Das; Dr. A.A. Ramasastry; Shri C.R.V. Raman; Dr. A.P. Mitra; Dr. R. Ramanadham; Dr. P. Koteswaran

M. Secy. Dr. D.K. Rakshit

Appointment

The Department of Science and Technology (DST) was interested in the Cyclone problem for some time. In 1979 Prof. M.G.K. Menon, Secretary of the DST brought the cyclone problem to the notice of Dr. Atmaram, the then Chairman of National Committee of Science and Technology (NCST). Prof. Menon suggested that a Cyclone Review Committee (CRC) should be set up under the auspices of the NCST to carry out a review of all aspects of the cyclone problem for consideration of the NCST which may be placed before the Prime Minister for subsequent implementation of the recommendations of the CRC. On the advice of Dr. Atmaram a Cyclone Review Committee was constituted by the Government of India on March 10, 1979.

Terms of Reference

1. Review of the storm warning systems existing in the country; assessment of the requirements of additional facilities and aids as used in different countries for improving the forecast accuracy.
2. Review of the telecommunication facilities existing in the country and improvement and modernisation thereof. Additional telecommunication facilities needed for improving and widening the

1. New Delhi, Department of Science and Technology, 1984, Vol. I, 480 p.

dissemination of informations.

3. Review of the present status of Community preparedness to anticipate cyclones and their impact, and review of the action plans for cyclone distress mitigation and recommend measures for improvement in these respects, where necessary.

4. Review the cyclone codes in operation in other countries.

5. To advise the Government with a comprehensive cyclone code to meet any situation caused by a cyclone.

Contents

Formation of the Cyclone Review Committee by the Government of India; Report of the Cyclone Review Committee—Arrangements of the recommendations and other matters; Organisation for the formulation, implementation and periodic review of the cyclone, Demarcation of the cyclone prone areas (CPARs) of coastal India and consideration of terrains and seasons; Cyclone detection, observation and tracking methods and facilities in India; The Cyclone Warning System (CWS) in India; Suggestions for formulation of a National Cyclone Code (NCC) for India and Cyclone Emergency Action Plans (CEAP) for the Coastal States; Suggestions for a community preparedness plan against cyclone (CPPC) threats and hazards for coastal communities in India; Cyclone Research and Training; Appendices; Recommendations of the CRC—Recommendations mainly for the Consideration of India Meteorological Department with respect to Cyclone Monitoring/Cyclone Warning Systems (CRC/1-CRC/107); Recommendations mainly for the consideration of Government of India and the Coastal States Governments with respect to; The National Cyclone and Code and the Cyclone Emergency Action Plan (CRC/108-CRC/231); The Community Preparedness Plan Against Cyclone (CRC/232-CRC/309), Recommendations for Research and Training (CRC/310-CRC/317).

Recommendations

3. *Rationale and Summary of the Recommendations of the Cyclone Review Committee (CRC)*

The Committee has proposed a Cyclone Plan for India for confronting cyclones from the moment they are detected up to the time when rehabilitation work ends. The Committee has suggested the formation of a high power standing Apex Cyclone Committee (ACC) for formulation, implementation and periodic review of the Cyclone Plan (CPL). It is hoped that this Committee will take up the work of the present Committee, after it has submitted its report, and advise the Government of India from time to time in all aspects of the cyclone problem and for all possible scenarios that may arise in a cyclone emergency. The Committee noted that certain parts of coastal India are very frequently visited by cyclones and it recommended that these be declared as Cyclone Prone Areas (CPARs).

The Committee has examined the very elaborate cyclone monitoring system, which has been established over the years by the Indian Meteorological Department (IMD), in particular of the radar horizon round coastal India and the satellite surveillance techniques that have been added in recent years. The Committee appreciated the introduction of all these new techniques for monitoring cyclones but felt that the standard ground observations from the normal meteorological observatories and ship observatories should not be neglected. All the various monitoring techniques should complement each other to arrive at correct assessment of cyclones because each method has its limitations. Indeed there has been instances when cyclones of strong intensities have been missed altogether by all the different methods. In order to interpret the radar and satellite pictures of Indian cyclones quickly in terms of their intensities (central pressure falls) and maximum wind speeds and their three dimensional structures it is necessary to develop accurate diagnostic techniques by correlating the normal observations with results of probing the cyclones by instrumented aircrafts. The central pressure fall is an important parameter for predicting storm surge heights. The Committee noted the establishment of a high density cyclone reporting network of surface observatories known as the Cooperative Cyclone Reporting Network (CCRN) on the eastern coast of India after the 1977 Andhra Pradesh Cyclone. It was however, felt that since there were not linked by WT links to the Area Cyclone Warning Centres/Cyclone Warning Centres (ACWC/CWCs), they would not be very useful when they are needed most, viz., during cyclones. With the introduction of the Data Collection Platforms (DCPs) and the INSAT communication network it should be possible in course of time, to replace these surface observatories of the CCRN by autonomous automatised DCPs. The Committee has recommended this.

The Committee noted that some of the Cyclone Warning Radars (CWRs) are not always located near the ACWC/CWCs so that the meteorologists who have to make on the spot assessments of the cyclones at the ACWC/CWCs, have the disadvantage of not being able to view the radar pictures continuously.

The Committee recommended that this lacuna should be removed as soon as possible. The Committee has recommended that all the cyclone assessment work should be centralised at a Cyclone Assessment Centre located at Delhi (CAC) though all the ACWC/CWCs should be empowered to take the final decisions about assessment/warnings. The Committee also noted that cyclone Assessment at Delhi could be done there easily because of the computer facilities at IMD units at Delhi, where all informations and observational data of a raging cyclone could be stored on real time and from where cyclone analysts at various warning centres of the IMD, including the ACWC/CWCs, could retrieve any information they desire in any format they may choose. The Committee has recommended that the radar horizon should be made more effective by the establishment of one more CWR on the Saurashtra coast and one more CWC to be located at Ahmedabad. The cyclone warning dissemination system appears to be quite complex, but it appears that there were doubts whether it worked efficiently. They logistic lacuna in the cyclone warning system seems to lie mainly in the vulnerability to cyclones of the land based telegram and telephone communication system.

The Committee recommended that the P&T Department should makes special efforts to keep the communication links at the highest level of efficiency during cyclone regimes. The existing system of using the AIR channels to disseminate the Cyclone Bulletins (CBs) including the Cyclone Warning Messages (CWMs) and the Cyclone Advisories (CAs) appears to work very well and must continue and indeed be strengthened, for these channels are well familiar to all cyclone warnees. The first stage 'Cyclone Alert' warning must be sent by the concerned ACWC/CWC by the traditional land line telegrams which should pose no problem when the cyclone is still far away. The subsequent CWMs and CAs must be monitored by the warnees from the broadcasts by the AIR. Often this will be the only channel of communication available because of snapping of other channels. The Committee felt that when it relates to Cyclone Codes (CCs) of the coastal State Governments and to Community Preparedness Plans against Cyclones (CPPCs), much remain to be done. To enquiries about how much has been achieved in this respect, the response from the coastal State Governments was very poor. A copy of the Disaster Plan of Tamil Nadu State was received and subsequently a similar document of the Andhra Pradesh Government was supplied by the Committee. The Committee realised that each coastal state has its own special features so that there can not be the same CC for all these states. The Cyclone Codes which is a set of rules and procedures which must be followed in cyclone emergencies must have different characteristics for different states and must be incorporated in their General Disaster Plans (GDPs). The Committee has laid down some guidance for setting up the CCs in particular the Cyclone Emergency Action Plan (CEAP) and for the preparation of the CPPCs. Other highlights of the recommendations of the Committee are the recommendations for the formation of the State Cyclone Committee (SCYC), which would formulate the CEAP for the State and supervise its implementation and operation, and indeed would be the kingpin in the Cyclone Distress Mitigation Organisation (CDMO) of a coastal state. District Cyclone Committees (DCCs) have also been suggested, which would work under the supervision of the SCYC and take all executive actions during cyclone emergencies. For long range plans for preparing the community against threats of cyclones the Committee recommended that for each coastal state a Coastal Development Authority (CDA) be formed and all such responsibilities be given to it.

The Committee has given some suggestions for formulation of the CEAPs and CPPCs and the functions of the CDAs. It is hoped that the coastal State Governments would find these suggestions useful in formulating their respective plans and in setting up of their CDAs. The importance of making the population of the CPARs aware of the nature and hazards of cyclones has been stressed. The Committee has also felt the need of continuing research on cyclones and resulting storm surges. All the recommendations of the Committee are serially numbered. The paragraph numbers under which they appear in the body of the report of the Committee are also given to enable their easy location in the main body of the report for understanding he background for making the recommendation. Many of the recommendations (marked X) are in the pipe line already. Some others (marked XX) have been implemented already but are included here for sake of completeness. The recommendations are collected and appear in the next paragraph 3.1. It will be seen that the recommendations are grouped in two groups : Group A : Recommendations mainly for the IMD with respect to the

CMS/CWS (CRC/1-1087) and Group B : Recommendations mainly for the coastal State Governments with respect to B. 1 The Cyclone Code (CRC/108-231) and B.2 The Cyclone Preparedness Plan (CRC/232-309) and Group C : Recommendations for Research and Training (CRC/310-317).

3.1 *Compilation of the Recommendations of the CRC*

Group A: *Recommendations mainly for the IMD with respect to the CMS/CWS (CRC/1-107).*

I. *Organisations for the Formulation, Implementation and Review of the Cyclone Plan (CPL)*

CRC/1: It is the responsibility of the Indian Meteorological Department (IMD) to study in collaboration with the World Meteorological Organisation (WMO) the most modern practices being adopted in the world for predicting cyclones and storm surges and review from time to time the technical aspects of the current Cyclone Plan (CPL) of the country to incorporate these late techniques in it to the extent necessary and possible. (Para 2.9)

CRC/2: An Apex Cyclone Committee (ACC) should be set up by the Government of India with the following terms of reference:

1. To implement the CPL in coastal India in particular to advise the incorporation of the Cyclone Code (CC) and the Cyclone Distress Mitigation Measures (CDMMs) in the General Disaster Plans (GDPs) of the coastal states of India. For this purpose the Committee may invite social scientists, public health experts and those organisations that have experience in rescue, relief and rehabilitation works.
2. To advise the coastal states on long-term measures for preparing the community against cyclones, some of which are improvements of dissemination systems for cyclones warning messages (CWMs), road and transport network, telecommunication network, establishing embankments against storm surges, improvement of water drainage and sewerage systems, construction of cyclone shelters, protection of agricultural products, improvement of public health systems, etc. Thus the ACC would help the coastal states to prepare their Community

Preparedness Plan against Cyclones (CPPCs).

3. To review periodically the CPL in the light of advance of scientific understanding of behaviour of cyclones and progress of techniques of cyclone monitoring and telecommunication.
4. To assess the extent of devastation caused by each cyclone in terms of loss of life and property after the cyclone has subsided.
5. To review the extent to which it was possible to monitor and predict the behaviour of each cyclone and assess the efficiency of the Cyclone Warning System (CWS) during its regime and to advise steps to remove lacunae if any.
6. To advise the Planning Commission to provide funds for additions of technological facilities as also for long-term preventive measures to prepare the community against ravages of cyclones as suggested in the CPL.
7. To advise the Government of India on various legislative measures that may be necessary for introducing the CDMMs and various aspects of the CPL. (Para 2.11)

CRC/3: The Government of India should provide adequate funds to the IMD for improvements of the Cyclone Monitoring and Warning Systems (CMS/CWS). (Para 2.13)

CRC/4: Legislative measures should be taken to cover.

1. Landuse and zoning laws to restrict or prevent industrial and/or residential development in areas where cyclone risks are high, e.g., low lying coastal areas exposed to storm surges. Such laws may cover taxation measures to stoor development away from the cyclone prone areas (CPARs). There may also be government actions to acquire land by compulsory purchases and to alter landuse.
2. Enforcement of suitable building codes setting out minimum safety standards in areas vulnerable to cyclones.
3. Soil and plant conservation measures to guard against erosion of land caused by storm surges.
4. Engineering measures related to management and control of rivers, roads, canals and embankments, water drainage systems protection of agricultural products and various other similar problems arising out of cyclones.
5. Public health measures and sanitation systems — against air water pollution and for waste disposals, and epidemic controls etc.

6. Putting into operation the emergency measures recommended in the CC — evacuation from danger zones, emergency transport requisition and control thereof, mitigation of distress caused by cyclones and storm surges, rescue relief and protection of life, immediate financial relief to distressed persons.
7. Long-term rehabilitation measures — restoration of buildings housing and installations, public service utilities including communications, transportations of all types, generation and distribution of electric power, repair of roads bridges dams dykes, embankments and harbours, immediate long-term loans to distressed persons.
8. Social security measures — preservation of social order, protection of property of evacuees, and prevention of crime, etc.
9. Replenishment of nationally owned stockpiles such as food, seed and medicine.
10. Utilisation of international credits and gifts and aids from abroad for mitigation of distress caused by cyclones.
11. Utilisation of various funds granted by the Government of India the concerned State Governments and charitable bodies for mitigation of the distress caused by cyclones. (Para 2.14)

II. *Demarcation of CRARs of Coastal India and Consideration of Terrains and Seasons*

CRC/5: In the pre-monsoon seasons the period April to June and in the post-monsoon season the period September to December may be declared as cyclone seasons when the coastal State Governments Gujarat, Maharashtra, Kerala, Tamil Nadu, Andhra Pradesh, Orissa and West Bengal should be generally prepared for cyclones. (Para 2.17)

CRC/6: Certain districts on coastal India as listed below may be declared as CPARs. Generally the CPARs may be demarcated be strips on the coast of width of about 25 km. The demarcation would depend on the topology, river systems, high lands/embankments and hydrodams near to the coast and should be done after the due consideration by the coastal State Governments. Landfall records of past cyclones reveal the following coastal districts of India as particularly vulnerable to such storms. While making the final declaration of the CPARs the IMD and the various flood forecasting centres of the Central/State Governments/IMD located in the concerned state may be consulted.

Cyclone prone districts

1.	Andhra Pradesh	East Godavari, Krishna, Nellore (including Prakasam), Shrikakulam
2.	Orissa	Balasore, Cuttack, Ganjam, Puri
3.	Tamil Nadu	Chingelput, Thanjavur
4.	West Bengal	Midnapore, 24-Parganas

This list is by no means complete and each coastal State Government should consider which other areas in the State may be declared as CPARs. (Para 2.20)

CRC/7: The flood forecasting centres of the Central Water Commission/State Irrigation Department/IMD should have at their disposals topological maps of the CPARs of the coastal regions of India prepared by the State Governments with contour lines at 1m intervals to prepare Storm Surge Risk Maps (SSRMs) to use for assessment from the storm surge height forecast in the Cyclone Warning Messages (CWMs), the possible extent of inundations, which information should be immediately available to the concerned public in the storm surge/flood forecasts and the Cyclone Advisories (CAs). This would enable the concerned District Cyclone Committee (DCC) to put into operation the appropriate measures. (Para 2.20)

III. *Cyclone Detection, Observation and Tracking Methods and Facilities in India*

III A *Cyclone Data Collection Systems (CDCSs)*

IIIA(1) *Surface Observatories (SOs)*

CRC/8: Since the most important parameters for cyclone assessment are pressure falls and wind velocities, all coastal surface observatories (SOs) of the IMD should be equipped with sturdy aneroid barometers and robust anemometers. Some selected SOs on the CPARs should be equipped with anemometers capable of measuring wind speeds up to 200 kmph. Efforts should be made by the IMD for indigenous development of such anemometers and towers for housing the capable of standing up to such winds. (Para 2.28)

CRC/9: The part time SOs (PSOs) on coastal India should be converted ultimately into departmental SOs (DSOs) and provided with distant reading equipments for measuring winds, pressures and rainfalls. Such instruments should be developed by the IMD in collaboration wherever possible with the research and technical development organisation in India. The IMD must ensure the completion of conversion of PTSOs to PSOs in 3-4 years. (Para 2.29)

CRC/10: As the pace of conversion of PTSOs to DSOs is too slow, and as the observational network will have to depend on the PTSOs for some time, academic organisations should be involved in the running of these PTSO stations for better performance. (Para 2.29)

CRC/11: A few SOs at selected sites on coastal India should be automatised and made self telecasting on an experimental basis. For this purpose the IMD should develop the necessary technology in collaboration, wherever possible, with the research and technical development organisations in India. (Para 2.30)

CRC/12: The densities of SOs in the CPARs areas on Kerala, Tamil Nadu, Andhra Pradesh, Orissa and West Bengal are inadequate and should be increased sufficiently to cover the needs of the CMs. (Para 2.32)

IIIA(2) *Upper Air Observations (UAOs)*

CRC/13: The Upper Air Observatory (UAO) network on the west coast may be usefully strengthened by converting immediately the pilot Balloon observations (PIBALS) at Bhuj, Veraval and Ratnagiri to Radiowind Observatories (RVOs). (Para 2.34)

CRC/14: Though the UAO network on coastal India may be just adequate, it is advisable to convert, in course of time all the coastal PIBAL observatories to RWO observatories or locate a few mobile RS/RW vans along the coast which can be moved into the affected areas. (Para 2.34)

CRC/15: The frequency of recording observations should be increased to four times daily at all RS/RW observatories when they come into the cyclone field. (Para 2.35)

CRC/16: Some of the METOX theodolites and the weather X-band radars at the UAOs are very old and have outlived their usefulness for wind determination at high levels of the atmosphere. They should be replaced by modern wind finding radars manufactured in the country by Bharat Electronics like Multimet radars, if their performance is satisfactory. Otherwise the replacements have to be done by import. (Para 2.36)

IIIA(3) *Data Collection Platforms (DCPs)*

CRC/17: The DCPs should have atleast ten primary meteorological oceanographic sensors for measuring: (1) air temperature, (2) wet bulb temperature, (3) relative humidity, (4) wind speed, (5) wind direction, (6) atmospheric pressure, (7) DCP housing temperature, (8) rainfall, (9) sunshine and (10) sea surface temperature. (Para 2.41)

CRC/18: After the INSAT-1 programme is satisfactorily implemented, some of the coastal SOs in the areas, where cyclone landfalls are more frequent may be converted into automatic Data collection Platforms (DCPs) if necessary. The collected meteorological data may be then transmitted via the INSAT system on real time to the various warning/forecasting centres and data collecting centres of the IMD: Area Cyclone Warning Centres/Cyclone Warning Centres (ACWC/CWCs) and the Regional/State Collecting Centres (RCC/SCCs). (Para 2.42)

IIIA(4) *Ship Meteorological Data (SMD)*

CRC/19: All meteorological data (SHIP) collected by the ships of the Voluntary Observation Fleet (VOF) plying in the shipping lanes of the Arabian Sea and the Bay of Bengal should be gathered through the INMARSAT system. The necessary transmitting/receiving equipments may be installed in the chosen ships of the VOF by the concerned Shipping Companies. The weather data so collected should be transmitted expeditiously to the ACWC/CWCs and the RCC/SCCs. (Para 2.43)

CRC/20: A Maritime Meteorological Organisation should be set up in the IMD and located at some suitable centre to provide the following meteorological services: (1) Weather routing of ships, (2) Forecasting of the state of the sea, (3) Forecasting of sea surface temperature, (4) Information about layer depths, and forecasting the sea subsurface temperature in the fixed layers and (5) Weather forecasting services for fishing operations. At present all these activities are carried out at various places. There is need to coordinate these activities at one place under one organisation. Apart from providing these services, this organisation should also take up research on all aspects of marine climatology and marine weather forecasting and serve as the nodal point for data collection from the Oceanographic Research Vessels (ORVs). (Para 2.44)

IIIA(5) *The Cyclone Warning Radars (CWRs)*

CRC/21: The Cyclone Radar Horizon (CRH) round the Indian coast may be made more effective on the west coast by installing a Cyclone Warning Radar (CWR) at a suitable location on the Saurashtra coast. (Para 2.51)

CRC/22: There should be direct transmission facilities for radar pictures from the CWRs so their respective ACWC/CWCs when they are not both located at the same site. The ACWC/CWCs and the collecting centres should be interconnected with voice grade communication links and video channels for transmitting radarscope imageries on real time. The ACWC/CWCs should be equipped with facilities for video taping and playback systems and equipments for digitising the radar informations and arrangements for storage retrieval of these imageries. (Para 2.54)

CRC/23: A cyclone which has crossed into the CRH set at 400 km. from the coast as determined by the normal range of the CWRs, should be kept under constant watch by these radars round the clock till it finally subsides. (Para 2.56)

CRC/24: While the capability of observation of wind structures within a cyclone by the Doppler radar is well realised, the technique is still under experimentation in USA and Japan and has not yet been put there into extensive operational use for cyclone monitoring. Moreover, its usefulness in estimating the wind velocities at different levels in a cyclone system has yet to be established. A ground based Doppler Radar for cyclone monitoring was therefore not recommended. However, as this was an emerging technique which may find many meteorological application for determination of velocities of wind and cloud masses, efforts may be made to make a beginning in the use of Doppler radar to study local storms like norwesters. (Para 2.57)

IIIA(6) *Cyclone Observation by Satellites*

CRC/25: The present Automatic Picture Transmission (APT) receivers manufactured by the IMD and employed in Satellite Monitoring of Cyclones (SMC) by the Polar Orbitting Satellites (POSs) need improvement and should be replaced by receivers of better performance to improve the quality of the cloud imageries received. It was noted that IMD has already entrusted the work to the Bharat Electronics (BEL). (Para 2.61)

CRC/26: The APT receivers at the ACWC/CWCs should be capable of receiving the infrared cloud imagery broadcasts by the POSs passing over the Indian region during night. (Para 2.61)

CRC/27: Since the pictures from the USSR meteorological satellites are received only at the Regional Telecommunication HUB (RTH) at Delhi, the IMD should arrange quick and prompt transmission of these pictures of the ACWC/CWCs. (Para 2.61)

CRC/28: The Very High Resolution Radiometer (VHRR) terminals set up at Satellite Application Centre (SAC) at Ahmedabad, the Meteorological Data Utilisation Centre (MDUC) at Delhi and the National Remote Sensing Agency (NRSA) at Hyderabad and any others that may be set up in the country, should be closely integrated with each other and with the neighbouring ACWC/CWCs for maximum efficiency for cyclone detection and assessment. (Para 2.68)

CRC/29: It is not advisable to set up VHRR terminals at the individual ACWC/CWCs. The expertise, analysis facilities and sophisticated technologies available at the various units of the IMD at Delhi are adequate for the purpose of analysis of satellite data on cyclones. The analysed data can be easily and immediately transmitted to the ACWC/CWCs by the telecommunication links of the IMD. (Para 2.69)

IIIA(7) *Aircraft Probing of Cyclones (APC)*

CRC/30: It is absolutely essential to prepare a classification of cyclones for the Indian region by correlating the measurements on the Indian cyclones by Cyclone Probing Aircrafts (CPAs) with the data from the cyclone imageries recorded by satellites and the CWRs. Such aircraft probing of cyclones (APC) are also important for micro-studies of all cyclone parameters and detailed analysis of their structures and for improving the forecasting capabilities of the ACWC/CWCs. It is expected that such studies would lead to deeper understanding of cyclone dynamics — their formation, development, movement and decay and the setting up useful cyclone models. (Para 2.72)

CRC/31: The CPAs should be long endurance aircrafts with maximum range of 2500 miles and must be aerodynamically suited to stand up to the stresses of flights through cyclonic conditions. Four engine turboprop aircrafts are usually used for cyclone probing and may be used to study Indian cyclones also. (Para 2.73)

CRC/32: The CPAs should have the capability of installing a belly radar in it. The following instrumental facilities were suggested for installation in the aircraft:

1. Instruments for measurement of meteorological parameters: (a) total/free air temperatures, (b) atmospheric pressure — static, (c) atmospheric pressure-differential, (d) pilot head, (e) flight level and wind, (f) dew point, (g) sea surface temperature, (h) wind, (i) temperature-vertical profile, (j) humidity-vertical profile, (k) pressure-vertical profile, (l) radar altitudes.
2. Instruments for cloud physics : (a) cloud liquid water contents, (b) total liquid water contents, (c) hydrometer size spectra (cloud droplets/hydrometers).
3. Suitable meteorological radars: (a) belly radar C-band PPI 360° scan (horizontal) fan beam radar, (b) nose radar for weather RCA AVO 30, (c) nose radar C-band PPI 240° scan (conical).
4. Onboard photographic systems : (a) sea state photography (looking down), (b) time elapse cloud photography (side looking), (c) data panel photography, (d) radarscope photography recording.
5. Onboard data recording system : (a) Two recording systems one dedicated to meteorological cloud physics, radiation sensors and On system, and the other to the nose and lower fuse lage, (b) a suitable onboard minicomputer and necessary peripherals. (Para 2.73)

CRC/33: For planning the Aircraft Probing of Cyclones (APC) a Directorate of APC should be established with the necessary support from the IMD to take decisions on probing flights, flight plans, installation/procurement/maintenance of instruments abroad the CPAs and to interpret the results of observations and to transmit the results to the forecasting centres including the ACWC/CWCs. (Para 2.73)

CRC/34: For telecommunication (TC) linkage with ground stations the IMD should be assigned special frequencies for use to establish two way communication between the CPAs and the base stations on ground. (Para 2.73)

CRC/35: The CPAs may be used during non-cyclonic seasons for other atmospheric studies like investigations of monsoon depressions, cloud physics, sea state studies, etc. (Para 2.73)

CRC/36: The maintenance and operations of the CPAs should be given to agencies like the national Remote Sensing Agency (NRSA) or to the Indian Air Force (IAF). (Para 2.73)

CRC/37: Proper training of the CPA mission scientists, technicians, and crew members should be organised as done in the Research Flight Centre (RFC) at Miami USA. The training should include flying the aircraft under cyclonic conditions, planning probing flight patterns in the field of the cyclones, conducting meteorological experiments under cyclonic conditions and interpreting data thus acquired and other similar tasks that would be necessary. (Para 2.73)

CRC/38: The CPAs may be acquired as expeditiously as possible. (Para 2.73)

CRC/39: More than one APC may be necessary for probing a cyclone. These may be acquired gradually in phases under the aegis of the WMO/ESCAP Panel on tropical cyclones as a part of a regional project. (Para 2.74)

IIIA(8) *Other Emerging Techniques of Studying Cyclones and Surrounding Neighbourhood*

CRC/40: There is need to develop expertise by the IMD on the investigation of the state of the sea by downward looking lasers by sending its scientists abroad for training. The instrument packet aboard the CPAs may be reinforced by the addition of these laser equipments. (Para 2.75)

CRC/41: The IMD may organise research programme with various research groups in the country to investigate the possibility of using a HF radar in the ionosphere scatter mode to study the state of the sea and correlate it with the parameters of a cyclone in the area. (Para 2.75)

CRC/42: Data on the swells on the sea as observed on ships should be regularly reported to the ACWC/CWCs when they are of a nature indicative of cyclone formation. (Para 2.75)

IIIA(9) *Rain Gauge/Storm Gauge Stations (RGs/SSGs) in Coastal India*

CRC/43: The Ordinary Raingauges (ORGs) used in the CPARs should in course of time be replaced by Self Recording Rain Gauges (SRRGs). (Para 2.77)

CRC/44: The tide measuring instruments set up at the Tide Gauge Stations (TGSs) on the coastal regions of India should be strengthened to be able to stand up to the fury of the cyclones. The instruments for measuring tide levels should be redesigned to be able to measure cyclonic storm surges. (Para 2.79)

CRC/45: For the purpose of cyclone assessment and warning more TGSs have to be installed particularly in the river estuaries and littoral areas and specially in the island groups in the river delta regions as also in the areas notorious for cyclone landfalls. (Para 2.80)

CRC/46: The intercommunication between the ACWC/CWCs and the Collecting Centres with the TGSs, should be improved so that they function without fail during cyclone regimes. (Para 2.81)

CRC/47: The IMD should collaborate with the National Institute of Oceanography (NIO) to design/develop/fabricate a new generation of self recording storm surge gauges (SSGs) capable of measuring: (1) maximum storm tide level reached, (2) direction of storm surge movement, (3) velocity of storm surge rush, (4) pressure exerted by storm surge, (5) wave structure of the storm surge, and (6) automatic timing of recording these data. The R&D should also involve the design/development/construction of structures on land/river/offshore sea, housing the SSGs capable of standing up to the violence of cyclone caused storm surges. (Para 2.82)

CRC/48: An important task of the ACWC/CWCs should be to collect and archieve in a routine manner the data on storm surges for the areas under their control. A cyclone storm Surge Research Centre may be established within the IMD to assess/analyse these data on storm surges collected by the ACWC/CWC for research investigations with objectives to understand the storm surges and improve the techniques of their forecasting. (Para 2.83)

IIIA(10) *Exchange of Informations with Cyclone Centres in Neighbouring Countries*

CRC/49: In the interest of better functioning of cyclone monitoring and warning systems established in India. It is desirable that close collaborations are established between the ACWC/CWCs of India and the CWCs of Bangladesh, Burma, Malaysia, Pakistan and Sri Lanka. (Para 2.84)

IIIB. *Statistical data on Cyclones in India and Climatology*

CRC/50: The frequency distribution of cyclone landfalls over coastal regions of India at 5 years interval should be periodically updated by the IMD. (Para 2,85)

CRC/51: Statistics of the return period of cyclones over each coastal regions of India with an assessment of the vulnerability of these localities to cyclones should be prepared by the IMD. (Para 2.85)

CRC/52: The Cyclone Atlas prepared by the IMD should be updated up to 1980 and may be widely circulated. It should show the tracks and include accounts of a selection of some particularly devastating cyclones occurring in India. (Para 2.85)

CRC/53: The IMD should prepare an Atlas of satellite imageries of Indian cyclones collected over the past decade and prepare individual analysis of structures/movements and classifications of those cyclones based on their satellite pictures. This would provide materials for preparing cyclone models in developing theories of cyclone formation/evolution. (Para 2.85)

CRC/54: The satellite pictures of Indian cyclones collected by the IMD should, in course of time, provide sufficient data to prepare a climatology based on the statistics of all cyclone eye formations in the Indian region, associated derived wind fields and pressure depths. (Para 2.85)

CRC/55: The IMD should build up an archieve of microfilmed informations on cyclones over the Indian region based on the earlier studies of the Department, on current observations carried out through whatever techniques employed and the microfilmed satellite cyclone imageries collected by USA and other countries for the period from 1960 onwards. The archieve should also contain the whole history/analysis of these cyclones and should be a reference centre for researchers on cyclones. (Para 2.86)

IV. *The Cyclone Warning System (CWS) in India*

IVA *Data Collection/Analysis/Forecasting Centres of the IMD for Cyclones*

CRC/56: Since the NHAC-Delhi receives all meteorological data from all Indian collecting centres and the ACWC/CWCs, the analysis of the data for cyclone assessment should be concentrated at this centre only. For this purpose it is necessary to ensure that all informations regarding cyclones from the Coastal Meteorological Observatories/Island Meteorological Observatories (CMO/IMOs), SO/UAOs ships, DCPs, CWRs and the satellites are promptly received at the NHAC on real time through the existing Message Switching Computer installed there. The NHAC should also have a computer of large storage capacity where all those messages can be stored and be instantly available, processed in any format desired by the cyclone analysis/user whenever needed for assessment purposes. (Para 2.89)

CRC/57: The IMD should advise the Apex Cyclone Committee (ACC) on various technical aspects of long-term measures for preparing the community for cyclones. It should also advise the ACC on the formulation of cyclone codes (CCs) for the coastal states and their updating in the Light of gathering experience. (Para 2.89)

CRC/58: The IMD should set up a Cyclone Assessment Cell (CAC) at Delhi dedicated to coordinating and evaluating the incoming data from the ACWC/CWCs and the Regional/States Collecting Centres (RCC/SSCs) and other data centres. (Para 2.92)

CRC/59: All the INSAT meteorological data processed at the Meteorological Data Utilisation Centre (MDUC) at Delhi should be transferred to all the Secondary Data Utilisation Centres (SDUCs) particularly to those situated at the ACWC/CWCs. (Para 2.95)

CRC/60: A Cyclone Warning Centre (CWC) may be established at Ahmedabad for more effectively operating the Cyclone Warning System (CWS) on the west coast of India. (Para 2.97)

CRC/61: Officers and other cadres working in ACWC/CWCs should be provided quarters within the premises of these centres. Questions of work leave, building up of reserve personnel and improvements of working conditions of the staff should be considered so as to minimise the fatigue of long hours of work. The consequent administrative problems arising should be solved by the IMD. Similar facilities may be provided to officials of other government agencies/departments involved in CMS/CWS.

CRC/62: As the tasks/responsibilities of the ACWC/CWCs are steadily rising, it is necessary to change the staffing pattern at these centres so as to strengthen the staff there and reduce the heavy pressure of work that has to be met. (Para 2.101)

CRC/63: Each ACWC/CWC should be equipped with suitable minicomputer to process the incoming data on cyclones from the CMO/IMOs for transmission to the CAC at Delhi. The minicomputer should also have automatic data and message handling capabilities, large storing facility and the peripherals for immediate display/print outs as required. (Para 2.102)

IVB *Cyclone Data Collection/Dissemination/Warning Systems*

IVB(1) *Centres for Dissemination of National/International Meteorological Data*

CRC/64: All the ACWC/CWCs should be equipped with RTT systems and facilities for receiving FAX broadcasts from the Regional Telecommunication Hub (RTH) – Delhi. (Para 2.109)

IVB(2) *Data Collection/Communication via INSAT-1 and the DCPs*

CRC/65: For the purpose of collection of cyclone data and dissemination of Cyclone Warning Messages it would be sufficient to establish via INSAT-1 S and C Band capabilities two way communication links between the MDUC, the ACWC/CWCs and the DCPs. The Earth Stations necessary for this purpose may be established. (Para 2.115)

IVB(3) *Telecommunication Systems Used for the Cyclone Warning System (CWS)*

CRC/66: Since the P&T TCCs form a vital part in the successful operation of the Cyclone Data Collection System (CDCS) and the Cyclone Warning System (CWS), the P&T Department should establish a special cell for improvement/maintenance/supervision of these TCCs so that these can function at the level of maximum efficiency. (Para 2.118)

CRC/67: The Cyclone Warning System (CWS, set up by the IMD should be progressively based on telecommunication systems (TCCs) like Wireless Telegraphy (WT) Radio Telephoney (RT) and Radio Teletype (RTT), Facsimile (FAX) transmission system, Very High Frequency/Ultra High Frequency (VHF/UHF) communication systems and Microwave systems all of which are comparatively immune to cyclones. The INSAT system should also be rapidly put into operation to supplement the other TCCs used in the CWS. (Para 2.120)

CRS/68: It would benefit the Cyclone Data Collection System (CDCS) and the Cyclone Warning System (CWS) of the IMD if the P&T Department establishes reliable cyclone proof TC linkages between the P&T communication centre in each coastal state and the various data collection/forecasting centres of the IMD of which the most important in the matter of cyclones are the ACWC/CWCs. (Para 2.120)

CRC/69: The P&T Department should provide to the IMD, UHF and Microwave telecommunication channels on lease, High priority for this project should be given to create a network for the Cyclone Warning System (CWS) in the CPARs of India. For this purpose considerations of economic viability should not stand in the way. (Para 2.121)

CRC/70: The Railway microwave network set up on the east coast and the Aeronautical Fixed Telecommunication Network (AFTN) system of the Civil Aviation and Tourism Department should be used in periods of extreme cyclone emergencies when all the normal TC channels have failed. (Para 2.122)

IVB(4) *TCCs for the ACWC/CWCs*

CRC/71: The weather telegraph offices (WTO) of the P&T should also be located within the premises of the CWCs as has been done for the ACWC. (Para 2.126)

CRC/72: When the proposed CWC at Gujarat is established it should be provided with reliable TC systems as the other ACWC/CWCs. (Para 2.129)

CRC/73: All the CMO/IMOs should in course of time be equipped with their own WT/RT facilities for communication with the corresponding ACWC/CWC for transmitting to it the meteorological data collected by them. The ACWC/CWCs also should be similarly equipped to communicate with the CMO/IMOs under their control. (Para 2.129)

CRC/74: The CWRs at Karaikal, Masulipatnam and Paradeep should be connected to the corresponding ACWC/CWCs by HF linkage. (Para 2.131)

CRC/75: During a cyclone regime, the P&T Department should position its maintenance staff within the ACWC/CWCs and other concerned meteorological offices for prompt and speedy rectification of faults in the telecommunication channels or their restoration in case of breakdown of communications. (Para 2.132)

CRC/76: The P&T and the AIR coastal Radio Stations with transmitters up to 10 KW power should have stand by diesel generator sets. The CMO/IMOs using IMD WT/RT channels may also be provided with similar stand by generators. (Para 2.133)

IVB(5) *TCCs for the Tide Gauge Stations*

CRC/77: If the experience of the DCPs telecasting their informations via the INSAT system to the ACWC/CWCs and the RCC/SCCs is encouraging, then the IMD may consider setting up its own network of automatised and self telecasting Tide Gauge Stations at selected points in cyclone prone areas which are vulnerable to storm surges. A beginning may be made with a few experimental stations in Andhra Pradesh and West Bengal'. (Para 2.134)

IV C *Cyclone Services*

IV C(1) *The Cyclone Warning Agencies/Warnees*

CRC/78: An organisation should be created and located at the IMD Headquarters at Delhi which is dedicated to coordinate/supervise the totality of the Cyclone Working Programme. A Cyclone Warning Directorate (CWDR) at Delhi may serve this purpose. One of the task of this body should be to guide the work of the Cyclone Assessment Cell (CAC) proposed by this Committee in CRC/61. (Para 2.135)

IV C(2) *Cyclone Warning Messages/Cyclone Advisories/Cyclone Bulletins (CWM/CA/CBs)*

CRC/79*: For the CWMs it may be more convenient for the public to grasp the magnitude of cyclones if they are classified under three categories according to wind speeds in the cyclone fields : (1) Depression (32-50 kmph), (2) Toofan (51-89 kmph) and 3) Severe Toofan (89 kmph and above). The use of the common Indian Word Toofan in place of the word cyclone is expected to be more effective and meaningful to the general categories of warnees. (Para 2.142)

CRC/80: All cyclones should be serially numbered : Cyclone : Year : X, Month : Y, Serial Number : Z, Later when the landfall point is known, the geographical characterisation of the landfall point may be added after the serial number : Landfall Point : A, State : B. (Para 2.143)

CRC/81: The CWMs and the Cyclone Advisories (CAs) should be drafted in layman's terms in the various local languages of the coastal states. A glossary of meteorological terms in these languages should be

* The IMD did not accept the classifications which does not conform to the international practice.

evolved for this purpose. (Para 2.144)

CRC/82: The CWMs and the CAs for the rural and the urban areas should be suitably reformated to suit the special needs of the local community and the special features of the terrain. (Para 2.145)

CRC/83: The various types of informations/advisories related to cyclones should be broadcast for the public in a cyclone affected area in two categories:

1. The Cyclone Warning Messages (CWMs) for special groups of warnees containing various informations/forecasts about an impending cyclone and accompanying storm surge. This part should be issued by the concerned ACWC/CWC and broadcast by the AIR.
2. The Cyclone Advisories (CAs) which should contain informations/instructions/orders about measures of precautions/protection/evacuation/rescue/sheltering and camping/relief/rehabilitation. This part should be issued by the concerned District Collectors at his Cyclone Control Room and conveyed to the different groups of affected population/action teams of the concerned State Government through various communication channels of the latter. Collectively the two parts should be referred to as the Cyclone Bulletins (CBs). (Para 2.146)

CRC/84: Forecasts of storm surges should be an integral part of the CWMs and CAs and these should be made areawise in the cyclone affected regions. Forecasts should specify clearly which areas are likely to be inundated under storm surges and also the times when such surges are to be expected. (Para 2.147)

CRC/85: The storm surge warnings/advisories broadcast during cyclone emergencies should be modelled on flood warnings/-advisories. (Para 2.148)

CRC/86: The CWM part of the CB may be put in the following format:

Format 1

Format for the CWM Part of the Cyclone Bulletin

1. Authority of issuance of the CWM
2. Serial Number of the Cyclone

3. Date/time of issuance of the CWM
4. Description of the Cyclone —
   (a) Classification of the cyclone
   (b) Last location
   (c) Direction of movement
   (d) Maximum Wind Speed
   (e) Expected landfall
      (i) Area
      (ii) Date/time
5. General Warnings to the public about wind speed (km./hr.) Rainfall (mm), Storm Surge (m) and state of the Sea Surface for (a) Area of Great Danger (AGD), (b) Area of Danger (AD) (c) Area of Alert (AA). (Para 2.150)

CRC/87*: The visual storm signals demonstrated at the sea ports should directly be correlated to the three classifications of cyclones : Depressions (32-50 kmph), Toofan (51-89 kmph) and Severe Toofan (89 kmph and above). (Para 2.151)

IV C(3) *Dissemination of Cyclone Warnings*

IV C (3.1) *Cyclone Warning Dissemination (CWD) by P&T TC Channels*

CRC/88: The first stage cyclone warning signal — Cyclone Alert must be sent by the concerned ACWC/CWC to all cyclone warnees by land based telegrams. It is important to ensure that this warning is transmitted to the Chief Secretary of the affected state without any wastage of time by "Weather Immediate" telegrams, which bear the priority code 000 and also by telephone so that the Cyclone Code (CC) can be put into operation immediately. The AIR, being the organisation ultimately responsible for dissemination of Cyclone Bulletins (CBs) containing the Cyclone Warning Messages (CWMs) and the Cyclone Advisories (CAs) to all cyclone warnees and the affected public, should be able to get the CBs at the highest priority from the concerned ACWC/CWC on the fastest TC channel available. The P&T Depart-

---

* As mentioned under CRC/81 the IMD did not accept this classification of storms.

ment must ensure that the communication links from the concerned ACWC/CWC to the office of the Chief Secretary and the AIR stations do not snap in a cyclone emergency, or if they do the P&T Department should repair/restore the communication link immediately or set up alternative TC links so that the dissemination of the CBs is not interrupted/impeded. (Para 2.166)

CRC/89: Though the ACWC/CWCs must make all attempt to disseminate the CBs containing the CWMs and the CAS to all cyclone warnees by whatever means that is available in a cyclone emergency as expeditiously as possible, it may be quite possible that it fails in doing this task because of the snapping of some TC link. After the first stage 'Cyclone Alert' signal has been received on the normal TC links from the concerned ACWC/CWC which will be generally possible because this signal will be issued quite some time before the cyclone arrives, the cyclone warnees should be advised to rely more on the CB broadcasts of the AIR for the latest up to the hour informations/advisories about the cyclone. The affected population should be advised that the CBs broadcast by the AIR are the only reliable informations about the cyclone that are available. (Para 2.166)

CRC/90: Since the Landline Telegrams (LLTs) are a vital part of the Cyclone Warning Dissemination System and since the general experience is that the Cyclone Warning Telegrams (CWTs) often fail to reach the warnees in the stipulated time not withstanding the priority codes marked on them, the P&T Department should examine the problem and remove the lacunae of the system and ensure that the communication system works efficiently. During the cyclone regime standby hot lines should be provided by the P&T Department between the ACWC/CWC, AIR, office of the Chief Secretary of the affected State, Cyclone Control Rooms at the district headquarters, and at the P&T coastal radio stations. (Para 2.166)

CRC/91: The ACWC/CWCs should established close liaison with the different Flood Forecasting Centres of various agencies in the State for prompt exchange of warnings so that they are in a position to assess the cumulative effect of the already standing waters and floods and the cyclonic storm surge, and then to utilise the data for the subsequent warnings. For this purpose it is essential that reliable TC channels are established between the ACWC/CWCs, the Flood Forecasting Centres and the Secretariat of the Irrigation Departments in the coastal states of India. (Para 2.167)

CRC/92: There should be standing orders by all coastal State

Governments, that their Police WT system is put at the disposal of the concerned ACWC/CWC without any loss of time for CWD work if such a request is made by the latter to the Chief Secretary of the State during a cyclone emergency. (Para 2.168)

IV C (3.2) *CWD through the INSAT System*

CRC/93: The Disaster Warning System (DWS) part of the INSAT programme should be established as early as possible to provide an alternative cyclone proof TC link between the ACWC/CWCs and the cyclone warnees. (Para 2.170)

CRC/94: The responsibility of providing the DWS receivers and their repair and maintenance must rest with the IMD. But the responsibility of daily operation of these instruments must rest with the concerned coastal State Government. (Para 2.170)

CRC/95: It would be very useful to link up the Police WT system with the DWS system to disseminate CWMs and advisories of Evacuation, Rescue and Relief (ERR) operations during a cyclone regime. (Para 2.170)

IV C (3.3) *CWD through All India Radio (AIR)/Doordarshan*

CRC/96: The first stage 'Cyclone Alert' warning signal should be broadcast 5 to 6 times daily as now, but when the cyclone has crossed into the CRH, the subsequent cyclone warnings should be broadcast hourly of half hourly round the clock for the benefit of listeners living in the areas where the landfall is expected (areas of Danger and Great Danger (AsD/AsGD). There should be more complete and up to the hour CBs broadcast from this stage onwards containing CAs from the State Authorities regarding precautionary measures to be taken by the public and evacuation/rescue/relief (ERR) decisions progressively taken by the State authorities. (Para 2.171)

CRC/97: After the cyclone has landfalled and weakened the ACWC/CWC must as soon as possible issue the 'Cyclone Dewarning' message to the AIR stations for broadcast to the public. (Para 2.172)

CRC/98: After the cyclone is over the AIR stations should continue to broadcast as long as necessary, the CAs of the concerned State authorities regarding Evacuation, Rescue, Relief and Rehabilitation (ERRR) measures taken by the State authorities. (Para 2.173)

CRC/99: When the cyclone has crossed the CRH, the frequency of broadcast of fishery warnings and coastal whether bulletins should be increased. It would be desirable to broadcast these warnings not only in the regular Home News Service of AIR in the regional languages of the coastal states but also, as and when necessary, from the local AIR stations in the affected states in the languages of the local speeches. 'Nil Warning' messages should be broadcast as usual. (Para 2.174)

CRC/100: Meteorological Liaison Offices should be established at maritime states to interpret to the fishermen/groups of fishermen/fishermen colonies/fishing cooperatives about the significance of the cyclone warnings issued by the ACWC/CWC over the AIR for fishing interest. (Para 2.176)

CRC/101: It should be imperative for each or groups of fishing craft to carry suitable transistor radios for receiving the CWMs and the CAs. These may be provided/let out under hire to these users by the concerned State Governments. (Para 2.177)

CRC/102: Designated officials in the State and Central Governments should possess facilities to monitor the CBs broadcast by the AIR stations. (Para 2.178)

CRC/103: For monitoring the CB broadcast of AIR Transistor radios should be provided to (1) designated officials of the coastal State and the Central Government located in the rural areas and (2) Headmen of hamlets and village Pradhans of Gram Panchayats and Sarpanches, who are entrusted by the District Collectors with the responsibility of disseminating CWMs and the CAs and various other tasks for protection of public life. (Para 2.179)

CRC/104: The range of audibility of the AIR stations in the coastal states should be reviewed periodically to the extent possible, to ensure that it is possible for all listeners in the CPARs on coast to receive clearly the CB broadcasts. (Para 2.181)

CRC/105: After the cyclone has crossed into the CRH it may become necessary for the AIR to broadcast its CBs to the public round the clock. The necessary arrangements should be made by the authorities of this organisation. (Para 2.182)

CRC/106: During a cyclone regime, the Doordarshan should show to the viewers satellite pictures of the evolution of the cyclone and its movement with time. After the cyclone has dissipated, the sequence of time elapsed pictures of the cyclone should also be shown. This is for all viewers in the cities and the village communities. In this way it is hoped that a greater awareness will be created among the public about the nature/hazards of cyclones. (Para 2.184)

IV C(3.6) *Periodic Testing of the CWD System*

CRC/107: To test the efficiency of the Cyclone Warning Dissemination System (CWDS), surprise mock tests should be carried out periodically jointly by the IMD, P&T Department, AIR, State Government and various agencies concerned with CWD, at least once a year during the non-cyclonic seasons. The results of such tests should be utilised to remove any lacunae of the system and strengthen the weak parts if any. (Para 2.189)

Group B.1: *Recommendations Mainly for the Government of India and the Coastal State Governments with Respect to the National Cyclone Code and the Cyclone Emergency Action Plans.*

V. *Suggestion for Formulation of a National Cyclone Code (NCC)*

V. A *Present Status of Cyclone Codes (CCs) in the Coastal States*

CRC/108: The Government of India should establish a National Cyclone Code (NCC) for the country by legislation in Order that the Coastal State Governments may use it for guidance for preparing their Cyclone Emergency Action Plan (CEAP). (Para 2.191)

CRC/109: The coastal State Governments who have yet to formulate their Cyclone Emergency Action Plans (CEAPs) should do so as early as possible for laying down rules/procedures for actions/measures to be taken in a cyclone emergency for mitigating the distress caused. The CEAPs may be based on the recommendations of the Committee with respect to a National Cyclone Code. The State CEAPs should be included as a chapter in the State General Disaster Plan. The coastal State Governments should publish their CEAP manuals for use any their officials during a cyclone emergency. (Para 2.194)

V. B *The Cyclone Distress Mitigation Organisation (CDMO)*

CRC/110: The coastal State Governments should each create a permanent cell under a Commissioner for Cyclone Rescue Relief and Rehabilitation (CCRRR) to supervise all Rescue/Relief/ Rehabilitation (RRR) operations required for a cyclone emergency. The Commissioner may be given the rank of an ex-officio Secretary in the State the

CCRRR Cell in collaboration with the proposed Coastal Development Authority may organise construction of roads/bridges/Cyclone Shelters/Cyclone Stores, enforce building codes and undertake the necessary operations for public health maintenance and supervise public health engineering measures to keep the community prepared for cyclones. (Para 2.199)

CRC/111: A senior officer from each of the departments of the State Government concerned with Evacuation/Rescue/Relief/ Rehabilitation (ERRR) works related to a cyclone emergency should be appointed to base with the CCRRR continuously in various matters arising at different times during the emergency. These liaising officers would relay appropriate advisories/orders from the senior officers of their respective departments to the field officers regarding the latter's duties/functions/specific tasks at all stages of the disaster, before/ during/after. (Para 2.200)

CRC/112: Each coastal State Government should set up its State Cyclone Committee (SCYC) which should be in the nature of a Standing Committee to implement/organise all the cyclone distress mitigation measures (CDMMS) in the coastal areas encoded in its CEAP to limit the loss of life and property under onslaught from cyclones and mitigate the distress brought about by them. The SCYC should be the Apex body controlling all aspects of cyclone distress mitigation work (CDMW) in the State. (Para 2.201)

CRC/113: The composition of the State Cyclone Committee (SCYC) should be as appropriate for the State on the lines indicated hereunder.

Chairman : Chief Secretary
Member Secretary : Commissioner - Cyclone Rescue Relief and Rehabilitation (CCRRR)

Members:

A. *State Government*

1. Agriculture and Community Development Department : Secretary
   Director : Agriculture
2. Animal Husbandry Department : Secretary
   Director : Animal Husbandry

3. Civil Defence Department : Secretary
4. Civil Supplies Department : Secretary
   Commissioner : Civil Supplies
5. Finance and Planning Department : Secretary
6. Fisheries : Secretary
7. Forest and Rural Development Department : Secretary
8. General Administration Department — Joint Secretary
9. Home Department : Secretary
10. Director : Home Guards
11. Irrigation and Waterways Department : Secretary Chief Engineer — Engineer — Major Irrigation
12. Panchayat Raj Department : Secretary
    Chief Engineer : Panchayat Raj
13. Police Department : Secretary
    Director General : Police
14. Power Generation Department : Secretary
    Chief Engineer : State Electricity Board
15. Public Health Department : Secretary
    Director : Medical and Public Health Services
16. Public Health Engineering Department : Secretary
    Chief Engineer : Public Health
17. Revenue Department : Secretary
    Commissioner : Land Revenue
    Chief Collector : Revenue
18. Chairman : Coastal Development Authority
19. Roads, Transport and Buildings Department : Secretary
    Chief Engineer : Public Works Department
    Chief Engineer : Roads
20. Refugee Relief and Rehabilitation Department : Secretary Commissioner : Relief.

B. *Central Government*

1. The Central Water Commission : Director of Flood Forecasting Organisation in the State.
2. Coast Guards : Director
3. Defence Establishments in the State —

   (a) Army Commander in the State subsector
   (b) Navy Commander in the State subsector

(c) IAF Commander in the State subsector

4. Indian Meteorological Department : Director of the concerned ACWC/CWC except during a cyclone emergency.
5. Indian Posts & Telegraph Department:

   (a) Director General — All India Radio (in the State Capital).
   (b) General Manager — Telecommunication (in the State Capital).
   (c) General Manager — Telephones (in the State Capital).

6. Railways : General Managers of the Railways passing through the CPARs of the State.
7. Shipping and Transport Ministry : Chief Officer of the Port Authority in the State.

C. *Legislature*

1. One member from the Loksabha from the State.
2. One member from the Bidhansabha.

D. *Voluntary Relief Organisations*

1. Chairman of the branch of the Indian Red Cross Society in the State.
2. Representative from other voluntary relief organisations active in the State. (Para 2.201)

CRC/114: The terms of reference of the SCYC should contain *inter alia* the following powers and responsibilities.

1. To set up standing District Cyclone Committees (DCCs) for taking emergency executive measures during cyclone regimes.
2. To establish and maintain snap proof TC channels of communication with the DCCs for dispatching advisories for precautionaries, instructions/orders for ERRR and for receiving back reports on the actions taken.
3. To formally declare areas of the coastal regions as Areas of Great Danger (area of likely landfall), Danger and under Alert : AGD, AD, AA.

4. To define and allot specific tasks to various departments of the State/Central Government and various agencies/voluntary organisations for the CDMW at various stages of the cyclone emergency and monitor on the progress of their efforts.
5. To mobilise the resources in men, materials and equipments of the State/Central Government and various agencies/voluntary organisations or that available from the public for the CDMW.
6. To advise the State Government about compulsive evacuation from identified AsGD during a cyclone.
7. To review periodically the Cyclone Emergency Action Plan (CEAP) for the concerned State in the light of the experience gained with the objective to remove the lacunae if any.

CRC/115: As soon as a cyclone emergency develops the Control Room General Administration (CRGA) should be placed under the control of CCRRR and manned by officers of the Departments of Revenue, Police and Defence, and representatives from the IMD if available during the emergency. The CRGA should be connected by reliable TCCs to the departments involved in Cyclone Distress Mitigation Work CDMW and with their field stations in the Cyclone affected areas. The CRGA should function as a monitor centre watching over the disaster and also as a command post for relaying the advisories/instructions/orders/requests of the authorities to the various officers engaged in CDMW. Large scale maps and all relevant informations like addressed of various officers/field units operating at the State Capital/District Headquarter Field positions in the cyclone affected areas, etc., should be available at the CRGA. The CRGA must in all circumstances keep unbroken telecommunication contacts with the concerned ACWC/CWC and the Flood-Forecasting Organisations in the State. (Para 2.203)

CRC/116: As soon as a cyclone threat develops the Chief Engineer (Major Irrigation) should set up a monitoring room in the Irrigation Department (MRID) at the State Headquarters to keep a close watch on the rainfall and the flood situation that may develop consequent to the cyclone. The MRID should be in unbroken telecommunication contacts with the CRGA, the Flood Forecasting Organisations in the State and the concerned ACWC/CWC. (Para 2.204)

CRC/117: District Cyclone Committees (DCCs) may be set up at the Headquarters of the districts in the CPARs. (Para 2.205)

CRC/118: The composition of the DCCs may be as follows:

Chairman : District Collector
Member : One member may be nominated from each of the following bodies.

A. *State Government*

1. Agriculture Department.
2. Animal Husbandry Department.
3. Civil Defence Department.
4. Civil Supplies Department: District Supply Officer.
5. Fisheries Department.
6. Forestry and Rural Development Department.
7. Information and Broadcasting Department: District Public Relation Officer.
8. Police Department: District Police Superintendent.
9. Public Health Department : (1) District Medical and Health Officer, (2) Superintendent, Government General Hospital.
10. Public Health Engineering Department: District Engineer.
11. Public Works Department.
12. Refugee Relief Rehabilitation Department.
13. State Electricity Board: District Engineer.
14. State Transport Department.

B. *Central Government*

1. The IMD representative if available in the District.
2. Coast Guards Department.
3. Defence Establishment in the District Headquarters — Army, Navy and Airforce : From units stationed in the District.
4. Post and Telegraph Department.

C. *Legislature* : One member from the State Bidhansabha from the District.

D. *Voluntary Organisation* —

1. Indian Red Cross Society.
2. Representative of other voluntary relief and rehabilitation organisation active in the district.

The office of the District Collector will do the Secretariat work and send out the executive orders of the DCC for Cyclone Distress Mitigation Work (CDMW) via the Cyclone Control Room (CCR). (Para 2.205)

CRC/119: The terms of reference of the DCCs should *inter alia* be:

1. To inform the public by organising beating of drums, or sirens or by flares (during night time) or by any other means about the threat of the cyclone.
2. To maintain a Cyclone Control Room (CCR) in the office of the District Collector to organise and correlate all executive actions by him. The CCR would issue to the public and special warnees instructions about precautionary measures to the taken and instructions/orders for evacuation/relief/rehabilitation to the cyclone victims.
3. To mobilise the local resources in manpower and materials like vehicles, powered launches for evacuation/rescue, drinking water, relief as food/clothes/blankets and medicines to combat epidemics of dysentery and cholera, etc., and maintain adequate stocks of these materials.
4. To utilise all the resources available locally or through the State Government via the SCYC or from other agencies and organisations and send them for this purpose to wherever they are necessary.
5. To organise evacuation and rescue operations in the Areas of Great Danger (AsGD).
6. To set up and run refugee camps till the affected people can be satisfactorily rehabilitated.
7. To organise protection from antisocial criminal elements of property in the (AsGD) from where people have been evacuated.
8. To make immediate assessment of cyclone caused damages in the district and report to Secretary of the Revenue Department. (Para 2.206)

CRC/120: The DCCs should meet at least twice a year in April and August just at the start of the pre-monsoon and post-monsoon cyclone seasons. At these meetings actions taken for preparing the community for cyclones and the success of the CEAP in fighting the cyclones of the immediately preceding period may be reviewed. (Para 2.207)

CRC/121: During a cyclone emergency a DCC in a cyclone affected region should set up a Cyclone Control Room (CCR) which will be in the nature of a monitoring/command post during the emergency. The organisation and the executive responsibilities of the Cyclone Control Room at the District Headquarters should be as follows:

Organisations

Officer in-charge of the Cyclone Control: PA to the District Collector of any other officer nominated by him.

Representatives from various organisations to be stationed at the CCR during a cyclone regime:

1. Police Department.
2. P&T Department.
3. Public Health Department.
4. Public Health Engineering Department.
5. Revenue Department: Tehsildars, Huzur Seristadars.

Responsibilities

1. To receive from the SCYC on behalf of the concerned DCC the orders/instructions for dissemination of CAs and evacuation/rescue orders/instructions and advisories about relief/rehabilitation measures for the victims in the cyclone affected regions, fishing boats at sea, and transports on road.
2. To transmit instructions/orders of its DCC regarding the CAs, and the evacuation/rescue/relief/rehabilitation advisories to various groups of people or organisations in the cyclone affected regions.
3. To monitor continuously during a cyclone the broad-coasts of the CWMs by AIR and pass on the informations to its DCC.
4. To establish direct communication with the concerned ACWC/CWC for obtaining the latest information about the cyclone and pass on the information to its DCC.
5. To establish communications with the Police Headquarters for conveying requests from its DCC for evacuation/rescue of cyclone victims from the AsGD.

6. To establish contact with local Defence authorities for any special assistance required by its DCC. (Para 2.208)

CRC/122: The District Collector should be given the power to activate the CCR after the first stage 'Cyclone Alert' warning is received by him. Normally the CCR should be deactivated after the cyclone has collapsed and the 'Cyclone Dewarning' signal is received by him. But he should have the discretion to keep the CCR activated in the interest of rescue/relief/rehabilitation of the cyclone victims. (Para 2.209)

CRC/123: During cyclone regimes after the 'Cyclone Alert' signal has been upgraded to 'Cyclone Warning' level, the CCRs should work round the clock and the consequent administrative problems should be resolved by the State Government. (Para 2.210)

CRC/124: At the taluk level standby Taluk Cyclone Committees (TCYCs) may be constituted with members nominated by the District Collector. These should be responsible for carrying out instructions issued by the CCRs of the DCCs. (Para 2.211)

CRC/125: At the village level, the Gram Panchayats would be sufficient to supervise the execution of the CAs/instructions/orders issued via the concerned TCYCs from the CCRs of the concerned DCCs. During cyclone regimes representatives of the P&T Department and the local Police should be associated with the Gram Panchayats to help these bodies. (Para 2.211)

CRC/126: At the city level with Municipal Authorities should organise, if necessary, emergency cells to meet the threats of an impending cyclone for the executions of the CAs/instructions/orders of the concerned DCC through their CCRs. These bodies should call upon other organisations for help if necessary. (Para 2.211)

CRC/127: The SCYC should have joint discussions with the representatives of Ministry of Defence for identifying the equipments which the Defence forces would need to help in a cyclone emergency and also the scale at which they should be distributed to the various administrative echelons within the State Government. Some equipments, which are required for cyclone emergency but can also be put to regular use for their own need by the Defence forces, could be purchased by the State Government and maintained by the Defence forces. (Para 2.212)

CRC/128: The DCC should have joint discussions with the representatives of the Defence Forces in the district after the cyclone warning has been upgraded, regarding the time and modality of seeking assistance from them. It is necessary that during these meetings, the specific tasks that the Defence Services would be required to undertake in a cyclone emergency, be clearly defined to them. (Para 2.212)

V.C. *TCCs for CDMW*

CRC/129: The CCRs should be equipped with Telephone/Telex and TP/WT channels and also with transistor radios to monitor the CBs broadcast by the concerned ACWC/CWC over the AIR stations in the State. Messengers on cycles and other vehicles should be put at the disposal of the CCRs. (Para 2.213)

CRC/130: On request from the concerned DCC mobile WT stations may be installed by the Police at strategic points in the declared Areas of Great Danger in the local Post Offices where telegram receiving and sending facilities are available. (Para 2.215)

CRC/131: It is advisable to appoint a temporary cadre of messengers/peons at the cyclone centres at the taluk/city/village levels, who can take messages/instructions/orders to various places on cycles/motor cycles/other means. (Para 2.216)

CRC/132: Each Cyclone Distress Mitigation Centre (CDMCN) at the taluk/city/village level should always have adequate stock of warning equipments : drums, tomtoms, mobile vans with loudspeakers. At various strategic places particularly in the cities sirens should be installed and these should be properly maintained so that they can be used when needed. (Para 2.216)

V.D. *Various Stages of CDMW*

V.D.(1) *Measures to be taken on Receipt of the 'Cyclone Alert' Signal from the concerned ACWC/CWC — The First Stage*

CRC/133: The coastal State Governments should prepare large scale suitable Cyclone Hazard Potential Maps (CHPMs) area wise based on contour maps referred to under CRC/7 and past experience gathered from the specific areas regarding devastations caused by storms and flood vulnerability and on risk analysis derived from these data. The maps should be made available to the SCYCs and all the DCCs of the coastal States. (Para 2.218)

CRC/134: As soon as the 'Cyclone Alert' signal is received by the Chief Secretary, a meeting of the SCYC should be called by the Commissioner of Cyclone Rescue Relief and Rehabilitation to discuss *inter alia* the following items:

1. Monitoring the CWMs broadcast by AIR by the CRGA round the clock till 'Cyclone Dewarning' signal is issued by the concerned ACWC/CWC.
2. Alerting the concerned DCCs about the impending cyclone.
3. Taking decisions on plans and strategies to meet the approaching cyclone.
4. The allotment of tasks and responsibilities to various departments of the State Government.
5. The issuance of requests for help to other agencies and departments of the Central Government like AIR, Defence, P&T department, etc.
6. To arrange transmission of CA part of the CBs to the various groups of warnees and designated State Government Officials assigned to CDMW over the communication channels of the State Government.
7. The creation of a cell responsible for drafting and issuance of the CAs.
8. Mobilisation of vehicles, road and water transports like trucks and buses of the State Transport Department, lorries, powered launches, country boats for possible evacuation/rescue operations.
9. Stocking reserve of various relief material — food grains, clothing, medicines for possible distribution amongst cyclone victims and medicines to stop epidemics that may follow in the wake of the cyclone.
10. Establishment of contact with the Flood Forecasting Centres in the State of the CWCM/State Irrigation Department/IMD and the concerned ACWC/CWC of the State for issuance of storm surge/flood advisories. The actual storm surge warnings will be issued by the ACWC/CWC to the SCYC after consultation with the Flood Forecasting Centres.
11. Maintenance by the P&T Department of reliable snap proof TC channels with the ACWC/CWC and the DCCs of the affected areas (via their CCRs). (Para 2.219)

CRC/135: On receipt of the 'Cyclone Alert' signal the Commissioner — Cyclone Rescue Relief and Rehabilitation should alert—

1. The Irrigation Department.
2. The Revenue Department.
3. The District Collectors in the threatened areas.

The concerned District Collectors should in turn warn the Municipal authorities, Panchayat Pradhans, Police establishments. Tahsildars in the threatened areas. The Tahsildars should warn the local officers/village committees and start arrangements for activating the public warning system. (Para 2.220)

CRC/136: All District Officers who are away on tour should be immediately recalled to District Headquarters to meet the District Collector. It must be seen that no officer is on tour or on leave during the period of the cyclone. (Para 2.221)

CRC/137: The Monitoring Room of the Irrigation Department (MRID) should be activated to watch over the development of the flood situation in the threatened districts. Inspection at close intervals of the state of water levels in the hydrodams, water reservoirs, rivers, etc., in the areas marked out in the Cyclone Hazard Potential Maps, should commence at this stage. (Para 2.221)

CRC/138: On receipt of the 'Cyclone Alert' signal from the ACWC/CWC, or from the Commissioner — Cyclone Rescue Relief and Rehabilitation of the State Government the first emergency meeting of the DCCs in the threatened districts should be called by the respective District Collectors to work out in advance the strategies to be employed. The DCC in any affected district should be more or less in continuous session when the Warning signal is upgraded there to the second stage 'Cyclone Warning' signal. (Para 2.221)

CRC/139: Though the period of 'Cyclone Alert' is the period of little actual danger for people residing on land, it may be the period of the highest danger for fishermen on sea particularly for those who are directly in the path of the cyclone. The CAs therefore contain detailed advisories for sailing, homing and sheltering to nearest identified ports, storing of boats and fishing equipments. The SCYC should directly issue these advisories through AIR broadcasts which should be monitored by the fishermen for taking appropriate safety measure. (Para 2.222)

CRC/140: The following items should be on the agenda for discussion/action in the first emergency meeting of the DCCs.

1. Activate their respective CCRs.

2. Establish immediate contacts with–

   (a) the Police Headquarters and the Thanas in the locality which are threatened by the cyclone, and alert them to standby for establishment of communication with the CCRs;
   (b) the P&T Department requesting them to bring up their communication system up to the talk, block and village levels to a full state of efficiency;
   (c) the Defence authorities in the districts and alert them to standby to help the State authorities in possible evacuation/rescue operations;
   (d) with the nearest AIR stations directly;
   (e) the local fire fighting units, coast guards, civil defence units, irrigation officials, PWD officials, Public health Officials, Public Health Engineering Officials asking them to be on the alert; and
   (f) the voluntary rescue/relief organisations that generally operate in the State asking them to be on the alert. If there are any lacunae in the communication systems with these bodies then to take immediate steps to remove them or provide alternatives.

3. To study the Cyclone Hazard Potential Map supplied by the State Government obtained from the SCYC/Revenue Department/Irrigation Department and review of the approach ways to the possible areas of Danger/Great Danger for possible subsequent evacuation and rescue.
4. Identification from the list of shelters : Temples, Mosques, Churches, Municipal High Schools, high grounds, special Cyclone Shelters (CYSHELs), previously selected by the DCC, for mention in the CAs as the recommended gathering points for the refugees and evacuees if the cyclone warning is later upgraded.
5. Identification of Health Centres and assignment of medical workers and provisions of drugs/medicines/vaccines at strategic points in the district for fighting epidemics, that follows in the wake of the cyclones, and planning of removal of affected persons from the scenes of disaster to these centres, and generally providing first aid for minor injuries to men and cattle.

6. Arrangements of messengers and despatch riders on cycles, motor, jeeps, motor bikes, horseback for communication with the officials of the TCYCs, City Municipalities, and Panchayat Offices at the villages to alert them of the impending cyclone.
7. Review the state of the Cyclone Shelters and bring them up to the level of preparedness to receive cyclone victims.
8. Review the state of the equipments at the Cyclone Stores for evacuation/rescue, debris removal, medicines for first aids/epidemic, etc., and send requisitions to the appropriate departments of the State Government—Public Works Department, Public Works Engineering Department, etc., and Agro Industries Complexes, etc.
9. Review the stock of the food grains, dry food commodities, clothing materials and fuels like kerosene and diesel oil, etc., that may be available for the cyclone victims, and send the requisitions for any deficit in this respect to the Department of Supplies of the State Government.
10. Assessment of vehicles — lorries, powered, launches, country boats needed for warning/evacuation/rescue for a requisition to be sent to the SCYC and mobilisation of what is available locally and dispatching the equipments and vehicles received or commandeered to wherever they are needed. Adequate stock of petrol/diesel oil should be assured for these vehicles and stocked at suitable strategic distribution centres.
11. Detailing all personnel for CDMW to their respective stations.
12. Requesting the PWD to inspect all roads, tanks, bunds, bridges, buildings marked for sheltering evacuees and refugees and to take steps to strengthen and repair them.
13. Requesting the PWD to remove also the dead and dying trees from the road side to prevent them from falling on people during the cyclone regime.
14. Issuance of CAs to local CDMO units at the taluk/city/village levels for warning and bringing them to the public by whatever means that is available.
15. Analyse the preliminary flood risk map received from the Irrigation Department/Flood Forecasting Organisations in the State to take decisions on the necessary steps.
16. Set up a large scale map of the threatened areas in the office of the District Collector for reference/guidance. (Para 2.223)

CRC/141: From the time the first meeting is held all communications sent/received from the SCYC, Departments of the State/Central Government, various Agencies/Voluntary Organisations, ACWC/CWC, Flood Forecasting Organisations should be preserved by the DCCs for record. (Para 2.223)

CRC/142: The respective CCR should constantly monitor the CWM broadcasts of AIR after the 'Cyclone Alert' signal is received by the DCC. (Para 2.223)

CRC/143: On receiving the 'Cyclone Alert' signals the officials in the local CDMO units at the taluk/city/village level should take immediate measures to warn the people in the threatened areas of the impending cyclone by whatever means that is available—by beating drums/tomtoms, coloured tethered orange coloured baloons/ pennants visible from long distances, mobile vans carrying public address systems, sirens, etc. (Para 2.224)

CRC/144: There are a number of urgent actions that must be taken at the 'Cyclone Alert' stage by the various departments of the State/Central Governments, agencies and voluntary organisations. Some of these steps are listed hereunder:

A. *State Government*

1. *Agriculture Department*

The Director of Agriculture should issue advisories to the farmers in the threatened areas to take precautionary measures to save the crops on the fields and store cut crops and agriculture products on raised platforms or covered sheds.

2. *The local CDMO units at the taluk/city/village levels in the threatened areas*

These should be in a state of alert and preparedness. In particular they should take prompt actions on the reports of the Municipal authorities/Major Panchayats.

3. *Fisheries Department*

(a) The Director-Fisheries will immediately arrange to issue advisories to the fishermen on the threatened coastal regions not to put out to sea and to secure their boats/nets in safe storage places to avoid damage;

(b) The fishermen living at particularly low lying places should be moved to safer places; and

(c) Arrangements should be made to give first aid/medical attention to injured fishermen who return.

4. *Irrigation Department*

(a) Flood Monitoring Room (FMR) should be immediately established in the office of the Superintendent Engineer's office to keep a watch on the local flood situation and feed the information to the MRID at the office of the Chief Engineer (Major Irrigation),

(b) The head regulators of the irrigation system serving threatened coastal areas should be closed and the water allowed to pass through to the river course.

5. *The Municipal authorities/Major Panchayats*

(a) They should review the stock of food/clothes from which supplies can be drawn when the actual emergency occurs;

(b) The Municipal authorities/Major Panchayats equipped with public water supply facilities should ensure that the maximum quantity of water is stored in overhead tanks/water towers. The water tankers with the Municipalities should be brought up to a state of useability and filled up with water;

(c) These authorities should instal emergency diesel sets for generation of electric power for installations needed for maintenance of essential services — pumps for lifting drinking water and removal of flood water, lighting at important units of the CDMOs;

(d) The Panchayat authorities should inspect the Cyclone Shelters (CYSHELs) and bring them up into a stage when they can be used. They should inspect the approach roads to the CYSHELs and report to their local unit of the CDMO;

(e) They should inspect the local health centres/hospitals and the stock of drugs/medicines/vaccines against epidemics and report to the local unit of the CDMO;

(f) They should inspect the stock of various materials/

equipments needed for CDMW : debris removing equipment/rescue equipments — boats/vehicles/floats/ladders/hooks, etc., at the cyclone stores (CYSTORs) and report to the local unit of CDMO;

(g) These authorities should inspect all possible sources of hazards — dying/rotten trees, unsafe building structures, etc., and report to the local unit of the CDMO;

(h) These authorities should inspect the state of the roads and bridges in their areas and report to the local unit of the CDMO; and

(i) They should inspect the state of water drainage and sewerage in their locality and remove any blocking/chocking of the pipes/channels so that they are in a good enough state to carry away flood water. If possible, pump sets should be set up at important points during the emergency for pumping out the water.

6. *Police Department*

(a) In most states the Police units are equipped with VHF/WT sets (Para 2.124). Mobile sets should be set up, if not installed already, at strategic points for transmitting informations relating to floods and cyclones. As has been stated already this is outside the normal scope of work of the Police Department (Para 2.168, CRC/92) but may be permitted during disaster emergencies. There should be standing orders that the officers of the Revenue Department and various units of the CDMO to use the WT/VHF sets during cyclone emergencies;

(b) During cyclone emergencies mobile vans stationed at important Police Stations should be equipped with VHF sets;

(c) When commandeering jeeps/vehicles, it is also necessary to draft Police drivers and kept on duty for driving the vehicles in case the drivers in the employment of State Government are not found; and

(d) The Police Department should insist on the prohibition of passage of all vehicles, as far as necessary, on the roads in the threatened areas to avoid the passengers from being stranded.

7. *The Power Department*

(a) The State Electricity Board/various Electric Supply Companies in the threatened areas should make arrangements to disconnect power in the threatened areas. Arrangements should be made to instal generators at important Municipal towns for only very essential purposes. A list should be maintained by the department of the locations from where such generators can be commandeered — cinemas/theatre halls, etc.; and

(b) The Executive Engineer — Power Department in the threatened area should keep himself informed by his counterparts from other districts about the power produced and available for his area and when it is possible to draw this power.

8. *The Public Health/Public Health Engineering Department*

(a) The Superintendent, Government General Hospital and the District Medical and Health Officer should keep teams of doctors ready with stocks of medicines/vaccines necessary for relief/prevention of epidemics. The District Medical and Health Officer should prepare a list of Government/Private medical doctors who can be called upon to serve during an emergency created by a cyclone;

(b) The state of the medical stores at the CYSHELs/Cyclone stores/other stores should be inspected by the District Medical and Health Officer and deficit of stock made up for the emergency. He should see that adequate stocks of drugs/medicines/vaccines/vitamins/chemicals for giving medical relief to cyclone victims and to control epidemics is available; and

(c) The District Medical and Health Officer should see that adequate number of ambulances are available for relief work and that they are positioned as strategic points from where they can move to the affected areas quickly without loss of time. If sufficient numbers are not available vehicles should be commandeered and put into use as ambulances. Drivers/maintenance technicians for the vehicles/ambulance attendants/para-medical men should be found for these emergency ambulance fleet.

9. *The Public Works Department*

(a) The PWD should inspect the weak bunds of all irrigation

sources near and around the villages and keep watch over the weak points for taking timely action against any possible breaches;

(b) The PWD should inspect the head gates of the irrigation channels and take necessary repair measures if needed. The Department should inspect the water drainage system and take necessary remedial measures; and

(c) The PWD should inspect all public buildings in the threatened areas and take reinforcement/demolition measures as necessary.

10. *The State Transport Department*

(a) The State Transport buses, private buses and lorries, jeeps, tempos should be requisitioned, put under the control of this Department and moved to strategic points near the threatened areas;

(b) Sufficient stock of petrol/diesel should be collected at convenient distribution points;

(c) Drivers and other support staff should be called in for duty during the emergency for driving the vehicles to the threatened areas for evacuation/rescue work; and

(d) When commandeering jeeps/vehicles, it is also necessary to draft Armed Reserved Police drivers and kept on duty for driving them in case the drivers in the employment of State Government are not found.

11. *Department of Supplies*

(a) The District Supplies Officers should make arrangements for withdrawal of food grains such as rice, wheat, etc. from the godowns of the Food Corporations of India, State Civil Supplies Corporation and similar organisations;

(b) The Department should maintain a stock of durable eating materials : breads, buns, puffed/pressed rice, chhattu, etc.; and

(c) The District Supplies Officer should obtain sufficient stock of petrol, kerosene, diesel in local distribution centres on Government account and keep them ready for use.

B. *Central Government*

1. *The Defence Establishment in the State*

(a) On being alerted by the DCC the Defence authorities should keep ready of vehicles/amphibians/powered boats that may be needed for evacuation/rescue operations;

(b) All equipments that may be necessary for evacuation/rescue operations in the second phase of the CDMW should be kept ready and available for use;

(c) The Defence authorities should keep ready a number of Helicopters for aerial survey/food dropping/rescue of sick people in the cyclone affected areas if requested; and

(d) The communication channels of the Defence establishments in the State should be held ready for CDMW if requested.

2. *Port Authorities*

(a) Arrangements should be made for safe berthing of ships in the ports. If necessary ships in the ports. If necessary the ships may be directed to move out to the open sea where they may be safer; and

(b) The Port Trust Authorities should be given the responsibility of evacuation/rescue work when water transports : powered launches/boats/country boats are needed. All such transports after collection by requisition/commandeering should be put under the disposal of the Port Trust Authorities. Sufficient stocks of petrol/kerosene should be reserved for this purpose.

3. *The Post & Telegraphs Departments*

(a) The Department should inspect its land based TC Systems that will be used for dissemination of Cyclone Advisories/-Bulletins/Informations and bring it up to a level that it can perform these tasks. If possible alternative communication channels in the form of VHF/UHF/microwave links should be provided;

(b) The Department should provide men and materials/-equipments at all units of the CDMW for restoring/repairing the communication system as and when needed; and

(c) The Department should keep in order the telephones of all officials connected with CDMW.

4. *Railways*

(a) All the trains on tracks passing through the threatened areas should be brought to a half at the nearest railway station;
(b) All personnel on duty at the stations located in the threatened areas should be warned to standby;
(c) Arrangements for food/medical attention should be made at all the stations for the period of the cyclone; and
(d) The Railway Microwave system should be available to the District Collector during a cyclone emergency if necessary. (Para 2.225)

V.D.(2) *Code of Actions to be taken on Receipt of the Cyclone Warning Signal — The Second Phase*

CRC/145: When the warning is upgraded to 'Cyclone Warning' the SCYC will constantly monitor the actions of the concerned DCCs and keep a watch on their urgent requirements of personnel/-equipments/materials and supply them at a moment's notice when requested. (Para 2.228)

CRC/146: It is important that the Control Room — General administration of the concerned State emergency CRGA should now be manned by designated officers of the State Revenue Department, Police Department and Defence Forces.

CRC/147: In all CDMWs in which the Defence Department is involved, the Department of General Administration of the State Government should take a leading part. The Defence Forces will be assisting the civil authorities in evacuation/rescue operations and running of relief camps. The Department of General Administration will be in overall charge of all this work which involve assistance from the Defence Forces and coordinate these operations.

CRC/148: When the 'Cyclone Alert' warning has been upgraded to Cyclone Warning the District Collector after discussing the matter at DCC will take the following actions:

1. Declare formally the areas of Great Danger (Land Fall point and neighbourhood), Danger and Alert (ASGD, ASD, ASA). In

the ASGD areas must be demarcated and declared to the public as being likely to be submerged and inundated by the in rushing storm surge. These areas would possibly be where evacuations may have to be enforced.

2. Put the Fire Brigade, Police, PWD and Public Health Department, P&T Department and the Defence Forces on alert round the clock during the remaining period of the cyclone regime for carrying out specific tasks at a moment's notice.
3. Stop all transport on roads passing through the ASGD at suitable places or direct them to safer routes if possible.
4. Establish communication system with the officials working on CDMMs, which are immune to cyclone : Police WT systems or the INSAT DWS system, if that exists in the state. The Superintendent of Police should instal one of the Police WT mobile vans at the CCR of the district for transmitting messages to the affected areas. There should be standing instruction that the staff of the CCR can use on a priority basis any telephone/telephone exchange that is in a working condition.
5. Declare local public holiday for all organisation in the AsGD and AsD. But the officials designated for CDMW and the Departments specially involved in such works do not come under this order. (Para 2.230)

CRC/149: On receipt of the 'Cyclone Warning' signal the Superintendent of Police should make arrangements to disseminate the warning through the TCCs of the Police Departments : WT, VHF, etc., so that all the Police stations up to the Thana level are alerted. It would be the responsibility of the Officer in charge of a Police Station to transmit the warning to all villages under the jurisdiction of that station. (Para 2.231)

CRC/150: The Divisional Engineer, Telephones must be communicate the 'Cyclone Warning' message to the various telephone communication hubs in the district. It would be the responsibility of the officer in charge of these communication hubs to transmit the message to Village Officers/Executive Officers/Block Development Officers/ Sarpanch/Panchayat Pradhans, etc. (Para 2.231)

CRC/151: If all TCCs to the villages fail during a cyclone or if no TCC : telephone, telegram, etc., exists up to some group of villages, then the Police Officers in charge of the Thana whose jurisdiction extends over these villages must, after close consultation with the concerned Tahsildars, communicate the 'Cyclone Warning' message through Police Constables/Special Messengers travelling on foot/ cycles/motor bikes/horses or by any other means. (Para 2.231)

CRC/152: In the final stages of the 'Cyclone Warning' phase, the village Munsiffs or some official of similar ranks should be given the responsibility of delivering the final warning in the AsGD by ringing the bells in temples/churches and public places which should be audible from long distances. (Para 2.231)

CRC/153: The Director of fisheries should direct his staff to spread the 'Cyclone Warning' message to the fishing community together with advisories for fishermen. (Para 2.231)

CRC/154: The Cyclone Advisories for AsD must be broadcast very frequently over the AIR. They should be concerned *inter alia* with the following instructions:

1. People should be requested to monitor with their radio sets, the CB broadcasts of AIR containing the latest warnings of the development/progress of the cyclone, and also the CAs broadcast locally by the State Government Officials and pass on the informations to others. The listoners should also be instructed that these informations are the most reliable that are available. Thus it is important that the radio receivers in the houses particularly the transistor sets should be fully operational and serviceable.
2. People should be requested to avoid listening to rumours and spreading them.
3. The people must be advised to keep calm and set example to others and help them.
4. Since it is difficult to predict the exact location of the landfall point and the intensity and extent of the storm surge, people should be requested to avoid generally low lying beaches named in the advisories.
5. In regions where there are streams and rivers or river dams, people should be requested to be on alert for dangers offlash floods or dam bursts and avoid possible routes of rushing water released in this manner. Such routes should be clearly named in the CAs by the State Government Officials.
6. If a house is well built and located on high ground in areas likely to be inundated, it is probably the safest place to stay in during the cyclone regime. The public should be so advised and

also instructed to stay on the upper floors and avoid the ground floor. But if the authorities advise evacuation from a particular place, then it must be abandoned without question.

7. People should be advised when going outside their residences to avoid trees, dilapidated/old houses and insecure structures and electrical transmission lines. If on road in a vehicle, shelter must be sought at the nearest house without wasting time. In general they should be advised to avoid going outside during a cyclone.
8. The most important thing, every body should be advised about, is examination of the state of the houses they are residing in. If the foundations/roof do not seem strong enough or the general condition of a house seem unsatisfactory it should be abandoned and the residents seek safer shelters.
9. People who stay on in their residences should be requested to board up glass windows or fix storm shutters in place. For this purpose good strong wooden planks should be securely fastened. Make shift and loose boards cause more damage, which fact must be pointed out in the CAs. For doors on outer surface of the houses and buildings strong supports must be provided. If wood planks are not immediately available, paper strips may be pasted on glass panes to prevent splinters.
10. People staying on in their residences should be advised to check loose objects in their houses which may be thrown about by the cyclone wind. Thus loose tiles should be secured by cementing. Doors/windows should be repaired. All articles and goods, which are likely to be blown off, should be tightly secured. In this category are : kerosene tins, cans, agricultural implements, garden tools, hurricane lamps, burning coals from chulhas, road signs and similar objects. These when blown may cause great danger to life and property and should be collected and stored in a room away from the rushing winds.
11. People staying on in their residence should be requested to provide for opening of doors and windows on the lee side of the house, i.e., away from the wind.
12. The area round the houses should be checked and dead/lying trees should be removed. Movable objects like lumber piles, loose zinc sheets/bricks, garbage, etc., lying outside should be anchored and secured.
13. Children, old people and sick persons and patients from hospi-

tals should be directed to go to identified safer places and the authorities should provide all assistance to them for this purpose. If that is not possible, as much safety should be ensured to them as possible under the conditions. Provisions should be made for special food and medicine that they may need.

14. People staying in their residences should be requested to make provisions for extra food : rice, wheat, flour, grams, potatoes, etc., specially of the kind which can be eaten without cooking or with very little preparation : pressed/puffed rice, Chhatu, powdered dal, etc. Reserve of cooking fuel and drinking water should also be kept to tide over the period of emergency.
15. Hurricanes/lanterns filled with kerosene, extra stock of kerosene and flash lamps with enough dry cells should be kept in reserve in case of power failures.
16. All householders should be requested to keep reserves of medicines and preventives against epidemics and they should be advised specifically about what items to keep in stock.
17. Valuable goods should be shifted to the upper floors, if these exist, to prevent damage from the flood water. All furnitures, professional/domestic implements, books, valuable clothes, etc., should be put in secure places.
18. The public must be informed that after the wind and rain during a storm, a full period may follow, which does not mean that the cyclone is over. It may be the result of the eye of the cyclone passing over the place, in which case there will be another period of wind in the opposite direction, perhaps with greater violence and more rain. So the public must be advised to be watchful and on the alert till the 'Cyclone Rewarning' signal is given.
19. If possible every body must keep contact with the Gram Panchayat Pradhan or the nearest Police Thana and the local Post Office which may have been selected to be local Cyclone Advisory and Operation Centres (CAOCs). (Para 2.233)

CRC/155: These CAs like all other will be broadcast by the State Government over its communication channels. The CAs in the AsGD must *inter alia* be concerned often with evacuation orders. Thus the advisories must contain the following type of instructions:

1. As soon as an area is declared as an AGD, people residing there

should be advised to leave the area sufficiently early before the approaches to the identified high grounds/the cyclone shelters and the relief/refugee camps are flooded and thus avoid being marooned.

2. Identification of place and time of gathering of people of a particular area in an AGD for collection by the Evacuation Authorities. These places should be made known to the concerned people by the personnel at the local CDMW/CAOC centre.
3. In case it is not possible for the Evacuation Authorities to approach immediately a particular locality, advice must be given to the residents of that locality to go to an identified place of comparative safety and wait there for further instructions.
4. As soon as the order for evacuation is issued by the District Collector for a particular declared AGD, people must be advised to lock up their residences and leave. For people hesitant to do so, forcible evacuation by the authorities must be carried out. This may be made known to all concerned.
5. The domestic cattle should be set free in time and allowed to seek shelters. The animals have a natural instinct to seek out the safest places. This is perhaps the easiest way of saving them from drowning. On no account should they be tethered or tied up at posts or locked up in sheds.
6. Advice must be given about what the evacuees can carry with them including cattles.
7. If upper floors are available, the valuable goods may be removed there before evacuation. Otherwise some possessions, particularly those made of metal can be saved by burying them below ground from where they can be retrieved later, when the storm water has subsided making it possible for the refugees to return. Such instructions may be issued by the District Collector in the CAs.
8. Arrangements should be made for the property of the evacuees to be protected against theft and plunder and the people should be assured of this.
9. Assurance must be given by the District Collector that food, medicine and relief would be provided for the cyclone victims and cattle at the cyclone shelters/refugee camps at all times during and after cyclone emergency.
10. At the evacuee camps at the place of shelters it must be insisted

that the instructions of the officers in charge have to be followed. All refugees will be under the camp discipline.

11. It must be insisted that no evacuee may leave the camp unless permitted by the camp commander.
12. People should be advised that they should keep calm at all stages and that the personal dangers would be minimised if the instructions are obeyed promptly. (Para 2.234)

CRC/156: Immediately after hearing of evacuation advisory of the State Government, the residents of the notified AGD would take the following actions.

1. Secure their movable valuable properties as best as they can storing in upper floors, burying some underground, if that is possible, and taking similar measures.
2. Let the cattle/poultry/pets loose and let them seek safer places by use of their natural instincts. The cattle should be marked/branded for later identification.
3. Collect and pack the goods/materials that are permitted to be taken by the authorities.
4. If the roads to the identified shelters are open, to proceed immediately with the family towards these destinations.
5. If the roads are cut off by flood water and if boats are available, to make use of them to go to the directed gathering points for collection by the Evacuating Authorities or to the shelters/refugee camps.
6. If the persons are already marooned, then they should make the best safety arrangements as are possible under the circumstances — finding and securing a local shelter, making provisions for emergency food/medicine, trying to arrange distress signals for drawing the attention of the rescue authorities so that they can rush through relief/rescue operations.
7. While at the shelters/refugee camps, the discipline there must be strictly obeyed. No body may leave the camps till permitted by the camp commander. (Para 2.234)

CRC/157: Adequate Police arrangements should be made at the Cyclone shelters/relief camps/gathering points to see that the refugees are protected against unruly/antisocial elements. (Para 2.234)

CRC/158: The following format may be used for CAs which are to be broadcast by the State Government over their communication channels.

Format 2

Format for the Cyclone Advisory (CA) Part of the Cyclone Bulletin

1. Serial Number of the Cyclone: Year X, Month Y, Serial No. Z.
2. Authority of issuance of the CA:
3. Serial Number of the Cyclone Advisory:
4. Date/time of issuance of the CA:
5. Description of Area under warning:

   Warning Status: Alert/Danger/Great Danger/Warning/Nil warning

   Particulars of Warning:

   Cyclone Advisory:

(a) Precautions against flying objects
(b) Precautions against storm surges
(c) Precautions against fire
(d) Protection and storing of movable property
(e) Advice about food stock, medicine, fuel for cooking and emergency lights
(f) Evacuation Orders: Including address/location of cyclone shelters/Refugee Camps/Gathering Points
(g) Advice about Rescue/Relief/Rehabilitation

6. Nearest Cyclone Advisory and Operation Centre (CAOC):
   Gram Panchayat Office
   Local Post Office
   Municipality Office
   Police Thana (Para 2.235)

CRC/159: Though all the facilities provided at permanent Cyclone Shelters can not be provided at the temporary Refugee Camps, the District Collector should ensure the following basic ones:

1. Storage tank for drinking water.
2. Emergency diesel generator set.
3. Public toilets and water closets.
4. Common Kitchen and common place of eating.
5. Adequate sewerage system immune to storm surge/floods.
6. First Aid centre, epidemic fighting centre with public health experts for inspection/advice medical care unit with trained doctors/nurses/attendants.
7. A TC system immune to cyclone like WT system/transistor receivers, etc.
8. A team of administrative/technical/medical personnel to care of all problems as they arise. A camp commander must be appointed by the concerned District Collector.
9. Some identifying mark — pennants/baloons in life saving orange colour which are visible from a long distance. (Para 2.236).

CRC/160: The District Collector after discussing the matter at the DCC will take the following executive actions in AsGD:

1. Move the evacuation and rescue personnel and equipments and vehicles of the State Transport System and other commandered transport vehicles : Cars, lorries, buses, boats, launches, etc., to the identified points in the district. If necessary the help of the Defence Forces may be sought at this point.
2. About 12 hrs. before anticipated land fall, forcible evacuation of people and cattle from the AsGD — low lands, littoral areas, deltas and estuaries and islands should start taking them to demarcated places of shelter. The agency mainly responsible for this will be the Police, but if necessary, the District Collectors may seek help from the Defence forces for men and equipments.
3. Persons in other areas should be informed in the CAs of their respective shelters and gathering points, health centres and relief distribution centres.
4. The houses and properties abandoned as result of evacuation should be protected against antisocial elements by mobile land and water police as soon as that is possible. Unless public confidence is generated in this matter, evacuation may have to be done only by applying force on reluctant people. The Police

Department should therefore be asked by the District Collectors to make all efforts to infuse such confidence in the public. If necessary local reliable persons could be mobilised to help in this operation.

5. The Organisation like the PWD in charge of public buildings should be requested to inspect them and take suitable actions like strengthening them against immediate dangers of collapse as a result of the fury of the cyclone wind/storm surge.
6. The public health workers should be moved to their stations and kept on the alert for rendering first aids to cyclone victims and to implement epidemic preventive measures especially in the AsGD where the problems are the same as those resulting from large scale floods caused by rivers or dam bursts. (Para 2.237)

CRC/161: As soon as the warring is upgraded to 'Cyclone Warning' the District Collector should take all steps to maintain essential services as much as possible. The following steps *inter alia* must be taken by him:

1. *Maintenance of power service:* During the actual time of passage of cyclone over any area, it may be dangerous to let the cables through high power transmission towers carry electric power. The State Electricity Board should therefore disconnect the supply of electricity to selected areas in AsGD to prevent accidents and injuries. Also there may be urgent need to have electric power in special public places where hospitals, cyclone shelters, relief/refugee camps and evacuation routes are located. Generators, already moved into places where they are urgently needed, should be worked by trained technical personnel. The PWD may be the agency for running these generator sets. The State Electricity Board and similar metropolitan electricity generating organisation should have a master plan according to which protective switches would be operated to take off power from the High Tension lines and rerouting the electric power along safe guarded High Tension lines with a high priority right of way to important places in a cyclone scene : Cyclone shelters, relief/refugee camps, public health centres/hospitals.
2. *Supply of drinking water:* If there are over head storage drinking water tank the public water distribution system should be maintained by lifting water to them. It should also be possible to

run deep tube wells in the AsGD/AsD through the entire 'Cyclone Warning' period.

3. *Supply of minimum food material :* At the cyclone shelters, the relief/refugee camps, public health centres/hospitals and for general public consumption, enough stock of rice, wheat, puffed/pressed rice, grams, potatoes, cooking media, etc., should be built up. The rationing system for distribution should be tightened up. The Department of Supplies should assign the highest priority to keeping sufficient reserve of food materials at the stores just outside the AsGD so that these can be transported to the CYSHELs/Refugee Camps/distressed people as soon as possible.
4. *Supply of kerosene, diesel oil, storage battery* : Enough stock of these materials should be available in the normal distribution system. Stocks should be available at the cyclone shelters, relief/refugee camps and public health centres/hospitals and for transport used for evacuation. The Department of Supplies should ensure that sufficient stock of these materials are available for distribution to all the above centres.
5. *Supply of medicine and drugs :* An adequate supply of the necessary medicines/vaccines/drugs/chemicals for prevention of epidemics should be rushed to the relief/refugee camps/public health centres/hospitals and the stock should be maintained all through the duration of the cyclones and for some time during the post cyclone phase till the camps are disbanded and the refugee return to their homes. Teams of medical men/epidemic experts/paramedical technicians should have by this time moved to their stations at the relief/refugee camps, cyclone shelters, public health centres and hospitals. The Department of Public Health should ensure that these materials are stocked at all the above centres well in advance of the cyclone.
6. *Maintenance of the evacuation routes and the essential roads and transport :* For purposes of evacuation/rescue the designated escape routes to the gathering points, relief/refugee camps, cyclone shelters, public health centres and hospitals should be kept open and maintained in usuable condition during this phase of the cyclone. The vehicles of the State Transport System and those mobilised from other sources should be maintained in good condition by teams of technical personnel and arrangements made for their garaging and the personnel and

found to drive them. The Department of Roads and Transports should be given all this responsibility. In particular the PWD should ensure that these roads together with the bridges on route are in good condition, or take remedial measures if they are not, well in advance of the cyclone. During the 'Cyclone Alert' phase the PWD would be expected to supervise all operations for keeping the roads clear of obstacles fallen trees, rubbles, etc. The State Transport should be given the special executive responsibility for moving the refugee to safe places.

7. *Vigilance over drainage/sewerage systems and river banks/irrigation channels/tanks/hydrodams :* It would be the joint responsibility of the irrigation Department and the Public Engineering Department to take all operational measures to prevent floods. The most important measures would be:

(a) To keep the head regulators of the irrigation system serving the AsGD closed and let the water flow down the river course;

(b) The Village Officers/Surpanches/Panchayat Pradhans would be alerted to intensify patrolling of river banks/irrigation channels/tanks/hydrodams and bring to the notice of the concerned engineers the anticipated locations/moments of possible breaches of the banks/hydrodams for corrective measures to be taken; and

(c) The Public Health Engineering Department should keep constant vigilance over the drainage/sewerage system round the places of habitation to prevent water logging and accumulation of flood water and remove promptly all debris blocking these systems. (Para 2.238)

CRC/162: As soon as the warning is upgraded to 'Cyclone Warning' all vehicles moving on the roads through AsGD/AsD should be directed to move and to wait in places of comparative safety, prepared in advance at the direction of the Chief Engineer — Roads and Transport Department. (Para 2.239)

CRC/163: When the warning is upgraded to 'Cyclone Warning' the trains passing through the AsGD should be brought to rest at the nearest railway station without any waste of time and berthed there till the warning is downgraded. (Para 2.240)

CRC/164: As soon as the trains passing through AsGD have been brought to the nearest railway stations, relief operations should be started by the Railway and Revenue authorities. An enquiry office should be started at these stations with a public address system. Stock of drinking water, rice, puffed/pressed rice, *channa, chapathis,* and lemon should be maintained at the stations and milk and biscuits for the children. Medical teams should be posted at the stations. The Station Masters should keep in close contact with appropriate Railway officials at local/divisional level. (Para 2.240)

CRC/165: On receipt of the 'Cyclone Warning' signal the Port Authorities should *inter alia* take the following actions:

1. All vessels should be brought into sheltered waters and marred firmly with the masts lowered down.
2. Some of the bigger vessels, if denied safe berths at the ports due to lack of space, may be advised to move out to demarcated areas on the open sea, if there is a time, where they may be safer than in the ports.
3. The general precautionary measures advised for cyclone safe guarding of electrical installations such as sub-stations, barricading of doors/windows/other openings in buildings and securing of movable objects, etc., should be immediately put into operation.
4. At the discretion of the Port Master, the electrical power may be cut off during the duration of the second phase of the emergency to avoid casualties from overturned electric poles and exposure to live wires. All transmission towers should have been strengthened during the 'Cyclone Alert' period or earlier.
5. Booms of all cranes and similar machineries should be lowered and put to rest on the ground.
6. All the general cyclone precuationaries recommended to make buildings safe against cyclones should be immediately applied to all godowns/sheds in the port.
7. The appropriate storm signal should be hoisted which should be kept up to date every time new information is received over the CBs broadcast by AIR or from the concerned ACWC/CWC or from the Port Meteorological Office (PMO) (Para 2.241)

V.D.(3) *Code of Post Cyclone Measures to be taken after the 'Cyclone Dewarning' Signal is Broadcast — The Third Phase*

CRC/166: After the cyclone has weakened, the ACWC/CWC should send the 'Cyclone Dewarning' signals to the SCYC, which in turn should relay the message to the concerned DCCs. The concerned CCRs should then issue the 'Cyclone Dewarning' signal to all the units of the CDMO which in turn should transmit the message to officials such as Gram Panchayat Pradhans, Chairman of the City Municipalities, concerned officers of the State Government — Police officers, etc., and the concerned officers of the Central Government — P&T Officers, Defence units working in the locality, etc. This would inform the 'Cyclone Dewarning' message broadcast directly by AIR. (Para 2.242)

CRC/167: After the 'Cyclone Dewarning' signal has been issued, the concerned ACWC/CWC should issue a summary of report of the various aspects of the cyclone through the medium of AIR so that the affected population and various groups of warnees are aware of all that has happened. (Para 2.242)

CRC/168: Immediately after the receipt of the 'Cyclone Dewarning' signal, the concerned District Collector should start the First stage Cyclone Damage Assessment (CDMA) which must be completed as soon as possible so that Rescue/Relief/Restoration works may start. The main object of this assessment is mainly to:

1. Review the state of the TCCs from the CCRs to the units of the CDMW in the affected areas up to the village/city levels that may have been snapped by the cyclone.
2. Locate the areas that have been cut off, i.e., which can be approached only by boats or after clearance of debris on the roads leading to them, and determine the number of marooned people/cattle in these areas.
3. Estimate the number of refugees already in the CYSHELs (Cyclone Shelters) Refugee Camps and quantify their basic needs: food/ clothing/medicine, etc.
4. Estimate the number/locations of the public utilities put out of operation where restoration is urgently needed for reviving the essential services.
5. Examine specially the public health engineering system and assess the locations where epidemic may break out.
6. Estimate the number and location of dead bodies lying on the roads and other places that have to be removed. (Para 2.245)

CRC/169: Since most of the areas where cyclone victims are marooned can not be approached if boats and powered launches are not available in sufficient numbers, the quickest method of locating these areas would be by aerial survey of the affected areas by the planes of the IAF. (Para 2.245)

CRC/170: The concerned District Collectors should send to the P&T Department the list of the TCCs in the units of the CDMW in the affected area that are non-operational and request the Department for prompt restoration of these channels. They should also make every effort to despatch inspectors to these units to receive the local reports on the TCCs and receive a first and impression of the damages done by the cyclone. (Para 2.245)

CRC/171: The District Collectors of the ravaged areas should set up at their respective CCRs Cyclone Damage Maps for the regions under their respective jurisdictions in order to have a firm basis for planning strategies for Rescue/Restoration works there. (Para 2.245)

CRC/172: Immediately after the 'Cyclone Dewarning' signal, the concerned District Collectors should start the First Stage CDMA and get the first reports of the locations of the marconed persons and damages caused by the cyclones. For this purpose assessment teams led by Tahsildars and Deputy Tahsildars should visit the spots indicated by aerial surveys. (Para 2.245)

CRC/173: All snapped TCC links—Telephone, Telex, TP, etc., should be restored by the P&T Department which should assign to this responsibility the highest priority. (Para 2.247)

CRC/174: The District Collector should ensure that immediately after a cyclone all rubbles and debris from collapsed houses and buildings, etc., should be removed expeditiously in the village/city areas to restore communication. The PWD Department should undertake this work. (Para 2.248)

CRC/175: Immediately after a cyclone the District Collectors should ensure that the Roads Transport Department take immediate steps to remove the fallen trees. The villagers may be permitted to gather and remove these trees if they can do that quickly so that roads can be cleared without loss of time. For cutting/sectioning these trees local labour/local equipments should be mobilised. The whole work would be done under the direction of the District Collectors who should be given absolute discretion in the matter. Mobile squads and vehicles should be commandeered to carry away these trees. (Para 2.248)

CRC/176: The PWD should set up immediately after the cyclone squads of engineers/workers with the necessary equipments/ materials to repair the damaged roads and bridges quickly at least on a temporary basis to permit resumption of transport systems by roads. The District Collectors in the affected regions must be informed by the PWD when the roads/bridges have been repaired. (Para 2.248)

CRC/177: The District Collectors of the Cyclone ravaged areas should issue suitable warnings to the public against playing with loose dangling electrical wires from electric lamp posts and high voltage transmission towers. The nearest authorities should be informed immediately when their existence is detected. The States Electricity Board/Other Electric Supply Organisation should take immediate steps on receipt the 'Cyclone Dewarning' signal to clear the roads of uprooted electric poles and fallen electricity transmission towers and restore supply of electricity to all consumers as soon as possible. The District Collectors of the concerned areas should be informed of all these actions as soon as they are completed. (Para 2.249)

CRC/178: The order of priority of restoration of electric power should be in the following order: (1) AIR, (2) Water Works, (3) Hospitals, (4) All Relief Camps/Cyclone/Cyclone Shelters/Relief Centres, (5) Public Health Engineering Works, (6) Railways and Parts, (7) Government Offices connected with the CDMW, (8) Private Residences, (9) Agriculture, (10) Commercial concerns — Markets/Stores, (11) Industries, (12) Public Utilities. (Para 2.249)

CRC/179: The concerned District Collectors should arrange installation of mobile pumps at strategic places/remote points to drain out the standing water from the fields and roads and places of habitation in the inundated areas, and route it into the drainage channels and river ways immediately after the cyclone has passed. (Para 2.250)

CRC/180: Squads formed by the Public Health Engineering Department should inspect all drainage installations in the areas ravaged by the cyclone to see that they are in good working condition. Any necessary repairs and technical problems that may arise therefrom should be solved by this Department so that the standing water can be removed promptly. (Para 2.250)

CRC/181: The District Collectors of the ravaged areas should collect informations about all the breaches of the water storage systems in these areas — hydrodams/water reservoirs/lakes/ tanks/bunds, etc., which are causing input to the standing water resulting from precipitation cause by the cyclone. Attempts should be made to repair these breaches, at least on a temporary basis, so that essential services can be restored. The concerned District Collectors should request to the PWD to undertake such repairs immediately. The Department of Supplies should provide all the materials necessary for these repairs. (Para 2.251)

CRC/182: Permanent repairs of the breaches of the water storage systems in the affected areas may wait till the second stage of Cyclone Damage Assessment has been completed so that an estimate can be made of the budgetary provisions that may be necessary. These repairs can be undertaken at a normal pace in due course. (Para 2.251)

CRC/183: The District Collectors of the affected areas should have completed informations about the whereabouts of the stranded trains and the schedule of moving them to their destinations. (Para 2.252)

CRC/184: The Railway Department should immediately inspect the nature/location of damage to the tracks caused by the cyclone and take prompt steps to repair them. (Para 2.252)

CRC/185: The Railway Department should restore normal traffic of passenger/goods trains as soon as possible. (Para 2.252)

CRC/186: As long as the Railway Department can not restore the normal running of the trains, it should consider each railway station in the affected area as a Relief Camp and provide all relief to the stranded passengers as is arranged in other Relief centres. It is important to have Public Address Systems installed in each of these stations to inform the public of the latest position about train movements/disseminate relief advisories. (Para 2.252)

CRC/187: The Railway Department should make every effort to start the trains moving from where they have been stranded after the tracks have been repaired or by diversions to alternative routes. A senior Railway Officer of the Division should be given the responsibility of taking all decisions about restoration of the Railway service. (Para 2.252)

CRC/188: The Railway Department should arrange trains wagons for movement of relief materials and cyclone victims to Relief Centres/Cyclone Shelters/Refugee Camps. (Para 2.252)

CRC/189: As soon as the cyclone ravaged roads/bridges have been restored, these should be opened to all the normal types of transports : lorries/buses/taxis/private motor cars, etc. In particular these roads can be used by the vehicles requisitioned for evacuation/rescue operations for the marooned persons. Road signs should be prominently displayed to inform the public whether the roads are useful or not. (Para 2.254)

CRC/190: The State Authorities should arrange normal trade and commerce to resume as soon as it becomes possible for goods and commodities to move freely by roads/railways/water ways to the normal market places. High priority must be given to bring into the market items like food/fuel/medicines and materials for repair of damaged houses: bamboos/cement/sand/bricks/agricultural seeds/professional tools, etc. (Para 2.255)

CRC/191: The Police should increase their vigil and patrolling and guard duties to ensure security to life and property of cyclone victims. (Para 2.256)

CRC/192: Identified anti-social elements should be rounded up during the period of the cyclone to prevent looting and plundering of property and commission of other crimes. (Para 2.256)

CRC/193: The District Collector should organise orderly return to their homes of the cyclone victims, evacuated to Cyclone Shelters/Refugee Camps. For this purpose all help must be given to the refugees, the most important of which is transport. The vehicles of the State Transport Corporation can be put to use in this operation. (Para 2.257)

CRC/194: As soon as the areas where the cyclone victims have been marooned have been detected from aerial surveys, the concerned District Collectors should if necessary appeal to the local Defence Authorities for help in rescuing the marooned people. (Para 2.259)

CRC/195: The concerned District Collectors should convene a meeting of their DCC after the 'Cyclone Dewarning' signal to discuss and prepare rescue plans. They should also prepare maps showing the location of the Cyclone Shelter/Refugee Camp to which the cyclone victims from a particular zone have to be transported. These Rescue Operation Maps should be put up at the CCRs. (Para 2.259)

CRC/196: Rescue teams should be formed promptly after the 'Cyclone Dewarning' signal from State Government Officials trained in rescue operations and units of the local Defence Organisation/ Civil Defence Department/Coast guards. All equipments necessary for rescue operations should be issued from the nearest Cyclone Store by the concerned District Collectors. (Para 2.259)

CRC/197: Transport vehicles : Buses/lorries/tempos/cars/or powered launches/boats/country boats which have been already commandeered should be put at the disposal of the Rescue Teams by the concerned District Collectors as and when demanded. The types of vehicles to be used should depend on the nature of the terrain and the state of distress of the cyclone victims. (Para 2.259)

CRC/198: The Department of Irrigation/the Defence Authorities should be able to provide sufficient number of powered launches/amphibian vehicles for Rescue/Relief Operations. Similarly the State Transport Department/Private Transport Organisations should be able to provide the buses/lorries/tempos needed for the same operations. The concerned District Collectors should make use of all these sources to collect the necessary transport vehicles and build up the Rescue/Relief Organisation quickly without loss of time. (Para 2.259)

CRC/199: The concerned District Collectors should call upon the local Defence Authorities to arrange aerial dropping of precooked food packets/medicines/chemicals for epidemic control and evacuate by helicopter those who are seriously ill/injured in areas which can not be reached by the rescue teams. Trained officials of the State Government can be transported by air to these areas to take control of the cyclone victims gathered there. (Para 2.259)

CRC/200: The State Authorities should call for help/direct participation from social welfare organisations and charitable bodies in the relief and rehabilitation work among the cyclone victims necessary after a cyclone and in particular for volunteers to work with the State Government officials. (Para 2.262)

CRC/201: If the preliminary assessments of the damages caused by the cyclone appear to be very large, the District Public Relation Officer of the concerned State Government should issue appeals for voluntary donations of money/relief materials and make arrangements to receive them. (Para 2.262)

CRC/202: Relief Centres should be established in close proximity of the Cyclone Refugee Camps or at the Cyclone shelters (CYSHELs) and put under the control of empowered State Government Officers. (Para 2.263)

CRC/203: All cyclone relief materials:

1. Stock of food materials : rice grains, wheat, flour dals, various vegetables — potatoes, cauliflowers, cabbages, etc., cooking spices/masalas — chillies, tamarind, turmeric powders, cooking media : oils of various types — mustard, coconut, rape seed oil, ground nut oil, cooking fuel : kerosene, coal, etc., cooking utensils and other accessories
2. Hurricanes, lanterns, hazzacs with adequate stock of fuels
3. Common medicines and medical treatment accessories
4. General medicines/chemicals for epidemic control should be stored by the Civil Supplies Department, Food Corporation of

India and similar organisations at the Relief Centres for distribution to the various Refugee Camps/CYSHELS. For distribution of the materials the lorries should be brought to the Relief Centres for loading and then the destination slips given to their drivers to take the materials to the Refugee Camps/CYSHELS and to those villages whose residents need these materials urgently. (Para 2.263)

CRC/204: The CCRs of the District Collectors should keep a close watch on the requests for the relief materials and their prompt distribution. It must be seen by the District Collectors that in such procurement/distribution no time is lost. (Para 2.263)

CRC/205: Relief Teams will be formed by the concerned District Collectors with State Government Officials and volunteers from Social Service Organisations/Charitable Bodies to carry out the actual Relief Work at the CYSHELS/Refugee Camps or at the actual villages ravaged by the cyclone. (Para 2.263)

CRC/206: All State Officials/Volunteers from Social Service Organisations/Charitable Bodies, and members of Rescue/Relief teams should report their activities to the concerned District Collector atleast twice daily and keep the CCRs/Tahsildars informed of their position/movement in the affected areas. (Para 2.263)

CRC/207: The concerned District Collectors in collaboration with the Police Department should form squads to remove/dispose of the dead bodies and carcasses of animals immediately after the 'Cyclone Dewarning' signal before their decomposition sets in. Attempts should be made by the Missing Person Enquiry Offices formed by the District Collector with the help of the village officials – Grampanchayat Pradhans and the local surviving people to identify the names of the dead persons before final disposal. Final disposal of dead bodies may pose difficulties and what may have to be ultimately done in mass burial/funeral. The concerned District Collectors should make all arrangements for such disposals — providing of transport for removal of bodies, fuel like coal/kerosene, etc. (Para 2.264)

CRC/208: The District Medical and Health Officer should send teams with the necessary drugs/vaccines/chemicals to the ravaged villages/Refugee Camps/CYSHELS for carrying out a programme of: (1) mass vaccination, (2) distributing the necessary palliatives and vitamins, and (3) implementing epidemic control measures specially against spread of cholera/dysentery. At the cities the city municipality authorities should take up this responsibility through their officials. (Para 2.264)

CRC/209: Wells and water tanks which may provide drinking water to the people living in the affected regions, particularly in the villages/Refugee Camps/CYSHELS, should be treated by the Public Health Engineering Department after the cyclone. These sources with polluted water should be clearly marked out by prominent notices and people warned against using them. A vigorous programme of chlorinisation of the water at these sources, should be undertaken immediately by teams of public health workers under the direction of the District Medical and Health Officer. (Para 2.264)

CRC/210: Enquiry offices should be set up by the District Collectors for giving informations about dead/injured/missing persons at all centres of CDMW/Cyclone Advisory and Operation Centres (CAOCs)/Cyclone Shelters/Refugee Camps/public places. As soon as the list of these persons can be prepared they should be exhibited at all these places. The work should start with the disposal of the dead bodies and preparation of list of refugees at the Cyclone Shelters/Refugee Camps and finish before the second stage of Cyclone Damage Assessment (CDMA) is started. The assessment of dead/injured/missing persons should be handed over to the second stage CDMA teams for entering into the Cyclone Damage Assessment Form 1 referred to in CRC/212. (Para 2.265)

CRC/211: After the refugees are well settled in the Cyclone Shelters/Refugee Camps, the concerned Divisional Revenue Officer should form Cyclone Damage Assessment teams to visit the ravaged areas for assessing the physical/economic damages caused by the cyclone. Each team should include a Gazetted Officer and another Officer not below the rank of Deputy Tahasildar. The assessment should be entered in prescribed forms supplied to the teams and submitted to the Divisional Revenue Officer. (Para 2.266)

CRC/212: The Cyclone Damage Assessment Formats cover the total damage caused by cyclones and tropical depressions and associated heavy rainfalls and the storm surges, floods and landslides, etc. There should be damage assessments to be recorded in two parts, both following the recommendations of ESCAP:

1. *Form 1*: to cover the description of the physical damages in terms of injury and loss of life and cattle, and damage of property caused by wind and water.

2. *Form 2*: to cover the damages in various sectors of the economy.

Both forms should be filled up by direct inspection to the extent possible and not from press reports not verified from authoritative sources, or from reports untrained observers. (Para 2.267)

CRC/213: The Cyclone Damage Assessment Form 1 (Physical Damage) should have the following format:

Format 3

Form 1

Physical Damages Caused by Cyclone

1. Cyclone Serial number
2. Cyclone Regime — Dates/time
3. Region of Survey:
   Geographic Description
   Number of villages
   Number of towns
4. Date of Survey
5. Sources of information
6. Casualties (Numbers)

A. *Human Lives:*
   (a) Number of Dead
   (b) Number of Missing
   (c) Number of Injured

Sub-total

   (d) People affected
   (i) Number of Families
   (ii) Number of persons

B. *Live Stock:*

   Cattle/poultry/pet
   (a) Number of Dead
   (b) Number of Missing

(c) Number of Injured

Sub-total

(d) Domestic animal
population affected
Cattle/poultry/pet

7. Crop destruction/damage
Name of crop destroyed

Area with the damaged crop (Hectare)

Total cultivated area
with the crop (Hectare)

Estimated damaged crop

Estimated potential yield

Sub-total

8. Loss of trees (in number)
(a) in orchards
(b) Others

Sub-total

9. House and Buildings damaged/
destroyed (number)
A. Huts
(a) Number completely destroyed
(b) Number damaged

Sub-total

B. Residential Buildings
(a) Number completely destroyed
for washed away

(b) Number partially destroyed or submerged above plinth level
(c) Number submerged below plinth level

Sub-total

C. Non-residential buildings
(a) Number completely destroyed or washed away
(b) Number partly destroyed or submerged above plinth level
(c) Number submerged below plinth level

Sub-total

10. Damage to Public Utilities
Type of utility damaged
Nature of damage
11. Loss to fishermen
Boats lost
Loss of fishing equipments
12. Inundated and/or area with damaged crop/houses (in hectare)
(a) Cultivated land
(b) House lots
(c) Others : Industrial complexes, etc.

Sub-total

Total

13. General Remarks

Signature of Assessment Officer

CRC/214: The following points should be kept in mind while filling up Form 1 of Cyclone Damage Assessment:

1. Casualties should be entered in rows 6A(a), (b) and (c). 'Dead' means confirmed deads or presumed to be dead (row 6A(a). 'Missing' includes who have not been traced after the cyclone but whose death can not be presumed (row 6A(b)). 'Injured' encompasses all those injured regardless of the seriousness of the injury (6A(c)). Population affected include thehomeless, evacuees and in CYSHELS/Relief Camps, i.e., those qualifying for assistance for relief and rehabilitation as also those whose routine of normal life has been snapped (row 6A(d)).
2. Casualties under rows 6B(a), (b) and (c) similarly include livestock : cattle, poultry and pet animals dead, missing and injured (row 6B).
3. Under row 7 the loss should be recorded under each type of crop : rice, wheat, potatoes, etc. Not only should the areas covering the total cultivated land in the cyclone ravaged areas be entered under 7, but also the areas bearing the crops damaged by wind and water must be entered. If possible the estimates should also be made of the total potential yield of a particular crop in the ravaged area as also of the damaged crop so that it is possible to speak in terms of percentage losses. The area of damaged cultivated lands should be used to estimate monetary value of crops damage by multiplying the area covered by the particular agricultural product direct if estimate can not be made of the damaged crops and the appropriate unit price of the commodity.
4. Loss of fruit bearing trees can be similarly converted (row 8(a) from the number lost into equivalent money value. Loss of other trees should also be recorded to assess the ecological disturbance (row 8(b)). Under row 8(a) would also come things like coconut trees/palms/casurina trees, etc., which dominate the landscape in the coastal regions. Also must be considered fruit trees like mango trees/banana plantations/ vine yards, etc., which are found all along the eastern coast.
5. Huts under 9A will be almost all in the villages Buildings affected (rows 9B and 9C) are classed as 'residential' and 'non-residential'. Under the classification 'residential' comes private houses, Government buildings, schools, libraries, community

centres, places of worship, hospitals, hostels, hotels, etc. Under 'non-residential' is included storehouses, garages, outhouses, etc. Under row 9(a) B & C those buildings are entered that can not be used any more and must be reconstructed. Row 9(b) A&B should cover those buildings that can be repaired for reuse.

6. Under row 10 will come description of damages to all public utilities — roads/bridges, electricity generation/transmission system, hydrodams/bunds/dykes/water/reservoirs/irrigation heads, water drainage/sewerage systems, etc. The physical, damages only would be recorded : total destruction, severe damage, light damage.
7. Under row 11 would come loss of fishing boats/fishing equipments like nets/navigation aids and fishing catches.
8. Under the heading 'inundated and/or area with damaged crops/houses' the most important item is that related to cultivated land (row 12(a) including paddy fields and those with various crops and house lots, industrial area and other areas inundated which should be recorded in row 12(b) and (c) for future guidance during re-construction when land zoning controls may have to be applied. Also valuable guidance can be obtained from this record for predicting storm surges and floods if this data can be correlated with cyclone parameters and rain falls. (Para 2.269)

CRC/215: The CDMA Form 2 (Economic Loss) should have the following format.

Format 4

Form 2

Cyclone Damage Assessment of Economic Losses (in Lakhs of Rupees)

1. Cyclone Serial Number
2. Cyclone Regime : Dates/Time
3. Region of Survey
   Geographic Description
   Number of Villages

Number of Towns

4. Dates of Survey
5. Sources of Information
6. Loss of Livestock
7. Loss of agricultural products/Loss to Agriculture Department Stores
8. Loss of private property
9. Loss of Government/local/municipal properties
10. Industrial loss
11. Loss of public work facilities : Irrigation/Electricity/Drainage/Roads/Bridges/Water Storage Systems
12. Loss of public utilities
13. Total loss in Monetary terms

Signature of Assessment Officer

(Para 2.270)

CRC/216: The items appearing in Form 2 of CDMA must be understood in following terms:

Row 6: Loss of livestock : Loss of livestock would include estimates of the price of all cattle/poultry/pets killed by the cyclone. The estimates may have to be indirectly estimated by judging the loss of cattle, etc., by drowning and burial under debris. A direct assessment based on reports from the surviving victims tend to overstress the losses.

Row 7: Loss of Agricultural Product: This item incudes the loss of:

1. Rice crops, vegetables, fruits,
2. Marine products,
3. Forest products,
4. Loss due to suspension of agricultural activities,
5. Materials stocked in Agriculture Stores — Cut crop/seeds/fertilisers/insecticides/fungicides/agriculture equipments, etc.

This group (Row 7) generally constitutes a high proportion of the total flood damage. The crop damage may be estimated by assessing the area under a particular crop damaged and the average loss of that crop per hectare and then summing up the amounts for all the crops. In estimated damage in terms of money the unit prices of various types of crops have to be considered. Crop damage must be estimated by assessing the extent of damage due to inundation and burial under debris. Loss of livestocks may be similarly estimated:

Row 8 : Loss of property : This includes:

1. Houses and buildings,
2. Household articles,
3. Stored goods : Tools and equipments or farmers, etc.

These should be estimated by surveys and listings. If possible the number of houses and buildings, their floor areas and the extent of damage which must be valued by some established norm of valuation for repair or reconstruction. Household articles include such things as clothes, furnitures, domestic appliances, water pumps, means of transports, books, etc. If percentage can be worked out for damages of household articles then the assessment may become simpler. Damage to stored goods — professional tools and equipments, etc., can be similarly estimated.

Row 9: Loss of Government/local municipal properties : This row should include loss to mining, construction, manufacturing and wholesale, retail and other properties. But loss to industries, agriculture, fishing, transport, communication and other public utilities should be excluded here.

Row 10: Industrial loss : The industries concerned should be requested to furnish the damages incurred. Indirect damage due to suspension of routine activities may be evaluated by sampling methods. The relevant data in this connection are the number of operational days lost, the number of workers affected, and the value added by industries (per worker per day). However often percentages are assumed for the total loss of general property and industry.

Row 11: Loss of public work facilities : This includes:

1. Agricultural lands
2. Irrigation and Drainage installations
3. Roads and bridges
4. Flood Control installations
5. Harbour, fishing and airport installations
6. Erosion control systems and land slides

7. Streets and roads, urban drainage systems
8. Other public works

All these include all facilities to restore which Government funds would be necessary including restoration of farm lands.

Row 12: Loss of public utilities : These include *inter alia* the following facilities:

1. State and private railways
2. Other land, air and water transportation systems
3. Telecommunication Systems
4. Power generation, transmission and distribution systems
5. Water supply systems
6. Gas supply

These mainly consist of organisations operated by the Central Government, State Government or autonomous agencies. Damages should be estimated in terms of buildings structures (excluding houses), rolling stocks, ships and boats, plants and machineries, and other capital assets and stocked materials and components, including losses incurred through the suspension in full or in part of operations.

CRC/217: After the Divisional Revenue Officer has collected all the CDMAs from the various areas ravaged by the cyclones, he should prepare a complete Second Stage CDMA report and send it to the Secretary, Revenue Department of the State Government for further processing for the request going from the State Government for financial assistance from the Central Government and advising the State Government about expenditures on financial relief to cyclone victims and the various expenditures on other heads requested at the various stages of the CDMW. (Para 2.272)

CRC/218: After the Cyclone, the Commissioner for Cyclone Rescue, Relief and Rehabilitation should prepare a final report on it, containing:

1. The success/failure of the Cyclone Monitoring System (CMS) as given by the report of the concerned ACWC/CWC.
2. The success/failure of the Cyclone Warning System (CWS).
3. The success/failure of the measures encoded in the Cyclone Emergency Action Plan (CEAP) of the concerned State

Government as prepared by the Revenue Department.

4. The total assessment of physical/economic damages and loss of life as given by the final report of the Second Stage Cyclone Damage Assessment (CDMA) prepared by the Secretary of the Revenue Department.
5. The total expenditures incurred in carrying through the measures encoded in the CEAP and how the financial problems were resolved as given by the final report of the Secretary of the Revenue Department.
6. The success/failure of the Community Preparedness Plan of the State against the cyclone (CPPC).
7. Plans for Rehabilitation/Reconstruction as prepared by the State Government.
8. Suggestions of remedial measures for any lacunae and for necessary long-term measures. (Para 2.273)

V.E. *Financial Management of Cyclone Disaster*

CRC/219: In general the expenditures for applying the CEAP in a coastal State during a cyclone would be very heavy. As the expenditures have to be met by both the State Government and the Central Government, it is necessary that adequate provisions are made by them in their financial outlays for the necessary funds. High priority should be given by both Governments to expenditures on this account. (Para 2.274)

CRC/220: The quantum of immediate subsistence financial assistance to cyclone victims should be considered by the Government of India for upward revision to enable them to survive with dignity. (Para 2.275)

CRC/221: The losses incurred by the cyclone victims should be classified under three broad heads. Under the first head should come those items for which the victim must make good the loss himself : his personal movable properties/professional tools, etc. The State Government may help him in this by giving loans on easy terms of repayment. Under the second head comes those losses which are the fruits of his labour or meant for trade like agricultural products, goods for commerce, etc. Much of this can be brought under in appropriate Insurance System. Under the third head comes such items as restoration of residences, restoration of agricultural fields, etc. For the technology of restoration R&D may be necessary and the results should be incorporated in the Community Preparedness Plan against Cyclones (CPPC). The State should undertake these reconstructions and the relocation of sites as a part of its CPPC as the expenses involved may be too much for individual victims. (Para 2.275)

CRC/222: The Government of India should encourage the Insurance Companies to cover the areas notorious for being areas of Danger and Great Danger and issue suitable directives, to them so that on payment of low premium rates, crops, lands, agricultural tools, live stocks : milch/drought animals and poultry/piggery, dwelling houses, tools and produces of small artisans and small scale industries, fishing equipments of fishermen, goods of small trading and business establishments and even human lives can come under insurance protection. Special arrangements should be made for assessment of damage and quick payments of the insured sums after a disaster. (Para 2.276).

CRC/223: The Government of India should set up a National Calamity Fund (NCF) by imposing levies. As soon as possible after the disaster, the cyclone affected State Government should make an assessment of the funds it would need for immediate relief and rehabilitation of the cyclone victims and make a request to the Government of India for liberal release of money from the NCF so that it can make the payment of the required subsidy and loans to the affected population. (Para 2.278).

CRC/224: The Government of India should have a scale measuring the severity of a disaster in terms of loss of life/property. Beyond a certain level in this scale (mild disaster) the State Government should be able to meet all the expenditures : Anticipatory/ Preparatory, Concurrent, Post disaster, from its own resources. Above this level and below another when the disaster can be termed severe, the present recommendations of the Seventh Finance Commission for Central Assistance should apply unchanged, i.e., the shares of the costs would be : Central Government 75 per cent, State Government 25 per cent. If this disaster is more severe the Central Government should be 100 per cent of the costs which would also include restoration/reinforcement of the facilities/preventives created by the State Government under its Community Preparedness Plan against Cyclone (CPPC). (Para 2.280)

CRC/225: Immediately after the occurrence of a natural calamity like cyclone, the Government of India can release some funds on an *ad hoc* basis after receiving the report of its Disaster Reconnaissance Team (DRT) visiting the affected State. With this assistançe immediate relief to individual victims and restoration activities can be taken up. (Para 2.281)

CRC/226: The Disaster Reconnaissance Team (DRT) of the Central Government should consist of technical officers *inter alia* from the following Ministries/Departments of the Central Government:

1. AIR
2. Central Water Commission
3. Central Power Commission
4. Central PWD
5. Post and Telegraph
6. Public Health
7. Public Health Engineering
8. Road and Transport Department
9. Ministry of Agriculture
10. Ministry of Finance
11. Ministry of Inland Waterways
12. Ministry of Shipping. (Para 2.281)

CRC/227: The DRT should visit the affected State immediately after invitation by its Chief Secretary. It should then have a series of meetings with the SCYC and discuss the Final Second State CDMA Report of damages caused by the cyclone as prepared by the Revenue Department of the State and make its own assessments by on spot inspections and interviews with samples of groups of victims in the AsD and AsGD. This will give the team an objective view of the disaster. (Para 2.281)

CRC/228: The final meeting of the DRT and the SCYC would be to consider the question of the ceiling of the legitimate Central Assistances to the affected State and also the quanta of fund allocations under different heads. (Para 2.281)

CRC/229: The DRT should submit to the Government of India its final report of the damages caused by the cyclone within three-four weeks after the 'Cyclone Dewarning' signal. (Para 2.281)

CRC/230: Through the process of discussion between the DRT and the SCYC outlined in recommendations CRC/225 to CRC/229, it is expected that the fears of the Central Government that the damages caused by the disaster have been over/exaggerated, would be dispelled. The report of DTA would assist the Government of India to establish the scale of the disaster and take decision on the quantum of financial assistance which can be given to the concerned State Government. (Para 2.281)

CRC/231: A National Finance Corporation for National Calamity (NFCNC) to mitigate disasters may be set up by the Government of India to provide long-term loans on easy terms and provide technical help to victims of cyclones and other natural disasters for reconstruction and rehabilitation for resuming their normal activities, reconstructing their damaged houses, acquiring various inputs for productions and reclaiming lands affected by disaster. (Para 2.283)

Group B.2: *Recommendations mainly for the Government of India and the Coastal State Governments/with Respect to — Community Preparedness Plan against Cyclone (CPPC).*

VI. *Suggestion for a Community Preparedness Plan against Cyclone (CPPC) for a Coastal State*

VI.A. *The Community Preparedness Plan against Cyclones (CPPC)*

CRC/232: The coastal states containing CPARs should include in their Disaster Plans, short- and long range measures to prepare the resident communities to face the threats and hazards of cyclones. All these measures should be incorporated into a Community Preparedness Plan against Cyclone (CPPC) for the State. (Para 2.284)

CRC/233: The Community Preparedness Measures against cyclones are for the benefit of the individual, the family, various sections of the population, residing in the CPARS of the coastal States, engaged in diverse economic activities — agriculture; fishing, trades and industries, etc., and various agencies of the Central and State Governments and those of private nature operating in these areas of the State — Defence, Post & Telegraph, Railways, Shipping, etc. The primary basic objectives of these measures are:

1. To reduce the risk potential of cyclone damage in the CPARs of the coastal state.
2. To educate the coastal community to respond to cyclones in a disciplined manner.
3. To train the State Administrative Officials to take control of a cyclone emergency by applying the CEAP of the concerned State swiftly without hesitation.

CRC/234 : The long-term aspects of the CPPC concerns with:

1. Installation of public utilities/facilities/organisations which help to protect the community against cyclones and providing an infrastructure for their maintenance.
2. Spreading the awareness of the hazards of cyclones among the public and educating them about the ways and means of meeting them.
3. Training the workers for CDMW.

The short-term aspect of the CPPC is:

1. To inspect all the public utilities/facilities/organisations at the beginning of the cyclone seasons every year to ensure that these are in a fit and proper condition to be used efficiently during a cyclone emergency. Any lacunae detected in these systems should be promptly remedied by the appropriate Department of the State/Central Government or the Coastal Development Authority.
2. To supervise and coordinate all repairs/reconstruction work after every cyclone disaster.

CRC/235: Implementation of the measures suggested in the Community Preparedness Plan against Cyclones (CPPC) and the maintenance of the various public utilities/installations set up in the State for it would need large outlay of funds. The State Government should provide for these outlays in their Five Year Plan Provisions as Plan Schemes and in their annual budgets to carry the schemes through.

VI.B. *Coastal Development Authority (CDA)*

CRC/236: Each coastal State should have its Central Development Authority (CDA) to prepare short and long range plans for development of the coastal areas in the State. Measures for reducing the dangers from cyclones for the community should form an important part of the task engaged to this body. (Para 2.289)

CRC/237: The management committee of the CDA may have the following composition:

Chairman To be appointed by the State Government.

Members Members to be nominated one from each of the following Ministries/Departments/Commissions/Authorities of the State/Central Governments.

A. *State Government*

1. Agriculture and Community Development Department
2. Education Department
3. Finance Department
4. Forest Department
5. Irrigation and Waterways Department
6. Panchayat Department
7. Planning Department
8. Police Department
9. Public Works Department
10. Public Health Engineering Department
11. Revenue Department
12. Roads and Transport Department
13. State Electricity Board.

B. *Central Government*

1. Agriculture Department
2. AIR
3. CPWD
4. Central Water Commission
5. Department of Environment
6. IMD — NHAC (Delhi)
7. Department of Ocean Development
8. Inland Water Ways Authority
9. Land Development Department
10. Ministry of Law — Legislative Department
11. P&T Department
12. Railways
13. Roads and Transport Department
14. Rural Development Department
15. Shipping Ministry. (Para 2.290)

CRC/238: Among the various tasks and responsibilities of the CDA of the coastal State the following would be relevant for the purpose of preparing the community for cyclones :

1. To establish close contacts with the SCYC for getting acquainted with the problems faced and the experience gained regarding the ravages of each cyclone landfalling in the State and to draw up long range plans for preparing the community against them after detailed risk evaluation by joint consultations.
2. To keep contacts with the ACC for consultation about the preparation of the CPPC of the coastal State.
3. To demarcate areas on the coastal strips where land zoning laws have to be enforced by it.
4. To demarcate areas on the coastal strips for which protection against storm surges may be possible by construction of bunds and be responsible for their constructions and maintenance.
5. To establish forest belts on the coastal strips for protection against cyclones and prevention of soil erosions caused by them.
6. To make arrangements for periodic dredging of rivers in the CPARs of the coastal State.
7. To formulate and implement plans for long-term soil and plant conservation in the CPARs.
8. To plan and implement an efficient drainage system in the CPARs to remove the standing flood water.
9. To establish a close network roads and bridges in the CPARs.
10. To formulate and implement plans for protection of agricultural products against cyclones and storm surges in the CPARs.
11. To lay down a set of buildings codes in the CPARs and act as consultants in this matter for private owners of house properties. The CDA should enforce the Building Codes for building.
12. To establish permanent cyclone shelters in the CPARs.
13. To plan, instal and maintain an efficient sewerage system in the CPARs.
14. To establish community hospitals at strategic points in the CPARs.
15. To introduce measures for protection of fishermen at sea.
16. To liaise with the P&T Department for installation of a snap proof TC system in the CPARs.

17. To prepare a detailed map of facilities/public utilities/installations in the CPARs of the coastal State available for CDMW showing:
    (a) Location of the forecasting centres: ACWC/CWC, FFOs of the CWCM/State Irrigation Department/IMD;
    (b) Locations of various departments of State/Central Government and various agencies involved in CDMW;
    (c) Agricultural lands;
    (d) Location of villages/towns;
    (e) Beeches;
    (f) Forest belts;
    (g) The TC network;
    (h) The road/bridge network;
    (i) The Waterways network;
    (j) The irrigation heads/hydrodams/lakes/water reservoirs and bunds/embankments/dykes for flood control, dredging points for rivers;
    (k) Areas prone to inundation;
    (l) The drainage system/location of drainage pumps — actual/possible sites;
    (m) Cyclone Shelters/possible sites for Refugee Camps;
    (n) Public hospitals, medical centres;
    (o) Stores of various types for disaster fighting;
    (p) Sewerage network;
    (q) Location of electric power houses and the electricity distribution network;
    (r) Tracks of Railways running through the CPARs together with the stations; and
    (s) Location of ports of various types, fishing ports, fishing villages.

18. To prepare Potential Cyclone hazard maps showing:

    (a) Possible breakdown of TCCs and alternative;
    (b) Possible areas of submergence under storm surges of a given height travelling in a given direction for a given landfall point;
    (c) Possible areas of submergence under a given amount/duration of rainfall;
    (d) Possible direction of water flow after dam burst/breach of

embankment, etc.;

(e) Possible areas where evacuation are generally necessary; and

(f) Possible locations of breakdown of road communications. (Para 2.291)

VI. C. *Highlights of a CPPC*

CRC/239: The concerned Coastal Development Authority (CDA) should examine the topology maps of the coastal strips in its State which were classified as CPARs in Recommendation CRC/6 and demarcate zones where housing/ industrial constructions have to be discouraged and controls have to be imposed on the construction of buildings and the pace and type of development activities. Also areas where raising of normal agricultural crops are hazardous should also be marked out. Such areas should be made known to the public with warnings that they come under land use and zoning laws which would be strictly enforced if it becomes necessary. (Para 2.292)

CRC/240: The State Governments through their CDAs should enforce punitive measures against violators of land use and zoning laws in the inundable areas in the CPARs such as imposing fines, penalties, demolition measures, high taxation measures, etc. If necessary the State Government may acquire by legislation lands through compulsory sales. (Para 2.292)

CRC/241: The great success of the traditional dykes and seawalls in Netherlands should be studied by the CDAs to consider whether similar measures could be introduced in India on an experimental basis at selected sites to save costal land from the onslaught of storm surges from the sea and prevent the growth of salinity in them. (Para 2.292)

CRC/242: The Department of Environment and the Department of Forestry of the Central Government may be consulted by the CDAs for the formulation and implementation of an afforestation programmes in selected coastal areas on an experimental basis with the objective *inter alia* of breaking the fury of the cyclone winds and storm surges. (Para 2.292)

CRC/243: The Department of Environment of the Central Government may be consulted by the CDAs for formulating the long-term measures that should be introduced for soil and plant conservations and to prevent large scale coastal erosions that become inevitable under the action of cyclones and storm surges. (Para 2.292)

CRC/244: The maps should be prepared by the State Irrigation Departments of the coastal States in consultation with the IMD and River Research Organisations in the State, showing various possibilities of the spatial extents and depths of inundations in vulnerable locations for a given direction of entry of a storm surge, intensity of rainfall, extent of standing water, conditions of flooding of nearby rivers and level of water in the hydrodams in the vicinity, local topology and other similar parameters. Model studies can be made by the various River Research Institutes in the State and also at the Central Water and Power Research Station at Pune for specific areas notable for frequent cyclone landfalls and storm surges, and the results of such model studies should be stored in the computers of the ACWC/CWC and the FFOs in the State for ready access/visual display for use as basis for forecasting. (Para 2.293)

CRC/245: The CDA should consult the Flood Forecasting Centres of the Central Water Commission/State Government/IMD to map out the path of water from the hydrodams situated near the coastal regions which may have to be released during cyclone regimes to prevent damages to these dams or which may be caused by dam bursts, and also the location/extent of areas which are likely to be inundated as a result. (Para 2.294)

CRC/246: The technical officers of the State Irrigation Department should make annual inspection of the flood control facilities before the onset of the monsoon/cyclone seasons and take remedial measures against any failures of these facilities. The inspection should in particular include looking into the state of the flood banks, dykes, embankments, hydrodams, etc. (Para 2.294)

CRC/247: There should be some research investigations by an appropriate Research Organisation for developing the methods which are best suited to reduce the fury of the incoming storms surges. The CDAs should try out these methods at selected sites on the coast on an experimental basis. (Para 2.294)

CRC/248: There exist some methods already which break the fury of storm surges — development of anchored inflated rubber tyres, cement cross pieces colosse/vertical piles and other types of obstructions to free flow of water along the beeches of the coast line. The CDAs should examine the effectiveness of these methods on selected points of the coast generally vulnerable to cyclonic storm surges and in the approaches to selected villages which are repeatedly ravaged by cyclones. (Para 2.294)

CRC/249: Since the rivers constitute a natural drainage system which should be able to carry away the greater proportion of the flood water, river beds and river mouths should be annually dredged by the Department of Inland Waterways before the onset of the monsoon/cyclone seasons and kept in a trim condition to drain off efficiently the flood/storm surge discharges and over precipitation of rain. (Para 2.295)

CRC/250: The CDAs should plan and establish a network of permanent water drainage channels not only to protect the agricultural fields in the CPARs but also to remove as much of the flood water as possible. These channels should also be maintained by the CDAs in proper condition and should be annually inspected. (Para 2.295)

CRC/251: Diesel driven pumps should be installed at strategic points to route the standing water to these drainage channels which would transport it ultimately to the main drainage system constituted by the rivers in the areas or directly to the sea, if that is possible. (Para 2.295)

CRC/252: If the CDAs establish their own TC systems, it would be a great help to the DCCs if these channels are made available to them during cyclone emergencies. (Para 2.296)

CRC/253: The CDAs should plan a cyclone proof TCC network for cyclone reporting and for CDMW, incorporating systems such as two way voice transmission WT systems, etc. and in course of time build up such a system with the help of the P&T Department and the IMD. (Para 2.296)

CRC/254: It is the responsibility of the Assistant Engineer, District Public Relation Officer and the Block Development Officer to ensure that the Community Radio Sets/TV receivers are kept in good condition to receive all occasions the CAs and the CWMs. Specific persons should be appointed to listen to these broadcasts at the village level and disseminate the messages to all villagers. The persons to be nominated will be in the category of Sarpanch/ Panchayat clerk/Executive Officer/Village Development Officer/ Headmaster of the Elementary Schools or persons of similar ranks/ class. (Para 2.296)

CRC/255: The CDAs should establish a close network of roads and bridges, connecting the villages and cities within 20-25 km. of the coastal strips. (Para 2.297)

CRC/256: The CDAs should develop waterways and landing piers for commuting between the coastal islands and the main land and travelling along the rivers. (Para 2.297)

CRC/257: The CDAs should also take the responsibility or maintaining these network of roads and waterways because their proper functioning is a very important part of any coastal development plan. (Para 2.297)

CRC/258: The CDAs should improve the quality of the coastal road network in gradual phases starting with kutcha roads and finally terminating with roads on which lorries and buses can travel. (Para 2.297)

CRC/259: The Railway Department may consider raising the railway tracks on artificially raised earth humps or bunds in areas where storm surges usually occur frequently. (Para 2.297)

CRC/260: The District Collector should have a list of diesel generators located at various cinema halls, and other places which can be requisitioned during cyclone emergencies. He should also keep a list of priorities for moving the diesel generators to various places where emergency power is needed: Refugee Camps/CYSHELs/hospitals/ CDMW centres, etc. Arrangements must be made to mobilise trained personnel at short notice to operate these generators. A rigid watch should be kept on these generators when put into emergency use, and they should be returned to their owners without fail, when the emergency has passed. (Para 2.298)

CRC/261: The State Electricity Board should set up alternative routes for power supply to places/installations with high priority for restoration of electric power when the normal transmission routes have been snapped by the cyclone. (Para 2.298)

CRC/262: The CDAs should consult experts on rural housing on the appropriate designs for cyclone and storm surge proof mud houses for the poor regarding effective measures to strengthen the existing ones. While designing such houses techniques should be developed to reinforce the traditional high incline roofs of the mud houses in Andhra Pradesh, Orissa and West Bengal which have shown remarkable success in standing up to the furies of cyclones. Cheap chemicals treatment of the mud walls should be developed to stand up against the hammering/erosion produced by floods/storm surges. (Para 2.299)

CRC/263: The Building Research Institute of the CSIR should formulate designs for low cost housings and buildings which can stand up to cyclones and storm surges or which if damaged can be easily repaired and made habitable again. (Para 2.299)

CRC/264: The people living in one storied pucca buildings in the CPARs should be advised to keep some bricks and mortar handy, or atleast enough sand bags, to seal up the doors and windows in the ground floor to prevent flood water from entering. If there are upper floors in these pucca buildings it may not be necessary to seal up the ground floors and it may in fact be wiser to keep the doors and windows there open and allow free movement of wind and water. (Para 2.299)

CRC/265: The public buildings, for which the ground floors are used for storing purposes, should have arrangements for quick sealing off all points of entry of water at the ground level. Special spurs may be designed on the outside walls of the ground floor to break the violence of the rushing waters. Points of access to these buildings at levels higher than the usual level of storm surges should also be provided. (Para 2.299)

CRC/266: The CDAs may consult various consultants, in particular with the Indian Standards Institution, to evolve building codes for industrial complexes in the CPARs to take care of special problems arising for them during cyclone regimes. (Para 2.299)

CRC/267: By legislative action, the CDAs should be given the authority/executive power to enforce the Cyclone Building Code (CBC) in the CPARs of the State with the powers to sanction proposed house/building constructions or demolish existing houses/buildings which are unsafe for human habitation in a cyclone regime or have been constructed in an unauthorised manner or not complying with the CBC. (Para 2.299)

CRC/268: The District Collectors and subordinate officers who tour the CPARs should inspect all temples, mosques, churches, schools and college buildings, and public buildings, etc., for their suitability as cyclone shelters. This selection should be done before the cyclone season starts. The location of the Cyclone Refugee Camps/Cyclone Shelters (CYSHELs) should be advertised to the public by maps affixed to notice boards in public places, schools, community centres, cinema halls, railway stations, ports, post offices, panchayat offices, etc., and also published in newspapers periodically. Special pennants and pennant type baloons in organge should be flown on these shelters so that they can be seen from a long distance. (Para 2.300)

CRC/269: In matters connected to construction and use of Cyclone Shelters (CYSHELs) the following points should be kept in view:

I. *Objectives and functions of the CYSHEL:* It is expected that the coastal population would know well in advance to which CYSHEL they would have to take refuge. The fury of the cyclone would rarely last more than a week, but the storm waters may be expected to stand for a month some times. The units set up for CDMW would be mainly stationed at the CYSHELs and these would be expected to take care of the refugees for a period of a month (phase 3 — post-cyclone period) by which time the water would recede and the refugees return to their homes. The medical/epidemic control units stationed here would not only take care of the refugees but also take preventive measures for epidemics in the locality. The relief in goods and money may also be given to the refugees at these shelters.

II. *Location*

1. In places where there is acute danger of flooding due to storm surges, the CYSHELs should stand well (at least 3m above) the highest water recorded in the locality.
2. The CYSHELs should be easily approachable during cyclone emergencies by the refugees and the cattle. These should therefore have alternative approach roads so that they are not cut off when some roads become non-passable due to debris and floods water. The CYSHELs should therefore be situated near the hubs of roadway networks.
3. The sites should be approved by the Collectors after detailed investigation or the environment and neighbouring population, which will use the CYSHELs built on them.

III. *Design*

1. The CYSHELs may be circular, octagonal or built on rectangular modules.
2. The framed structure should be designed to stand up to a wind speed of 250 kmph and gust winds of 270 kmph in addition to dead and live loads as per National Buildings Code and should have an infilling of local bricks.
3. It should be a two storied building with a basement. The basement should enclose a fully protected well or bore well of required yield covered with movable inspection covers and space to house pumps/tube wells/diesel generating set/fuel and storing space for groceries and grains. The ground and first floors should accommodate mainly the dor-

mitories. Sufficient space should be allotted here for Cyclone Relief Administration/Security and Police/Wireless Communication Monitoring Units/Weather Observatory/Essential Health and First-aid Medical Facilities and an Epidemic Fighting Centre with provisions for a few beds for victims needing medical attention and common kitchen and canteen/public toilet facilities. The water tank should be under the roof level to avoid wind blast, or suitably protected against it.

4. The shelter should have minimum openings. Such windows that must be put in, should be provided with wire meshes on the outer surface and wooden shutters inside. For use of the shelters during the non-cyclone season a certain minimum number of windows have to be put in.
5. There should be at least four screen walls integrated to the frame of the main structure so that at any time during a cyclone regime at least one leeward doorway can be left open for late entrants.
6. The roof should have a slight camber at the rim for streamlining and the central area should be sufficiently reinforced to serve as a helipad for delivery of essential commodities and transportation of men by helicopters.
7. The basic design is a two storied RCC building framed structure — for circular designs dimensions 15m diameter and 7m high are capable of taking 500 refugees. But in may areas CYSHELs capable of taking 1000 people may be required.
8. The CYSHELs should be located on a site of area of about one hectare. A space of 22.5m may be kept clear round the building to facilitate movement of vehicles for transporting men and materials during cyclone emergencies. Adjacent to the CYSHEL, space for weekly market/shandy (67.5m x 36m), space for cattle, agricultural products, hay, etc. (67.5m x 60m) may be provided.

IV. *Management and other Units Stationed at the CYSHEL : The following Units may be Stationed at the CYSHELs*

1. Office of the CYSHEL Commandant in charge of the CYSHEL and management staff

2. Security
3. Telecommunication office
4. Weather office
5. Office of the Medical Officer and his staff/Epidemic Control Centre
6. Office of the Revenue Department for giving relief to the refugees — this should be in the vicinity if not actually in the shelter.

V. *Facilities:* The following facilities should be provided:

1. Water tank, water pump, tube well
2. Emergency Diesel generator set
3. Public toilets and water closets
4. First and centre, epidemic fighting centre, medical care unit, a few beds for emergencies with a stock of commonly needed medicines and epidemic preventives
5. Common kitchen and common place for eating
6. Adequate sewerage system immune to storm surges
7. Rescue gadgets like inflatable boats and light bridges, jeeps, ambulance cars, etc.
8. Adequate stock of grains, groceries and fuels to last a month
9. Adequate stock of medicines and epidemic preventives for refugees not only sheltering in the CYSHEL but also the residents of the locality.

VI. *Special communication channels:* The police communication network should be available at the CYSHELs. If the present Police WT/UHF systems are replaced with UHF systems then each CYSHEL should be equipped with an UHF manpack transreceiver.

VII. *Use of CYSHEL in non-cyclone seasons:* It is quite obvious that the CYSHELs should be continuous community use throughout the year and yet should be available and ready as a cyclone shelter within hours of receipt of the 'Cyclone Alert' signal. Without such continuity of use round the year the shelters would fall into decay and disrepair. The type of use evidently must be such that it can be halted at a short notice and the shelter transformed to be ready for its real use. Thus use as community hospitals, school/college laboratories, libraries must be avoided. However us as class rooms of elementary/ high schools, lecture halls in colleges/mahila mandalis/ Balawadis/mangal karyalayas, etc., are appropriate community use of CYSHELs.

VIII. *Funds for Stock at the CYSHELs and their maintenance:* Adequate funds are necessary to keep the CYSHELs in proper state to receive the refugees at a very short notice. It is therefore, necessary for the Commissioner Rescue Relief and Rehabilitation be provided with special funds out of which he may allocate money to appropriate agencies to carry out the required tasks. Without this special funds the CYSHELs would not be able to serve the purpose for which they are built.

IX. *Construction Agencies:* As most of the CYSHELs would be located at the rural areas, the appropriate construction agency on behalf of government would be the Panchayat Raj Engineering Department, or when there are special reasons, by the Roads and Buildings Departments.

X. *Agency for maintenance:* In the rural areas the Panchayat Raj Engineering Department would be the proper agency for maintenance of the CYSHELs. Any other Department of the Government may also be give this task if necessary. (Para 2.302)

CRC/270: The State Public Health Engineering Department should take the responsibility of establishing an efficient sewerage system in the CPARs, which should be maintained and periodically repaired. A detailed sewerage map of the CPARs should be prepared by this Department. (Para 2.303)

CRC/271: The CDAs of a coastal state should have its units for disposal of bodies of victims of cyclones and dead animals which should cooperate with similar units of the concerned State Governments. The CDA should be able to establish common burial/cremation grounds for mass disposal of corpses and dead animals at a short notice. (Para 2.303)

CRC/272: The State Public Health Department should have units at permanent health centres with expertise to fight all kinds of epidemics. At these centres arrangements should be quickly set up after the cyclone emergency has passed, to go into operation a mass inoculation programme to prevent outbreak of cholera, dysentery and similar epidemics. (Para 2.303)

CRC/273: The CDA of coastal state should insist on the implementation of the land zoning laws against unrestrained agricultural use of lands in areas liable to be periodically inundated under saline water brought in by storm surges from the sea. These lands may be permitted to be used for raising such agricultural crops which can grow under saline conditions and under prolonged submergence by flood waters. The Indian Agriculture Research Institute (IARI) may be requested to advise on this matter. (Para 2.304)

CRC/274: Cut crops which have been already removed from the fields in the low lying inundated areas have to be stored on artificially raised platforms to protect them from storm surges. These platforms should be designed to stand up to the fury of cyclone winds and storm surges. The State Agriculture Department should also provide storing space for cut crops in shed in the rural areas which can stand up to cyclones and storm surges. (Para 2.304)

CRC/275: Mobile community driers, perhaps using solar energy should be provided whenever needed in the CPARs for use by the farmers to dry their crops and thereby cut their loss. The appropriate CSIR national laboratory may be requested to develop such low cost mobile driers and the concerned State Agriculture Department may put them to field trials. (Para 2.304)

CRC/276: The Department of Environment should be consulted by the CDA of the coastal States regarding measures to desalinate the lands submerged under storm surges from the sea and implement them where necessary. (Para 2.304)

CRC/277: The CDA of a coastal State should establish a system of closely spaced fishing ports which need not be very elaborately equipped except that they may have storage space for fishing equipments, boats, some homing signal system and an emergency medical care unit which can be quickly set up during cyclone emergencies. During such emergencies the homing signals should guide the fishing boats to these ports where shelter can be sought and medical care given to injured fishermen. Persons should be trained to manage these ports. (Para 2.305)

CRC/278: To facilitate rescue operations, the fishermen should be advised to fit bright orange coloured sails on their boats and generally wear shirts, vests, turbans or scarves in the same colour, which can be seen from a large distance from land air or the sea. (Para 2.305)

CRC/279: There should be R&D work on designing fishing boats which may capsize in cyclones but which would not sink easily. (Para 2.305)

CRC/280: The State Department of Fisheries should have an arrangement of keeping a master roll of fishermen at sea at any given time and should, in course of time, have their own launches and helicopter to carry out search and rescue operations. (Para 2.305)

CRC/281: As a part of the CPPC the State Government should establish stores of various types for materials/equipments needed in a cyclone emergency at strategic points distributed over the CPARs of the State. (Para 2.306)

CRC/282: The stock of materials/equipments at these stores should be reviewed annually at the beginning of the cyclone seasons and replenished if necessary. (Para 2.306)

CRC/283: One of the first steps to be taken by the District Collectors is to build up the stocks at these stores to the degree necessary as soon as the 'Cyclone Alert' signal is received by them. The materials/equipments have to be requisitioned from different Departments of the State Government/Central Government and different agencies. At the end of emergency a close accounting should be done of materials/equipments used and the commandeered goods released to their original owners. (Para 2.306)

CRC/284: Accumulation of large stock of valuable goods at one place leads to corrupt practices which should be prevented by strict vigilance by District Collector who should be in administrative control of most types of stores used for cyclone emergencies. (Para 2.306)

CRC/285: The location of the stores used in cyclone emergencies should be in close proximity but outside the parts of the CPARs which are notorious for being AsD/AsGD. This would ensure that the stored goods would remain in good condition and not be destroyed by the cyclones, and yet can be moved quickly where required as soon as the emergency conditions have relaxed a little (phase 3 — Post cyclone period). (Para 2.306)

CRC/286: Cyclone Stores for evacuation/rescue (ER—CYSTOR) should store the following materials/equipments :

1. Inflatable boats, rubber tyres, life buoys
2. Emergency floating bridges of light structure
3. Grapping hooks, expandable ladders
4. Nylon/jute ropes, wires, chains, spades, crow bars
5. Other life saving equipments
6. First aid kits.

CRC/287: The CYSTORs for relief/rehabilitation (RR-CYSTOR) should be equipped with the following materials which are necessary for setting up emergency Relief Camps or to supply the CYSHELs if required:

1. Tents, tarpaulines, cc sheets, asbestos sheets, polythene sheets which can be used for providing temporary covers,
2. Tent pegs, ropes — jute/nylon, steel poles, bamboos, slotted angled iron frames,
3. Carpenters tool kits, general all purpose tool kits,
4. Buckets, mobile pumps, water tanks,
5. Equipments for community kitchen/canteen — large cooking vessels,
6. Almirahs/storage bins,
7. Emergency lighting equipments, hurricane with kerosene, diesel generators,
8. Blankets, clothes, dhotis, saris, etc., and
9. TC sets — in particular transistor receivers, VHF units, ordinary cycles for messengers. (Para 2.306)

CRC/288: Flood Stores (FLOODSTORs) should generally store all equipments necessary for repairs of embankments and breach filling machineries. The machineries for breach filling should include:

1. Proclain, 2. Dozer, 3. Tippers (with rocking bodies), 4. Jeeps with wenches. (Para 2.306)

CRC/289: Medical Stores (MEDSTORs) should generally stock general medicines for nervous breakdown, excessive exposure to wind and water, intenstinal disorders, vaccines and vitamins. The stock should be furnished by State Public Health Department. (Para 2.306)

CRC/290: Epidemic Control Stores (ECSTORs) should generally stock all types of drugs/medicines/chemicals for control of epidemics like cholera/dysentery and remedies for water pollution : chemicals like alum and filtering equipments. (Para 2.306)

CRC/291: Agricultural Stores (AGRISTORs) should generally store various types of seeds/agriculture tools/mobile crop driers which can be loaned to the refugees or given as outright grant for rehabilitating them. (Para 2.306)

CRC/292: State Transport Department Stores (STDSTORs) As the State Transport Department is expected to play a big role in evacuation/rescue operations, it is advisable to set up a number of garages/workshops/spare part depots all grouped under the class STDSTORs at appropriate places in the CPARs. These can be the collecting points of the requisitioned vehicles as well as the places where they can be maintained and repaired during the emergency. (Para 2.306)

CRC/293: Since the PWD is expected to play a major role in clearing debris from the roads and knock down damaged buildings which are sources of danger to the public during a cyclone emergency, the Department should set up their stores (PWDSTORs) at appropriate places in the CPARs. These stores should stock equipments like bulldozers/tractors with winching arrangements, perhaps obtained during the emergency from the Agro Industrial Complexes in the State. These stores should also contain sufficient stocks of building materials : bricks/cement/sand, etc., for carrying out expeditiously the programme of restoration of public life. There should be also in these stores sufficient sand bags which can be used to seal up water entry points of important public buildings/utilities.

CRC/294: Very important from the point of all disasters are the Food Stores (FOODSTORs). The purpose of helping the victims is not doubt served by the various Siloes of the Food Corporation of India and the similar stores of the State Government. But from the point of view of cyclone emergencies the time available to move the food materials to the danger points is very limited. Thus extra FOODSTORs should be set up in the CPARs stocking.

1. Food grains like rice/wheat/dal, etc.
2. Precooked/preprocessed food materials like puffed/pressed rice/flour, powdered dal, etc.
3. Cooking media like mustard oil/coconut oil/ground nut oil
4. Cooking masalla of various types
5. Simple vegetables like potatoes which can be stored without much trouble over short intervals of time
6. Fuel for cooking : wood/coal/kerosene, etc. (Para 2.306)

CRC/295: Fodder Stores (FODSTORs) should be established at appropriate places in the CPARs at close intervals. Every year a part of the fodder harvested should be set aside by the State Government and stored in the FODSTORs for use during the cyclone and other emergencies. (Para 2.306)

CRC/296: Those commandeered/requisitioned land vehicles for

which place can not be found gathering/parking at the STDSTORs should be parked at other places where permanent structures for these purposes should be provided by the State Government as a part of its CPPC. (Para 2.307)

CRC/297: The Irrigation and Waterways Departments of the State Government should set up gathering places along the river sides, at the sea coasts and at the various ports for the commandeered/requisitioned water vehicles. The necessary structures for this purpose should be built by the State Government as a part of its CPPC. (Para 2.307)

CRC/298: The CDAs of the different coastal States should establish close liaison with the ACC through the concerned SCYCs for generating the legislative measures necessary for preparing the Community against cyclones. The CDAs should be assigned the task of enforcing the laws laid down for all aspects of coastal management/ development and given the necessary power/authority. (Para 2.308)

CRC/299: The coastal States should build up a pool of officials specially trained in the techniques of cyclone management in all its aspects and other disaster managements, out of which personnel can be drawn and allotted special tasks in a cyclone emergency for mitigating the distress caused. The items and methods of training should be carefully selected and constantly updated in the light of experience gained. The Government of India should come to the assistance of the State Governments in the Disaster Management training programmes. (Para 2.309)

CRC/300: The Film Division of the Ministry of Information and Broadcasting should prepare with the help of the IMD, a series of documentaries and video tapes on cyclones, to inform the viewers about the nature of cyclones, their hazards and the devastation they cause, the ways and means to confront them and what to do during cyclone emergencies. These documentaries and video tapes can be shown to the general public just before and during cyclone seasons in cinemas, through Doordarshan and rural community TV circuits of the INSAT. In particular the films and tapes advising the public what they must do in emergencies, should be shown very frequently to viewers in the CPARs. The State Public Relation Department may be given the responsibility of organising the presentation of these visual materials to the public. (Para 2.310)

CRC/301: The AIR should arrange frequent broadcasts of suitable programmes about cyclones — their nature, their hazards and the devastations they cause, how to confront them, and what should the people do during cyclone emergencies. These broadcasts should be arranged just before and frequently during the cyclone seasons taking special care that they are directed to listeners in the CPARs. The broadcasts can be included in the schools broadcast programmes and in community programmes directed to rural listeners. (Para 2.310)

CRC/302: The State Public Relation Department may seek the help of the local newspaper media to inform the public about cyclones, their origin and nature their hazards and the devastations they cause, how to fight them and in emergencies what to do. This should be done through articles written by experts of the IMD, which should appear frequently in the newspaper during cyclone seasons particularly in those circulating in the CPARs. (Para 2.310)

CRC/303: The State Public Relation Department should circulate booklets/pamphlets on cyclones in the rural areas in the CPARs through the Gram panchayats. These booklets should contain specific informations for the rural population how to meet cyclones and in particular what to do during cyclone emergencies. The booklets may be prepared with the help of the IMD. They should be in local languages and should be available at nominal prices from government stationery shops, book shops, Railway stations and prominent places where people assemble. (Para 2.310)

CRC/304: The CDAs should prepare cheap pamphlets for circulation among the public in the CPARs containing advisories and codes of constructing cyclone proof huts/buildings. (Para 2.310)

CRC/305: The IMD should establish a publicity cell in each ACWC/CWC which will work in collaboration with the news media, AIR, Doordarshan, and the State Publicity Department to educate the public of the CPARs about cyclones — their nature, hazards, measures for community preparedness, and instructions required to be followed in emergencies. (Para 2.310)

CRC/306: The Directors of Public Instruction (DPIs) in the coastal States should ensure that the syllabi of Indian schools at the secondary level include the subject of cyclones in very elementary and descriptive terms with informations about some famous Indian cyclones and also regarding what to do during cyclone emergencies as has been done in Burma, Phillippines and other countries. The National Council of Educational Research and Training (NCERT) should arrange the publication of suitable text books for the schools to cover these topics. (Para 2.311)

CRC/307: Frequent seminars should be arranged by the State

Government in collaboration with the IMD and other agencies at schools on subjects covering the causes of natural disasters, their prevention, mitigation of distress caused by them to people including measures for relief rehabilitation reconstruction and restoration of normal life. State Officers in charge of relief and other experts should be invited to give talks on these subjects at these seminars. (Para 2.311)

CRC/308: To generate interest in cyclones, Cyclone Clubs should be formed in the coastal States. An important activity at the Cyclone Clubs should be to monitor the CWM broadcasts over the AIR, and to keep records of tracks, movements and other parameters of various cyclones like wind speeds and pressure depths and also of various other informations like the extent and categorisation of damages caused by them in these states. These clubs should also arrange group discussions on the cyclone problem. In times of cyclone emergencies they can contribute directly by volunteering in cyclone distress mitigation operations. The work of these Clubs would help to a very great extent to spread the awareness of the cyclone problem among the general public. (Para 2.312)

CRC/309: The recommendations of the State CDMCs should be reviewed specially with respect to CEAPs of these states and their CPPCs in the light of subsequent experience gained of cyclone disasters and the recommendation made by the Cyclone Review Committee. While formulating the CEAPs the established administrative practices prevalent in the concerned state should be kept in view. (Para 2.313)

Group C : *Recommendations for Research and Training*

VII. *Cyclone Research and Training*

CRC/310: It is important to organise continuous research on Indian cyclones to improve the forecasting capabilities and methods of detecting and tracking them. (Para 2.314)

CRC/311: The Cyclone Warning Research Centre at Madras should be expanded into a National Cyclone Research Centre which should be responsible not only for research on Indian cyclones but also for development/assessment of forecasting techniques. (Para 2.314)

CRC/312: There is need for the Indian Universities, Indian Institutes of Technology and various research agencies in India to organise research projects on tropical cyclones. (Para 2.315)

CRC/313: There should be well supported research projects on cyclone caused storm surges, their origin and their identification of various parameters determining their origin nature and effects. This may be organised by the IMD in collaboration with the Department of Oceanography. (Para 2.316)

CRC/314: Model studies on the rivers in the CPARs should be undertaken by the IMD in collaboration with the Central Water Research Station at Pune, to understand the interaction of the state of these rivers with the storm surges, and to devise techniques for forecasting the extent of inundations caused by rainfall, wind action and storm surges induced by cyclones in various sectors of the CPARs, taking into consideration the state of the rivers and other conditions there during cyclone regimes. (Para 2.316)

CRC/315: A national multi-disciplinary and multi-institutional projects may be initiated by the DST for aircraft probing of cyclones/other weather disturbances like thunder-storms/norwesters. The aircrafts can be used also to monitor and study the behaviour of clouds and monsoons. (Para 2.318)

CRC/316: A team of experts may be sent to visit countries like USA/Japan where the technique of probing aircraft has reached a high level of perfection with the objective to find out the economic viability, aspects of training/operations and the potential for research in this technique. (Para 2.318)

CRC/317: For successfully operating the Cyclone Plan suggested by the Committee, quite a large number of specialists should be trained abroad and in this country in cyclone forecasting/warning work, techniques of interpretation of data obtained by different techniques of cyclone observations, who would in turn in course of time, generate a band of competent meteorologists needed in the Cyclone Plan. (Para 2.320)

10

WORKING GROUP TO REVIEW THE SYSTEM OF CASH CREDIT, 1979 — REPORT[1]

Chairman Shri K.B. Chore
Members Shri S.P. Chandavarkar; Shri V. Mahadevan; Shri R.P. Vaidya; Kum. M. Tyagarajan
M. Secy. Shri M.L. Inasu

Appointment

Following his meeting with bankers, the Governor, Reserve Bank of India, advised all scheduled commercial banks on the 30th November, 1978 that they should "so plan their future expansion of non-food credit that the incremental gross credit (non-food) — deposit ratio for the period December 1, 1978 to end-March 1979 would be well within 40 per cent". While reviewing the monetary and credit trends in March 1979, the Governor again stressed the need for exercising continued restraint on further expansion of credit. He also indicated in the meeting the need for considering certain long-term issues relating to banking operations. In his letter dated the 16th March, 1979 to all scheduled commercial banks, he indicated:

> "I would like to initiate action on certain structural matters which need further examination. It is necessary to take a fresh look at another major problem faced by banks in implementing the credit regulatory measures viz., the extensive use of the cash credit system. Its drawbacks have been pointed out by various Committees in the past including the Tandon Committee, which suggested the bifurcation of credit limits into a demand loan and a fluctuating cash credit component. Although the banks were advised to implement this recommendation, I am afraid, the progress achieved has

---

1. Division of Publication, Reserve Bank of India, Bombay, 1979, p. 81.

been very slow. Clearly, this problem needs to be looked into further and for this purpose I propose to set up immediately a small Working Group, to report to me. . . on the reforms to be introduced".

It was in this context that the Reserve Bank appointed the Working Group to review the system of cash credit in all its aspects.

In pursuance of the decision taken at the meeting which the Governor had with Chairmen of some of the major banks on March 15, 1979, the Researve Bank of India appoints the above persons to constitute a Working Group to review the system of cash credit by banks in all its aspects.

Terms of Reference

(i) To review the operation of the cash credit system in recent years, particularly with reference to the gap between sanctioned credit limits and the extent of their utilisation;

(ii) In the light of the review, to suggest:

(a) modifications in the system with a view to making the system more amenable to rational management of funds by commercial banks, and/or

(b) alternative types of credit facilities, which would ensure greater credit discipline and also enable banks to relate credit limits to increases in output or other productive activities; and

(iii) To make recommendations on any other related matter as the Group may consider germane to the subject.

Contents

Introduction; Compliance by banks with the credit policy instructions of the Reserve Bank – end-November 1978 – end-March 1979; Gap between the sanctioned limit and utilisation; Advantages and disadvantages of different styles of lending – Recommended lending system; Proposed amendments to the lending system; Discount House; Other Recommendations; Summary of Recommendations; Appendices from I to VI.

Recommendations

1. The advantages of the existing system of extending credit by a combination of the three types of lending, viz., cash credit, loan and bill should be retained. At the same time it is necessary to give some directional changes to ensure that wherever possible the use of cash credit would be supplanted by loans and bills. It would also be necessary to introduce necessary corrective measures to remove the impediments in the use of bill system of finance and also to remove the drawbacks observed in the cash credit system. (Para 4.22)

2. Bifurcation of cash credit limit into a demand loan portion and a fluctuating cash credit component has not found acceptance either on the part of the banks or the borrowers. Such bifurcation may not serve the purpose of better credit planning by narrowing the gap between sanctioned limits and the extent of utilisation thereof. It is not likely to be voluntarily accepted and it does not confer enough advantages to make it compulsory. (Paras 5.2 and 5.4)

3. The need for reducing the over-dependence of the medium and large borrowers — both in the private and public sectors — on bank finance for their production trading purposes is recognised. The net surplus cash generation of an established industrial unit should be utilised partly at least for reducing borrowing for working capital purposes. (Para 5.7)

4. In order to ensure that the borrowers do enhance their contributions to working capital and to improve their current ratio. It is necessary to place them under the Second Method of lending recommended by the Tandon Committee which would give a minimum current ratio of 1.33:1. As many of the borrowers may not be immediately in a position to work under the Second Method of lending, the excess borrowings should be segregated and treated as a working capital term loan which should be made repayable in instalments. To induce the borrowers to repay this loan, it should be charged a higher rate of interest. For the present, the Group recommends that the additional interest may be fixed at 2 per cent per annum over the rate applicable on the relative cash credit limits. This procedure should be made compulsory for all borrowers (except sick units) having aggregate working capital limits of Rs. 10 lakhs and over. (Para 5.9)

5. While assessing the credit requirements, the bank should appraise and fix separate limits for the 'normal non-peak level' as also for the 'peak level' credit requirements indicating also the periods

during which the separate limits would be utilised by the borrower. This procedure would be extended to all borrowers having working capital limits of Rs. 10 lakhs and above. One of the important criteria for deciding such limits should be the borrowers' utilisation of credit limits in the past. (Paras 5.10 to 5.12)

6. If any *ad hoc* or temporary accommodation is required in excess of the sanctioned limit to meet unforeseen contingencies the additional finance should be given, where necessary, through a separate demand loan account or a separate 'non-operable' cash credit account. There should be a stiff penalty for such demand loan or 'non-operable' cash credit portion, at least two per cent above the normal rate, unless Reserve Bank exempts such penalty. This discipline may be made applicable in cases involving working capital limits of Rs. 10 lakhs and above. (Paras 5.13 and 5.14)

7. The borrower should be asked to give his quarterly requirement of funds before the commencement of the quarter on the basis of his budget, the actual requirement being within the sanctioned limit for the particular peak level/non-peak level periods. Drawings less than or in excess of the operative limit so fixed (with a tolerance of 10 per cent either way) but not exceeding sanctioned limit would be subject to a penalty to be fixed by the Reserve Bank from time to time. For the time being the penalty may be fixed at 2 per cent per annum. The borrower would be required to submit his budgeted requirements in triplicate and a copy each would be sent immediately by the branch to the controlling office and Head Office for record. The penalty would be applicable only in respect of parties enjoying credit limits of Rs. 10 lakhs and above, subject to certain exemptions. (Paras 5.15 to 5.20)

8. The non-submission of the returns in time is partly due to certain features in the form themselves. To get over this difficulty, simplified forms have been proposed. As the quartely information system is part and parcel of the revised style of lending under the cash credit system, if the borrower does not submit the return within the prescribed time, he should be penalised by charging the whole outstandings in the account at a penal rate of interest, one per cent annum more than the contracted rate for the advance from the due date of the return till the date of its actual submission (Para 5.21).

9. Requests for relaxation of inventory norms and for *ad hoc* creases in limits should be subjected by banks to close scrutiny a agreed to only in exceptional circumstances. (Para 5.22)

10. The banks should devise their own check lists in the light of

the instructions issued by the Reserve Bank for the scrutiny of data at the operational level. (Para 5.23)

11. Delays on the part of banks in sanctioning credit limits could be reduced in cases where the borrowers co-operate in giving the necessary information about their past performance and future projections in time. (Para 5.24)

12. As one of the reasons for the slow growth of the bill system is the stamp duty on usance bills and difficulty in obtaining the required denominations of stamps, these questions may have to be taken up with the State Governments. (Para 5.25)

13. Banks should review the system of financing book debts through cash credit and insist on the conversion of such cash credit limits into bill limits. (Para 5.26)

14. A stage has come to enforce the use of drawee bills in the lending system by making it compulsory for banks to extend at least 50 per cent of the cash credit limit against raw materials to manufacturing units whether in the public or private sector by way of drawee bills. To start with, this discipline should be confined to borrowers having aggregate working capital limits of Rs. 50 lakhs and above from the banking system. (Paras 5.27 and 5.29)

15. Banks should insist on the public sector undertakings/large borrowers to maintain control accounts in their books to give precise data regarding their dues to the small units and furnish such data in their quarterly information system. This would enable the banks to take suitable measures for ensuring payment of the dues to small units by a definite period by stipulating, if necessary, that a portion of limits for bills acceptance (drawee bills) should be utilised only for drawee bills of small scale units. (Para 5.30)

16. To encourage the bill system of financing and to facilitate call money operations an autonomous financial institution on the lines of the Discount Houses in U.K. may be set up. (Paras 6.1 to 6.11)

17. No conclusive data are available to establish the degree of correlation between production and quantum of credit at the Industry level. As this issue is obviously of great concern to the monetary authorities the Reserve Bank may undertake a detailed scientific study in this regard. (Para 7.2)

18. Credit control measures to be effective will have to be immediately communicated to the operational level and followed up. There should be a 'Cell' attached to the Chairman's office at the Central Office of each bank to attend to such matters. The Central

Offices of banks should take a second look at the credit budget as soon as changes in credit policy are announced by the Reserve Bank and revise their plan of action in the light of the new policy and communicate the corrective measures to the operational levels as quickly as possible. (Para 7.3)

19. Banks should give particular attention to monitor the key branches and critical accounts. (Para 7.4)

20. The communication channels and systems and procedures within the banking system should be toned up so as to ensure that minimum time is taken for collection of instruments. (Para 7.5)

21. Although banks usually object to their borrowers dealing with other banks without their consent, some of the borrowers still maintain current accounts and arrange bill facilities with other banks, which vitiate the credit discipline. Reserve Bank may issue suitable instructions in this behalf. (Para 7.6)

11

COMMITTEE ON FORWARD MARKETS, 1980 — REPORT[1]

Chairman Dr. A.M. Khusro
Members Shri L.S. Venkataramanan; Shri B.N. Kapre; Dr. Vijay L. Kelkar; Dr. P.N. Kaul
Co-opted Member Shri V.N. Lokur
M. Secy. Shri M.G. Jawle

Appointment

The Government of India have decided to set up a Committee to look into the operations of forward markets and the role of the Forward Markets Commission to effectively regulate the futures trading and futures markets in various commodities with a view to curb unhealthy trends, and also to implement the Government's decision prohibiting forward trading in specified commodities. Vide Government of India, Ministry of Commerce, Civil Supplies and Co-operation, Department of Civil Supplies and Co-operation Order No.10(3)-IT/77 dated March 27, 1979.

Terms of Reference

(i) To review the role that forward trading has played during the last 10 years;

(ii) To assess the role that forward trading can play in the prevailing economic conditions and marketing/distribution system in the commodities in which forward trading is possible, particularly in commodities in which resumption of forward trading is generally demanded;

---

1. Delhi, Controller of Publications, 1984, p. 108.

(iii) To examine the extent to which forward trading in commodities in which such trading may be permitted could be of direct or indirect benefit to producers and consumers of the commodities;

(iv) To examine the extent to which forward trading has special role to play in promoting exports;

(v) To suggest measures to ensure that forward trading in the commodities in which it is allowed to be operative remains constructive and helps in maintaining prices within reasonable limits;

(vi) To suggest amendments to the Forward Contracts (Regulation) Act in the light of its recommendations particularly with a view to efficient enforcement of the Act to check illegal forward trading when such trading is prohibited under the Act; and

(vii) To suggest measures for strengthening the Forward Markets Commission to achieve the objective of making futures trading socially purposeful.

Contents

Approach to Futures Trading; Theory and Practice of Futures Trading; Regulation of Forward Trading in India; Commodities Suitable for Futures Trading under Present Conditions; Basic Requisites for the Regulation of Futures Trading; Non-transferable Specific Delivery Contracts; Amendments to the Forward Contracts (Regulation) Act, 1952; Strengthening of the Forward Markets Commission; Summary of Conclusions and Recommendations; Annexures from I to XV.

Recommendations

Approach to Futures Trading

The Committee first addressed itself to the task of laying down its approach to futures trading in the light of the prevailing economic conditions and marketing and distribution system prevailing in various commodities.

2. It noted that not all commodities are fit for futures trading. A commodity to be eligible for futures trading must be homogeneous, capable of being standardised in one or more grades and its supply and demand should be so large that even the biggest purchase and sale of the largest speculators constitute a fraction of the total market. It should be free from substantial control either by a Governmental or

public authority or a private organisation, cartel, association, corporation or individual. Its supply and demand should be uncertain and it should neither be a perishable commodity nor subject to changes in style and fashions. Lastly, leading segments of the production and trade sectors handling the commodity and prepared to use it for hedging should come forward to organise futures market. (Paras 1.2 to 1.8)

3. While it is a necessary condition for a satisfactory operation of futures markets that supply and demand should be large, the Committee noted that in India – unlike the major cereals, in particular, wheat, and cotton which have undergone a substantial technological change – other foodgrains, especially the inferior foodgrains and almost all industrial raw materials produced in agriculture have been stagnating owing to lack of technological breakthrough. As more resources are bound to be concentrated in these commodities in the future, supplies are most likely to respond to growth in demands, and the markets for almost all agricultural commodities, except cereals, and in particular inferior cereals, are bound to grow. Indian conditions are most likely to become more and more favourable for forward trading in these commodities as a result of the expansion of the volumes of demands and supplies. In the case of most of these agricultural commodities almost the entire production is for marketing. The expansion of the market size generally goes with improvement in market sophistications which would also be a favourable circumstance for the operation of futures market. (Paras 1.10 and 1.11)

4. As regards the existing marketing and distribution system in commodities, the position is that in rice and wheat and some other foodgrains, there is a complex system of regulation and control involving support prices, procurement and a vast network of public distribution agencies. This social necessity involves the Government in a complex and costly distributive apparatus which ties up a great deal of Governmental resources. These mechanisms cannot be extended for commodities other than the most urgent ones. In this context the question arises as to what other methods could be used to regulate the prices of these other commodities, many of which exhibit a high degree of price fluctuations. The Committee is of the opinion that in such a context futures trading can be considered as a possible measure, in suitable cases, for dampening the peaks and lifting up the valleys of prices; in fact, in some cases, such a measure may turn out to be a necessity. (Paras 1.12 and 1.13)

5. As for the benefit of futures trading to producers and con-

sumers, the Committee's considered view is that if the gains from futures trading accrued only to those who traded in the futures market and to nobody else, or indeed, if the gains to futures traders were accompanied by losses to producers, manufacturers, consumers and other social interests, this Committee would not recommend resort to futures trading at all. However, futures trading, under suitable conditions and when properly regulated, can be of immense help to growers and various other functionaries. (Paras 1.14)

6. The cultivators who grow commodities in very large quantities can use futures markets for hedging their crops or stocks. This enables them to spread out the sales of such stocks over a period and obtain a better price for their produce. Even if the cultivators do not participate in the futures markets directly, such markets are beneficial to them as an advance indicator of the expected levels of prices during the marketing period, enabling them to undertake proper crop planning. In the absence of futures market in appropriate commodities, the traders and manufacturers attempts to cover their risks by charging a higher price to the consumers or by paying a lower price to the producers. In other words, the margin between what the producer receives and what the consumer pays is widened just because no adequate method to cover risks of traders and manufacturers is provided. It is obvious that in the absence of futures trading and risk minimisations, as the farmer gets less, his motivation to produce more and, indeed, his investment capability gets reduced. On the other side, in the absence of futures trading as the consumer pays more, demands may get constrained and the final retail market does not get widened as it would when, in appropriate cases, futures trading exists. Thus futures trading, in appropriate cases and suitable conditions, makes the return to the producers higher and the price to the consumer lower. (Paras 2.27, 2.28 and 1.16)

7. As regards the role of futures trading in promoting exports, the Committee has come to the conclusion that hedging facility is of invaluable help to exporters. It enables them to make hedge purchases against the overseas sale contracts. Besides, the futures markets supply quotations for different future delivery periods based on the expert assessment of the anticipated future supply and demand which enables them to quote to foreign buyers, for different shipment periods. Further, being assured of normal profits because of the insurance service provided by the futures market, the exporters are in a position to trade on a smaller margin of profit which increases their competitive

capacity in the world markets. Futures markets can, therefore, be considered as one of the instruments of export promotion. (2.30 and 2.31)

8. There is no scope for futures trading in any commodity if there is complete control of the State on its supply and distribution. However, if the private trade is free to procure a large part of the supply and handle its marketing or if the State procures entire supply from producers but sells it to the private trade for its distribution, the trade interests would need hedging facilities. Under the price support programme, the State or its agencies are committed to purchasing the commodity when the price of the commodity tends to fall below the prescribed support prices. Futures trading is not incompatible with such programme because there is considerable scope for determination of fair competitive prices above these minimum levels and their is no reason to deprive the farmers of such higher prices. Similarly, buffer stock schemes are also not incompatible with futures trading if the major part of the crop is to be marketed by the private trade. In fact, the existence of futures markets in commodities in which management schemes have been introduced will be helpful to the proper implementation of the schemes, since the agencies operating the schemes have generally to face the same problems, as faced by the private trade, in the management of the stocks procured by them. The availability of futures prices would also enable them to decide their buying and selling policies and the quantum of stocks to be held. (Paras 2.33, 2.34 and 2.35)

Commodities Suitable for Futures Trading

9. The Committee has considered the desirability of permitting futures trading in different commodities under present conditions. The commodities considered for this purpose are those in which there has been a tradition of futures trading and in some of which such trading has been suspended from time to time and also those commodities in which there has been a demand for introducing futures trading. Our conclusions and recommendations in respect of various commodities are as follows: (Para 4.1)

(i) Foodgrains – Cereals and Pulses

Foodgrains being commodities of mass consumption have been subjected, for very good social and economic reasons, to fairly thorough regulations and controls through such measures as support price fixing, retail price fixing, procurement, buffer stock operations and organisation of ration shops in an extensive public distribution system. As our criteria have shown, such commodities cannot be a fit material for trading in the futures markets. The Committee, therefore, recommends that unless this sector has developed large surpluses to the extent of enabling the country to undertake regular exports, it would not be advisable to permit futures trading in foodgrains. (Para 4.6)

(ii) Cotton and Kapas

(a) *Cotton*

The supply position of cotton has considerably improved in recent years as compared to the position in 1966 when futures trading was prohibited. There have been no imports during the last two years. Exports of selected varieties have been permitted. Although consumption of cotton by mills has been increasing, large stocks of it have to be carried forward by the functionaries in the trade. Despite the operations of the CCI, the MSCMF and the co-operative sector over a number of years, the cotton economy has remained a market oriented economy, as more than 50 per cent of the cotton is still marketed by the cotton trade and fluctuations in the prices of different varieties have remained quite large. The MSCMF needed the facility of futures trading in cotton in view of the large stocks it had to handle exposing it to the risk involved in price fluctuations. The Committee, therefore, recommends that futures trading may be resumed in cotton at a few well selected centres. (Paras 4.16, 4.17 and 4.18)

(b) *Kapas*

The marketing of kapas is seasonal, as in that form it remain in the market only for about three to four months. Moreover, tradition of futures, trading in kapas in only in certain parts like Punjab and Saurashtra. The Committee, therefore, recommends that futures trading may be permitted in kapas at a few centres where there has been long tradition of such trading and where functioning of competitive futures markets if possible. (Para 4.19)

(iii) Raw Jute and Jute Goods

(a) *Raw Jute*

The supply of raw jute (including mesta) is large and sizeable stocks have generally to be carried forward from season to season. The demand for jute is exclusively from jute mills and it is reckoned around 75 lakh bales annually. Exports have been negligible so far but may have to be allowed in larger quantities to support prices in view of the increased surplus. The statutory minimum prices and the operations of the JCI have not brought adequate relief to the farmers and often transactions are reported to be taking place at less than the statutory minimum prices. This indicates the need for supporting the existing mechanism. Taking into account the supply and demand position in raw jute and the existing marketing arrangements the Committee is of the view that futures trading in raw jute can play a useful role to bring benefits to growers, stockists and other functionaries in the trade. The facilities of Transferable Specific Delivery (TSD) and Non-transferable Specific Delivery (NTSD) contracts serve the purpose of entering into long-term commitments and carrying adequate stocks safely if such facilities are coupled with futures trading facilities also. The Committee, therefore, recommends that futures trading in raw jute should be permitted. (Paras 4.21 and 4.25)

(b) *Jute Goods*

Sacking: The main items of production in jute goods are hessian and sacking and there has been tradition and demand for futures trading only in these items. The facility of futures trading in sacking has been made use of by the dealers, who sell to the domestic consumers, and the shippers who sell to the overseas buyers. The hedge market in sacking is also used for hedging stocks and PDOs. The sacking futures market has functioned satisfactorily. The Committee, therefore, recommends its continuance. (Para 4.30)

Hessian: The bulk of the production of hessian is exported. Immediately after the conclusion of a export deal, it is not possible for the exporters to get the required goods through TSD contract, since the construction of quantum required may not be readily available. This makes it necessary for the exporters to cover their export commitments in a futures market simultaneously with the export sale. The absence of futures trading facilities results in loss of export business and in some cases export markets. Hedging facilities would increase the competitive capacity of the exporters against other jute goods producing countries and synthetic substitutes. Further, the competitive prices quoted in the futures market help to reduce monopolistic tendencies in the internal market. The Committee, therefore, recommends that futures trading in hessian should be permitted. (Para 4.31)

Carpet Backing: Carpet backing is produced by the mills as per the specifications of the foreign buyers and supplied to them directly. There is no domestic market in it and there has not been any demand for futures trading. The Committee, therefore, does not consider it necessary to permit futures trading in carpet backing for the present. (Para 4.32)

(iv) Edible Oilseeds and Oils

Although the total production of major edible oilseeds and oils is large in absolute terms, a serious secular shortage of these commodities in relation to the demand has emerged in this country. This has resulted in large, violent and frequent fluctuations in process of major oilseeds and oils. Under, these circumstances, in our opinion, edible oilseeds and oils are not, in the present stage, commodities fit for being permitted for futures trading as it is not clear whether social gains through futures trading will be larger than private gains. The Committee, therefore, recommends that futures trading in edible oilseeds and oils should not be permitted for the present. The Committee would like to point out that it is extremely important to augment the supplies and to reduce the fluctuations in availability and indeed to restrain demand to the extent possible. As the primary cause of restricted supplies in relation to high demand is the absence of any major break-through in the production technology of these commodities, it is to be recommended that large resources, e.g., research and development, should be devoted to edible oilseeds. Until this happens, the Committee further suggests that the regulatory mechanism already in operation should be continued and further strengthened. Only when supply is augmented, an important condition for the operation of futures market might emerge in these commodities in future. (Paras 4.37, 4.38 and 4.39)

(v) Castorseed

A study of the price behaviour indicates that there is no direct relationship between the prices of castorseed/castor oil and those of groundnut oil and that the ban on futures trading in castorseed had not helped in exercising a stabilising influence on the prices of groundnut oil. This is mainly because the total annual production of castor oil, a non-edible commodity as distinct from groundnut oil, forms only an insignificant proportion of the total production of groundnut oil. Being export oriented with about 50 per cent of castor oil produced finding an outlet to the overseas markets, the prices of both castorseed and castor oil are determined to a great extent by the developments taking place in the international markets. Taking into consideration this important aspect as also the pleadings made by the various concerned interests including STC, the Committee recommends that futures trading in castorseed should be resumed. (Paras 4.44 and 4.46)

Castor Oil: The facility of futures trading has been sought by all the concerned interests only in castorseed and not in castor oil. Besides, the market for castor oil is quite narrow and futures trading in this country has been conducted only in castorseed. Further, the need for hedging in castor oil can be met through the facility of futures trading in castorseed. The Committee, therefore, recommends that there is no need for futures trading in castor oil. (Para 4.47)

(vi) Linseed

The rise in the production of linseed, emergence of sizeable carry-over stocks in recent years, and the absence of any direct relationship between the prices of linseed oil and edible oils are points in support of futures trading in linseed. Further, since as much as about two-thirds of the production of linseed oil is used for non-edible purposes, viz., industrial use, the argument that futures trading in linseed should not be permitted because linseed oil is used for edible purposes does not carry sufficient conviction. Futures trading in linseed had been permitted uninterruptedly for about 20 years till it was banned in February 1977. Futures trading in this commodity had functioned satisfactorily. We, therefore, recommend that futures trading should be permitted in linseed. (Para 4.53)

Linseed Oil: Exports of linseed oil are at present banned and there has neither been any tradition of futures trading in linseed oil nor any demand for such trading from the concerned interests. Moreover, the market for linseed oil is quite narrow. Hence, we do not consider it necessary to permit futures trading in linseed oil. (Para 4.54)

(vii) Oilcakes

Oilcakes may be broadly grouped into major and minor oilcakes. In the case of minor oilcakes such as mahua oilcake, neem oilcakes, etc., not only their production is quite small, but also there is no assured supply of even a minimum quantity. In view of this and the extremely small size and unorganised nature of the markets in minor oilseeds, the Committee considers that there is no case for permitting futures trading in any of the minor oilcakes at present. (Para 4.60)

As regards major oilcakes such as groundnut, cotton-seed or rapeseed oilcakes, the Committee has looked at the whole question primarily from the point of view of promoting exports of extractions. The expeller oilcake contains six to seven per cent oil and it is in the interest of not only the domestic consumers of edible oils but also of the extraction industry that this oil is extracted within the country itself. The Government of India have already banned the exports of all expeller oilcakes. Further, futures trading in groundnut expeller cakes, which in terms of production accounts for the bulk of the total production of expeller oilcakes, was banned due to rising prices of the groundnut group of commodities. In respect of other expeller oilcakes such as rapeseed cake, linseed cake, such trading was banned because of their misuse for trading in banned commodities. In view of the position as aforesaid, we consider that there is no need for permitting futures trading in expeller oilcakes for the present. As regards extractions, the supply is quite large, the demand for it, which is mainly from overseas buyers, is uncertain and the international market for it is highly competitive. The quantum of exports of extraction is sizeable. The commodity is also suitable for futures trading. Properly organised futures markets in major extraction cakes would be useful for promoting their exports. Since, on the basis of production and exports, groundnut extractions have been found to be eminently suitable for being traded on a futures market, the Committee recommends that initially this facility may be extended in respect of groundnut extractions and extended to other major extractions such as rice branoiled cake. However, the actual opening of futures markets should follow the coming into existence of a representative association at a suitable centre. (Paras 4.62 and 4.63)

(viii) Pepper

The supply of pepper during a season is fairly large. Out of an annual production of about 35,000 tonnes, the domestic consumption forms only about one-third and the rest is available for export. The overseas demand for the commodity is susceptible to wide variation causing undue price fluctuations which results in hardships to the producers, stockists and exporters. The facility of futures trading in pepper is extensively used by exporters and stockists. Taking into account all these factors, the Committee recommends that futures trading in pepper should be continued. (Para 4.67)

(ix) Turmeric

Due to large variability in supply and inelastic demand, turmeric prices are susceptible to wide fluctuations. This would necessitate hedging facilities for those who carry large stocks of the commodity in the process of marketing. Futures prices by serving as advance indicators have exercised, during periods of sharp fall or rise in the ready prices, a restraining influence on them. The dealers and exporters benefited from the futures market in turmeric, the former by hedging their stocks and the latter by purchasing on the futures market against their actual export commitments. The experience of regulation of futures trading in turmeric has been satisfactory. The Committee, therefore, recommends that the facility of futures trading in turmeric should be continued. (Paras 4.70 and 4.71)

(x) Sugar and Gur

(a) Sugar

In view of large variations in the supply of sugar and the demand for it continuously rising, sugar has been subjected to control of one form or the other. Taking into account the special circumstances in which the market in sugar functions, the Committee recommends that there is no need for futures trading in it. If, however, the present pattern of marketing of sugar is to give place to a system of free market, then the case for futures trading could emerge as a mechanism which would provide the advantages of such trading to the various functionaries in the trade. It would also then be of benefit to the producers and consumers. (Paras 4.73 and 4.74)

(b) Gur

Gur has neither been subjected to any fixed price nor to any other form of control at any point of time, while a major portion of sugar coming under the levy scheme has remained controlled at various points from time to time. Hence, in periods of shortages when the demand for sugar exceeds its supply, the price of levy sugar does not change but the excess demand is transferred to the gur market, which is free leading to a sharp rise in the prices of gur. Conversely, in times of surplus, the controlled sugar prices do not register much of a downward move, but the full impact is transferred to the gur market leading often to an undue fall in the prices of gur. Such wide fluctuations in gur prices seem to make a strong case for futures trading in gur. However, the factors in respect of gur which required special consideration are that despite the tradition of futures trading, there are no well-defined and acceptable standards in respect of gur and hence the grades as understood in different markets do not have close relationship with one another. Further, gur cannot be stored for long without deterioration in its quality. In view of these factors, we consider that while there is an inherent need for futures trading facilities in gur, such trading would require much closer supervision both by the recognised associations and the Forward Markets Commission. We recommend that futures trading in gur should be permitted as a policy on a continuous basis save in exceptional circumstances brought about by acute shortage of sugarcane, when the Government of the Forward Markets Commission might, if the situation so warrants, suspend it for the time being. Such suspension, however, should be temporary and futures trading should be restored as soon as possible. At the same time, when futures trading is permitted in the commodity, it should not be for any specified period since that leads to uncertainty and speculation having unhealthy effect on the working of futures markets. Further, the associations recognised for gur should be such as to be able to deal with the special problems of the commodity, particularly those relating to standardisation and grading, and should have qualified personnel and resources to deal with such problems. (Paras 4.76, 4.77 and 4.78)

(xi) Silver

India's production of silver is negligible and its supply is limited. Silver has become a very important industrial material and has also acquired strategic importance. As a result, the stocks of silver are getting depleted over the years. Exports of silver are not permitted. Silver market has also become volatile, of late, with very abnormal variations in prices and these abnormal conditions are expected to continue in the foreseeable futures. Taking all these factors into consideration the Committee is of the view that there is no case for permitting futures trading in silver at present. (Para 4.82)

(xii) Other Commodities

Futures trading in India has, so far, been confined to certain commodities in which there has been a long tradition of such trading. However, it was represented to us that there has been a substantial increase in the production of many other commodities in excess of internal demand, necessitating their exports in large quantities and if futures trading in those commodities could be organised, it would serve as an advance indicator of the future trend of prices to producers who would then plan their production and offer hedging facilities to other functionaries. The commodities indicated in this regard were cardamom, coffee, tobacco, tea, ginger, chillies, onion, potatoes, apples, etc. While the Committee could not study all these commodities for lack of time, the position in regard to some of the them, which could be studied in some detail, are as follows. (Para 4.83)

(a) Cardamom

Although production of cardamom is not very large in absolute terms, in value terms the commodity assumes importance. From the export angle, the commodity is significant since the bulk of the production is exported and the foreign exchange earnings from it are quite sizeable. However, there are no adequate cold storage facilities under which condition alone the quality of it can be fully preserved. As a result, stocks are not carried forward on any large scale beyond a period of three months or so. We are of the opinion that these difficulties are not insurmountable and with the building up of the necessary infrastructure this commodity would become suitable for futures trading. We, therefore, recommend that the Commission should keep this commodity under watch and advise the Government regarding introduction of futures trading in it at appropriate time. Once this happens, further developments in the marketing structure may get accelerated. (Para 4.85)

(b) Coffee

Coffee is, no doubt, suitable for futures trading as it has standardised grades. However, the functioning of a board futures market, within the present institutional arrangements for marketing in our country, is not possible since the release of coffee are controlled and no body except the registered traders is permitted to purchase coffee. The question of introducing futures trading in coffee can be considered only when free trading in coffee is introduced. (Para 4.87)

(c) Tobacco

The supply of tobacco is large and there have been wide fluctuations therein. Further, the demand is uncertain since a part of it comes from overseas buyers. Fluctuations in the prices of the commodity are quite large and the growers generally do not get remunerative prices. Though the present system of gradation is not fully satisfactory, the commodity is amenable to a proper system of gradation. However, the present market structure in tobacco is imperfect in the sense that the manufacturer-buyers are limited in number and they are in a position to dictate the terms to the sellers. There are no organised markets for ready and forward transactions. In the above context, the Committee is of the view that the commodity being suitable for futures trading, it would be advisable for the Tobacco Board and the concerned interests to take early steps to provide a proper system of ready and futures market in the commodity. (Para 4.90)

(d) Tea

The production of tea in the country is large and a substantial quantum is exported. There are also gluts and shortages in this commodity leading to large variations in its prices. The commodity being export oriented, the facility of futures trading would be to the advantage of the exporters and will contribute to export promotion. Although there are innumerable qualities of tea, it should be possible to evolve a suitable futures contract. However, the necessary institutional framework would have to emerge before the actual opening of futures trading. The Committee, therefore, recommends that the Tea Board and the concerned interest should work towards the evolution of such a framework so that futures trading in tea is possible. (Para 4.92)

As regards commodities such as potatoes, onions, apples, ginger, chillies, etc., the supply position in them has been comfortable in recent years owing to significant increases in their production. In fact, in some of them like potatoes, onions and apples, there have been gluts leading to uneconomic prices to the growers and subsequent short-fall in production leading to high levels of prices for the consumers. The existence of futures markets will enable the stockists and dealers to act as a cushion in periods of excess production and shortages since they would be able to cover their own risks in the futures markets. The introduction of futures trading may itself help to some extent the process of building up the necessary infrastructure required for efficient marketing. The Committee, therefore, recommends that these commodities too should be kept under watch by the Commission so as to take timely steps for introducing futures trading in them. (Para 4.93)

Basic Requisites for the Regulation of Futures Trading

10. The maintenance of competitive character of a futures market should be the most important consideration in the regulation of futures trading. The location of centres for establishing future markets, selection of suitable associations for conducting trading at the centres, rules and regulations subject to which such trading should be permitted, regulatory measures that may be introduced by the Commission to contain excessive speculation, etc., need to be considered from this point of view. (Para 5.2)

(a) As regards choice of a centre for the location of a futures market, we recommend that, as far as possible, the number of recognised futures markets in any commodity should be limited to the minimum necessary to avoid dispersal of hedge and speculative business over a number of markets making them in the process thin and less competitive. This would also facilitate more effective regulation of the recognised markets by the authorities concerned. (Para 5.6)

(b) The present provision in Section 15(4) of the FC(R) Act of permitting members to appropriate the business of non-member clients, although with their consent, is not conducive to maintaining the competitive character of futures trading. We, therefore, recommend that the present provision of permitting members to appropriate non-member's business outside the trading ring should be deleted and the FC(R) Act as well as rules and regulations of the recognised associations should provide that all business of non-members shall be put through in the ring by an outcry and any member of the association should have an opportunity to enter into an opposite transaction with the non-member at the most competitive rate offered in the ring. (Para 5.7)

(c) We feel that since the futures markets are primarily established to offer hedging facilities, the Commission's measures should not be such as to impair the utility of these markets for the purpose of hedging. We are of the view that while reasonable restrictions on speculative open positions as opposed to hedge open positions and reasonable limits on periodical fluctuations in prices are in conformity with the basic purpose for which futures markets are established, very stiff special margins linked with the futures price levels and maximum and minimum prices only in respect of futures contracts should be examined critically and in any case used sparingly. (Para 5.9)

11. At present the Commission requires the members of recognised associations to the submit returns normally on weekly basis and, in special circumstances, on daily basis. The present system of reporting is defective in many ways. First, it does not bring out the most vital information regarding the extent of hedging for which the markets are established. This information can be obtained by requiring each operator to disclose the break-up of his open position as hedge position and speculative position separately under a statutory requirement. Secondly, the present practice of requiring members of indicate the trading details of their non-members clients is not likely to bring forth correct information. We, therefore, recommend that periodical return on the lines indicated in the proforma given in Annexure XIII may be prescribed by the Commission and all operators – members as well as their non-member clients – should be required to submit it to the Commission. (Para 5.10)

12. We recommend that in a commodity in which more than one futures markets have been established initially, even when such markets are few, their continuance should be periodically reviewed on the basis of the extent to which the established markets have been used for the purpose of heading. (Para 5.11)

13. Since many of the manipulative tendencies in the futures market arise through trading in the name of non-members, it is desirable to have a more direct control on the activities of non-members than at present. This can be achieved by requiring all non-members desirous of trading in a futures market, to register with the Commission through the concerned recognised association subject to

such rules and conditions as may be prescribed by the Commission for the purpose. We also recommend that the recognised associations should be required to lay down in their rules, certain minimum margin or deposit, ranging between say 5 to 25 per cent of the value of the contract, to be obtained by a member from each non-member. In order to protect the non-members in respect of such margin or deposit, it should be laid down in the FC(R) Act that the amounts collected by the member should be held in segregation by the member concerned and not commingled with his own funds. (Paras 5.13, 5.14 and 5.15)

14. On many occasions, running hedge contracts under the auspices of the recognised associations are suddenly closed out by the members acting in concert or by the Boards of recognised associations before the actual due date of the contract, at rates arbitrarily decided upon. The Committee recommends that the rules and regulations of the recognised associations should make special provisions to prevent these types of malpractices and such activities on the part of any association should be considered serious enough to justify the withdrawal of recognition of such an association. (Para 5.16)

15. Having recommended continuation or immediate resumption of futures trading only in such commodities in which it is economically and socially desirable and also introduction of a proper scheme of regulation, we recommend that the Government should adopt a long-term policy in respect of futures trading. Once it is permitted, it should be continued without any interruption except in very abnormal situations when it might be necessary to suspend it in a particular commodity for a short period. (Para 5.17)

16. We suggest that it should be the endeavour of the Government and the Forward Markets Commission to develop the associations recognised for futures trading in the country into modern commodity exchanges. We hope that the existing associations will take heed of these suggestions and strive towards such institution building. (Para 5.18)

Non-transferable Specific Delivery (NTSD) Contracts

17. The need for the facility of NTSD contracts to various trade interests arises mainly for ensuring in advance a smooth and assured supply of and demand for the commodity in the future period. A large proportion of buying and selling in the commodity markets is through the medium of NTSD contracts of duration of two to five months though

contracts of much longer duration, particularly in manufactured commodities such as cloth or steel or tools, are also often entered into. (Paras 6.4 and 6.6)

18. The experience of the Forward Markets Commission showed that NTSD contracts were used for camouflaging futures trading in banned or regulated commodities. In a large number of commodities NTSD contracts were either prohibited by applying Section 17 of the FC(R) Act or were not permitted to be traded in the commodities to which section 15 of the Act had been applied. We have come to the conclusion that permanent ban or prolonged suspension of NTSD contracts is no solution. The prolonged prohibition of NTSD contracts is causing genuine hardships to important functionaries in different commodities. We have already recommended in Chapter 7 that the present scheme of the FC(R) Act enabling the Government to regulate NTSD contracts, when necessary, should be retained. We consider that, along with other amendments suggested by us, this is an adequate safeguard to control any possible use of NTSD contracts for speculative purposes. The Commission's experience of regulating NTSD contracts has been very satisfactory. Taking all these factors into account, we recommend that the prohibition imposed on NTSD contracts in important commodities (like major edible oilseeds such as groundnut, mustardseed and cottonseed and their oils, coconut oil and foodgrains, which are no more subjected to zonal restrictions) should be lifted and such contracts in them should be permitted under the auspices of properly selected recognised associations representing different functionaries dealing with the actual commodity. (Paras 6.8 to 6.11)

19. The principles followed by the Commission in selecting associations for recognition in respect of NTSD contracts have been stated in the Commission's Report on the Recognition of Association in respect of NTSD contracts in Indian Cotton submitted to the Government in April 1972. We are generally in agreement with these principles and would, therefore, recommend that the Commission should proceed on the basis of these principles for regulating NTSD contracts in important commodities in which such contracts cannot be permitted freely. The need for continuing regulation of these contracts in the commodities in which they are regulated should be examined by the Forward Markets Commission at regular interval and necessary recommendations made to the Government. (Para 6.12)

20. In the case of commodities other than the major commodities mentioned above, we recommend that trading in NTSD contracts may

be permitted freely after the amendments proposed in this report to the definition of NTSD contract and other related matters have been carried out. The Forward Markets Commission should keep a watch on the working of such contracts through its Enforcement Directorate. If the facility for free trading in NTSD contracts in any of these commodities is found to be misused by unscrupulous elements for speculative purpose, the question of bringing them under regulation should be considered by the Commission as and when necessary. (Para 6.13)

Amendments to FC(R) Act

21. There is no need to change the present scheme of classification of contracts or regulation as the experience relating to the enforcement of the FC(R) Act has clearly indicated that the present approach is broadly correct. To ensure that NTSD contracts are not used for (i) camouflaging speculative trading to evade ban or restrictions imposed by the Government on futures trading in the commodities, or (ii) acquiring pre-emptive hold on large future supplies of the goods concerned, it is necessary to provide for their regulation, whenever necessary as at present. There is, however, a strong case to amend the definition of NTSD contract to make it precise and to provide for certain facilities required by genuine trade. (Para 7.12)

22. We feel that in order to make the Act effective, it is necessary to prevent illegal forward trading in regulated or banned commodities conducted in the guise of unregulated or unbanned commodities. We therefore, recommend that the Act should be amended to provide that (i) all trading in transferable contracts (i.e., forward contracts other than NTSD contracts), which is not regulated or controlled by an association, shall be illegal, and (ii) no association regulating and controlling transferable contracts shall to so without obtaining a certificate of recognition from the Government except when the Central Government has specifically exempted any commodity from this requirement of recognition. The net effect of these two provisions in the Act would be that trading in all transferable contracts (and in NTSD contracts when such trading is specifically regulated) will be under the auspices of recognised associations only and there will be no need for a separate category of registered associations. The possibility of conducting illegal futures trading in the name of so-called party to party contracts would thus be eliminated. In our view, these restrictions cannot be construed as unreasonable for reasons mentioned in paragraph 19 of

Chapter 7. (Paras 7.17 to 7.22)

23. The Commission had suggested to the Government a number of amendments to the Act in October 1978 (Annexure XV). These amendments were referred to this Committee for its views. We agree with the amendments suggested by the Commission such as (i) to definitions of ready and NTSD contracts, (ii) to tighten the penal provisions by increasing the maximum and minimum fines and imprisonment, to provide for compulsory imprisonment for the first offence and to remove discretion to the Magistrate to release the offenders under the FC(R) Act by taking recourse to provisions of the Probation of Offenders Act, and (iii) to make presumption under Section 22B applicable to seizures effected both with or without a warrant, and others except those for powers for search and seizure. This is because none of the Commission's Officers except the Director of Enforcement, is equipped by training and temperament to exercise such powers and if such powers are vested in the Commission, the police authorities may no longer consider themselves solely responsible for investigation for offences under the FC(R) Act and their full co-operation may not be easily forthcoming. (Paras 7.25 to 7.33 and 7.37 to 7.43)

24. The amendments suggested by the Commission to the definitions of the terms association, registered association and in respect of other matters relating to registered associations will not be necessary if the amendments suggested by us in paragraph 22 above are accepted as in that case, the category of registered associations would stand abolished. The amendments suggested by the Commission would, however, be necessary in case our suggestions are not accepted. (Paras 7.34 to 7.36)

25. The Commission had made a proposal for adjudication of offences under the Act by the Commission. We recommend that instead of providing for adjudication of offences by the Commission, the offences under the Act should be made compoundable with the sanction of the Commission. This would enable the Commission to get quick disposal of a large number of cases pending for long in law courts without the need for setting up a cumbersome and costly adjudication machinery which will have to remain idle for most of the time. (Paras 7.44 to 7.46)

26. We have also recommended amendments for (i) registration of all non-members trading in futures markets, (ii) submission of periodical returns by all operators, members as well as non-members directly to the Commission showing the volume of trading and break-

up of the open position as hedge and speculative positions, (iii) requiring all business of non-members to be put through trading ring of recognised associations by public out-cry, and (iv) requiring each member of the recognised association to obtain from his non-member client a minimum margin or deposit which should be held in segregation without commingling with his own personal funds. (Para 7.47)

Strengthening of the Forward Markets Commission

27. If the recommendations of the Committee in respect of various matters are accepted by the Government, it would substantially enlarge the role of the Commission. The Committee notes that two posts of Member out of four provided under the FC(R) Act have remained unfilled for long. It is necessary that the vacant posts be filled so that a better division of labour regionally, functionally and commodity-wise and better handling of the volume of work can be brought about. As the Commission has to deal with persons and agencies of the highest standing in the trade, commerce and manufacture, it is important that the official standing of its Members and Chairman should be of a high level. It is, therefore, recommended that the Chairman of the Commission be given the status of an Additional Secretary and the Members of a Joint Secretary in the Central Government. (Paras 8.1 and 8.2)

28. The staff strength of both the Commodity and the Enforcement Divisions of the Commission will have to be appropriately strengthened in the light of our various recommendations to enable the Commission to discharge its functions more comprehensively and efficiently. Having regard to the selective approach to futures trading which we have recommended, the magnitude of illegal forward trading in the country and the potential for anti-social elements devising ingenious methods to conceal such trading, we fee that the present enforcement arrangements in the office of the Commission are totally inadequate to cope with the task of combating illegal forward trading. The major pockets of illegal forward trading are located in the States of Gujarat, Rajasthan, Punjab, Haryana, Uttar Pradesh, Madhya Pradesh and the Union Territory of Delhi and the Cities of Bombay and Calcutta. Taking into account the above factors, we recommend that Regional Offices of the Commission may be established, in addition to the one already at Calcutta, at Delhi, Ahmedabad and Lucknow to begin with. These offices should be under the charge of a gazetted officer who should be assisted by supporting staff at the level of

senior/junior research assistants and necessary subordinate staff. The establishment of such small Regional Offices would be feasible economically and assist in the efficient discharge of the responsibilities of the Commission under the FC(R) Act. (Paras 8.4 to 8.7)

29. There is no regular research unit manned with staff having adequate statistical and econometric qualifications in the office of the Commission to undertake specialised studies. The Commission should undertake research activities to cover various aspects of futures trading since the potential for such research studies is quite wide. (Para 8.8)

30. The timely publication of the data regarding recognised futures markets in the Forward Markets Bulletin brought out by the Commission would be of much help to the Government in framing its policies and also to the trading community in adopting a responsible approach towards futures trading. (Para 8.9)

12

RAILWAY ACCIDENT INVESTIGATION REPORT ON THE OCCURRENCE OF FIRE IN A TRAILER COACH NO. 72169 OF NO. S-9 DOWN BOMBAY (VT)-KARJAT SUBURBAN TRAIN AT KM. 54/9-18 BETWEEN KALYAN-KARJAT ELECTRIFIED DOUBLE LINE BROAD GAUGE SUBURBAN SECTION OF BOMBAY DIVISION, CENTRAL RAILWAY AT ABOUT 14-10 HOURS ON APRIL 11, 1979 – REPORT[1]

One Man Commission Shri P.M.N. Murthy

Appointment

The Commission was constituted under Ministry of Tourism and Civil Aviation (Commission of Railway Safety) in accordance with Rule 4 of the Statutory Investigation into Railway Accidents Rules, 1973 Vide Notification No. RS 13-T(8)/TI dated April 19, 1973 on April 11, 1979.

Terms of Reference

To enquire into the occurrence of Fire in Trailer Coach No. 72169 of No. S-9 Down Bombay (VT) – Karjat Suburban Train at Km. 54/9-18 between Kalyan-Karjat Electrified Double Line Broad Gauge Suburban Section of Bombay Division, Central Railway at about 14-10 Hours on April 11, 1979.

Contents

Summary; Inspection and Inquiry; Relief Measures; The Train; Local

1. Delhi, Controller of Publications, 1981.

Features; Summary of Evidence; Observation and Tests; Discussion; Conclusions; Remarks and Recommendations; Annexures; Railway Board's Comment on various paras of the Report.

Conclusions

Clause

43. (a) On careful consideration of the available evidence and based on the results of analysis of the burnt debris furnished by the State Forensic Science Laboratory, Bombay, I have reached the conclusion that the Occurrence of Fire in Trailer Coach No. 72169 of No. S-9 Down Bombay VT-Karjat Suburban train between Kalyan and Vithlwadi stations on the Kalyan-Karjat Suburban Section of Bombay Division of Central Railway at about 14.10 hours on 11th April, 1979, was the result of a highly inflammable material such as gun or blasting powder carried by one of the passengers in the 2nd class compartment of the coach being ignited by contact with a lighted '*bidi*' or cigarette.

Responsibility

(b) The responsibility for this accident must rest with the passenger who carried the hazardous material with him in violation of Section 59 of the Indian Railways Act and with the commuter who it a 'smoke' ignoring the notification prohibiting the same in suburban trains.

44. *Relief Measures*

Apropos Section II of the Report the relief measures were adequate.

Recommendations

The following Immediate Recommendations which were appended to my Preliminary Report on this accident are repeated herein for necessary action:

"(a) Intensive raids (along with renewed educative propaganda through the available media) must be undertaken by the Railway Administration and the Railway Police to enforce the ban on smoking (which was introduced in Suburban trains with effect from 1-6-1976, pursuant to a recommendation made by the Commission of Railway Safety) and the carriage of inflammable/explosive materials by commuters in defiance of Section 59 of the Indian Railway Act.

"[It is noted that no checks whatever were carried out on Suburban trains by the Central Railway pertinent to Section 59 of the Indian Railways Act after February, 1977].

"(b) Legislative measures to bring these commissions under the category of 'cognizable offences' [within the purview of Section 131 of the Indian Railways Act] may be hastened, as these constitute grave safety hazards, more so in Suburban travel."

It had been recommended by the Additional Commissioner of Railway Safety, Northern Railway on 31st October, 1974 that "The passenger who was carrying the 5205 of 14 Down Upper India Express between Bharwari and Manoharganj stations of Northern Railway on 31st October, 1974 that "The passenger who was carrying the highly inflammable material in gunny bags is reported to have remarked that she had been doing this regularly. This is a hazardous practice which has to be stopped. It is not a practical proposition for the railway administration to arrange for inspection of the luggage of all passengers to prevent their carrying such dangerous articles. It should, however, be possible for the Government to legislate suitably so that the sale of such hazardous materials is made only by licensed dealers and it is ensured that these materials are packed in suitable containers which would preclude any fire hazard." On this the Railway Ministry had expressed the following views vide their O.M. No. 74/Safety (A&R)/1/16 dated 21-11-1975: – "Production, sale and movement of dangerous and hazardous goods are controlled by the Chief Inspector of Explosives as such things fall under the purview of the Indian Explosives Act. Section 59 of the Indian Railways Act also prohibits persons from carrying any dangerous or offensive goods upon the Railways without fulfilling the conditions laid down for their carriage. The Act also provides that the Railway may refuse to carry such goods for carriage for stop such goods in transit if it has been carried without the permission. For violating the provisions of this Section 59, a person is punishable with a fine which may extend to Rs. 500 and shall also be responsible for any loss, injury or damage which may be caused by reason of such goods having been so brought upon the Railway. This punishment is prescribed under Section 107 of the Indian Railways Act." Apparently, the question of packaging of such materials for safe marketing and conveyance was not pursued. It appears very necessary that appropriate legislation is soon enacted making it obligatory on Manufacturers and Stockists of highly inflammable materials to pack them in suitable, containers so as to obviate any fire hazard during transit, as recommended by the Commission.

It came to notice during inspection that 6 out of the seven 5 amps. fuses in the Relay-cum-fuse panel of coach No. 72169 were oversized. Suitable corrective action may be taken to prevent recurrence.

Railway Board's Comments on Various Paras of the Report

Para 45 (a): The Railway administration have re-iterated instructions and renewed massive educative campaign through all available mass media against carrying inflammable/explosive materials and smoking by commuters. During the period March 1977 to March 1978, 204 persons were prosecuted under Section 110 of the Indian Railways Act for smoking and 2 persons prosecuted under Section 107 for carrying inflammable/explosive materials. Also during the period April 1978 to April 1979, as many as 329 persons were prosecuted for smoking and one for carrying inflammable/explosive material.

The Railway administration are being asked to give wide publicity to the prosecution and conviction of offenders detected as a result of the checks conducted.

Para 45 (b): With a view to making railway travel safer and to minimise accidents on Railways, carriage of explosives, inflammable and dangerous goods in coaches, as luggages, is not permitted. The booking of such goods governed by the rules and regulations laid down in Red Tariff No. 19. These rules are laid down in consultation with the Chief Inspector of Explosives, Government of India, Nagpur, who prescribes the necessary packing conditions, mode of conveyance, etc., after taking into consideration the nature of the articles. Keeping in view these conditions, necessary provision is also made in the Coaching and in the Red Tariff of the Indian Railways regarding carriage of such articles.

Fire prone articles like varieties of dry grass, leaves, waste papers, etc., are also not booked as luggage.

Under Section 59 of the Indian Railways Act, no person shall be entitled to take with him upon a railway dangerous or offensive goods without giving due notice to the Railways of the nature of such goods to the Station Master or other railway servant. It is also laid down that no person shall tender or deliver any goods for carriage on a Railway without distinctly marking their nature at the outside of the package containing such goods. In all these cases, Railway has a right to refuse such goods for carriage.

Section 107 of the Indian Railways Act lays down punishment for violating the provisions of Section 59 of the Act mentioned above. If a person takes with him any dangerous or offensive goods upon the Railway or tenders or delivers any such goods for carriage upon a Railway in contravention of the provisions of the Section 59, he shall be punished with a line which may extend to Rs. 500 and in addition he shall be responsible for any loss, injury or damage which may be caused by reasons for such goods having been so brought on the Railways.

In addition to the above, a campaign of education through posters, advertisements, etc., is carried on by the Railways informing the people of the dangers of carrying such goods by passenger trains and also the punishments that will be inflicted for violation.

Legislative measures to prevent carriage of dangerous and offensive goods in contravention of Section 59 has already been taken in hand and the amendment is being processed alongwith the revision of the Indian Railways Act, 1890. The amended provision provides for imprisonment for a period of three years for the carriage of dangerous goods; penalty of fine upto five hundred rupees in the case of offensive goods has been retained. It is also proposed to make carriage of dangerous or offensive goods in violation of Section 59, a cognizable offence.

As regards smoking, it may be mentioned that smoking is still permissible and will continue to be so under the revised-Act except wherever it may be specially prohibited Smoking being generally permissible and not being hazardous in itself it would not be proper to bring it within the category of cognizable offences and legislation to this effect may be termed void.

Para 46: As for legislation with regard to conditions of packing of dangerous and offensive goods so as to obviate the hazards during transit, it may be mentioned that the carriage of these articles is governed under rules contained in I.R.C.A. Red Tariff in which conditions of packing are provided for each and every such commodity. These conditions being compulsory, there is no necessity for any further legislation on this issue.

Para 47: Instructions with regard to use of fuses of appropriate size already exist. These have been re-iterated by the railway administration. Coach No. 72169 has been put back into service with proper size of fuses.

The Railways is being asked to investigate the matters as why fuses of improper size used in Coach No. 72169, and take up with the defaulting staff.